A PASSION FOR THE GAME

A PASSION FOR THE GAME
REAL LIVES IN FOOTBALL

Tom Watt
Foreword by Alan Shearer

Best wishes

MAINSTREAM PUBLISHING

EDINBURGH AND LONDON

First published in 1995 by
MAINSTREAM PUBLISHING COMPANY (EDINBURGH) LTD
7 Albany Street
Edinburgh EH1 3UG

ISBN 1 85158 714 4

A catalogue record for this book is available from the British Library

Typeset in Palatino
Printed and bound in Great Britain by Butler & Tanner Ltd, Frome

CONTENTS

ACKNOWLEDGMENTS

A Passion For The Game would never have got off the ground without the help, advice and address books of Tony Stephens, Steve Stride and Richard Payne. As the book progressed I received valuable help from everybody I asked, whether it was filling in background detail; furnishing introductions or helping track down pictures: Peter Gordon, Peter Gilham, Tony Ward, Terry Murphy, Joan Hill, Phil Carling, Bill Harvey, David Smith, Gordon Banks, Teresa Coneely and Peter Bishop all offered assistance for which I'm very grateful. The writing of *A Passion For The Game* was made much easier by the support of companies such as Hilton National Hotels, Fred Perry Limited and KangaRoos UK, and individuals – Bill Hamilton, Paul Windle, Alex Halpern and Adam Harrison – who took on trust what the book (and me!) were all about. Many hours and no little support came from the world's best typist, Judi Spector, her husband, Simon, and my illustrator, the estimable Peter Boggon. I'd like to thank everyone for all their help. I must acknowledge, too, the contributions of an unwitting Studs Terkel, whose book *Working* suggested a model for *A Passion For The Game*, and my publishers, Mainstream who – perhaps unwitting, too – commissioned the book from me in 1994.

The real acknowledgment due, of course, is to the 90 people whose stories are told here. Thanks are in order not only for the time they gave up to talk to me about their lives but also for the help they all gave in passing me on to other people in their own fields or elsewhere. Not only was everybody involved important in their own right, but their generosity was also the cement that holds the whole together. I hope they'll feel the book does them and the game they love justice. They have my gratitude, my admiration and my respect. For the same reasons, I'd like, too, to thank Alan Shearer for contributing his foreword.

A Passion For The Game is dedicated to those whose stories it recounts. And to my wife, Ann, the best thing to ever happen in the course of my own story.

FOREWORD

Alan Shearer, Blackburn Rovers and England

In the North-east, as soon as you can walk someone throws a ball at your feet! And I was no different. I know now that perhaps I should have studied harder at school – my teachers were always telling me that the chances of making it as a footballer were very remote! – but it was what I always wanted to do. I suppose I dreamt then about playing at the level I do now. I was very lucky to have parents who were prepared to go without so that I could have what I needed. If I needed a pair of boots – and when you're a kid you don't want any old boots, you want the best, don't you? – they went without so I could have them. When I first started playing football as a boy my parents were great.

When I was about 12 I was playing for a city side,

Newcastle Boys I think. At a game one afternoon there was an old bloke on the touchline: Jack Hixon. There were a few scouts there and Jack hadn't come to watch me: he was just taking in a game like he still does every weekend. After the match, Jack went over to my dad and said: *Do you mind if we have a look at your son further, take him down to Southampton?* My dad said: *You're asking the wrong person. You'd better ask him!* And that was it. You know, I still talk to Jack every two or three days. It doesn't often happen like that, as far as I know. Usually, a scout will hand you on to a club and then disappear into the background. But that's never been the case with me and Jack. I'd like to know how much I've spent in phone bills talking to him over the years! It's great: Jack's a good bloke, a nice man and he's family now, to be honest.

At 13, Southampton were ready to let me go! They didn't think I was going to make it but I had one last game for them and managed to score a hat-trick – so they took me on schoolboy forms at 14! At a club like Southampton, you're passed through the staff and teams as you get older. From 14 to 16, I was with Bob Higgins, the Youth Development Officer. Then it was the youth and reserves with Dave Merrington and Ray Graydon and, finally, the first time with the manager Chris Nicholl and the first-team coach, Dennis Rofe.

I think I was particularly lucky – we all were – that between 16 and 18 my age group had Dave Merrington as Youth Team manager. Dave was an ex-player: in fact, Jack Hixon signed him for Burnley when Dave was a boy! Dave was a Geordie, too, which was a help for someone like me who, at just turned 16, had come 350 miles down the motorway, leaving home for the first time to come to Southampton. He was very strict – I remember one afternoon I left the tap running in the boot room and flooded the medical room: Dave found out who it was and had us all do 50 laps of the pitch in a snowstorm the next day! – but with all the discipline and toughness he was good to us too. He kept the pressure off us and made sure we all got on well. We had plenty of laughs and jokes which you need at that age, don't you? It wasn't all serious – he took us away on some great trips – but, when the work had to be done, Dave wanted it done right. He was really good for all of us, kept our feet on the ground.

I got my chance in the first team very early. I was only 17 when I made my debut – I knew nothing about it until the manager told me I was playing a couple of hours before the match – and scored a hat-trick against Arsenal. There was a really good set of pros at the Dell. You'd train with the first team maybe once a week, and you'd be in awe of players like Peter Shilton, Mark Wright, Steve Williams and Danny Wallace. But they used to take the younger lads out – for a game of snooker or a drink – and that helped us along. It's why Southampton have done so well: it's a very close-knit club. There's the same feeling behind the scenes too. We used to meet up and go out with the office staff as well.

I was 21 when the Southampton manager at the time, Ian Branfoot, told me that there had been enquiries about me from other clubs. I asked to be kept informed, which Ian was very good about doing. In the end, I was told that the club had accepted an offer worth £3.3 million from Blackburn Rovers and that I was free to contact Kenny Dalglish to discuss it. I drove up to Blackburn with my wife, Lainya, and I spoke to Kenny while his wife, Marina, took Lainya out for the afternoon. How I found Kenny – he was just himself and very straight about things – and how he treated both myself and Lainya had a lot to do with why I decided to come here. Before I left Blackburn I told him I would let him know within 24 hours but an hour after we got home I phoned and said I wanted to sign!

What's happened at Blackburn is unbelievable. When I first came here, there was an old wooden stand along that side and standing behind both the goals. The money that Jack Walker's put into Blackburn Rovers is amazing. Here's a man who's worked hard for every penny he's got, who's just a football fan at heart and wants to see his team doing well. He's in the dressing-room before every game to shake your hand and wish everybody the best and – win, lose or draw – he's back after the match as well! Everyone at the club means something to him and he treats us all equally, whether it's me or the tea-lady. I was pleased for Mr Walker more than anybody when we won the Premiership last May.

I'm only 24 now and I know I've still got a lot I can learn. When you think you know everything is the time you should be thinking about quitting! If you know everything, you should be winning everything, shouldn't you? I think I've got things I can learn from all sorts of people. On the football side, one of the reasons I came to Blackburn – and it's still the case – was that I knew I'd learn a lot from the management team: Kenny Dalglish and Ray Harford. And I'm lucky, too, that if I need someone to talk to, I've got people like my parents and Jack Hixon to turn to. I couldn't ask for better.

INTRODUCTION

'Don't be daft. It's only a game after all.'
Ian in An Evening With Gary Lineker *by Arthur Smith and*
Chris England

Early summer of 1993, I was in the middle of a long run in *An Evening With Gary Lineker*, a comedy about football fans in which I played the one character who wasn't one. This seemed like a good idea at the time. Pretending to be a person whose life didn't revolve around football was something of a professional challenge: they might as well have asked me to play a Martian. And spending each evening timing crass jokes at the England team's expense while the 1990 World Cup semi-final flickered away on the onstage telly was by way of a break from the day job – a hobby, I suppose, that got out of hand – compiling an oral history of Arsenal's late North Bank terrace.

Acting's a great way to make a living. Like playing football, it's a career that gives you every chance of waking up in the morning and actually looking forward to going to work. You'd enjoy doing it even if you weren't being paid to. My only problem with the chosen profession is that, unlike the unfortunate Ian in *An Evening With Gary Lineker*, I don't spend much time not thinking about football. If you don't know it yourself from experience, you'll have picked it up from *Fever Pitch*: once you're hooked, the game insinuates itself into just about every waking hour. If you're working Saturday afternoons and weekday evenings during the season, there's an obvious conflict of interests.

Now and again, flushed with confidence or a run of repeat fees, you can see your way clear to letting football come first. After watching Arsenal win 3–0 at Villa Park on New Year's Eve 1988, I was so sure of what 1989 had in store that I turned down flat any job that might have meant me missing a game, home or away, until the Championship had been pirated so memorably at Anfield the following May. The rest of the time, though, you're between a rock and a hard place: miss games or miss the mortgage. It's not very clever, onstage or on a studio floor, when there's a game crackling away on the radio in your dressing-room. You're late for entrances, rush the serious bits, forget your lines and overact or mumble incoherently, depending on the latest score.

Anyway, two summers ago there was a week's break in the schedule, between a tour and a season in the West End. Good, a comedy with timing: I'd be at Wembley for the FA Cup final against Sheffield Wednesday. What's more, I'd be able to turn out in four games myself in the eight days before we moved into the Vaudeville Theatre. The second of these was a testimonial at Colchester United on the Wednesday evening. Just right: big crowd, warm night, plenty of players over 40. About 15 minutes in, I turned – not quickly, I never turned quickly in my life – after clearing a corner. My heel decided to stick where it was, in a comfortable divot, and I went down to sniggers from the crowd behind our goal and a sound a bit like slow-tearing velcro. That was a ruptured cruciate ligament in the right knee, and I've not kicked a ball since. I decided a proper footballer's injury was the closest I was ever going to come to being a proper footballer.

I was never any good: skinny legs, no physical courage and a sense of balance that makes Mr Bean look co-ordinated. Charity football suited me down to the ground. I had the chance, during what passed for my playing career, to play with and against some of my boyhood heroes. Lining up alongside Frank McLintock or tackling George Best are the kind of things you can die happy having done. People could come along, admittedly not so much to watch as to laugh and point. There was even the excuse that it was all in a good cause, although that wore a bit thin with my girlfriend after 60 or 70 games a season for the best part of eight years. The truth was I'd found a way of getting a game every weekend in spite of – even because of – being useless. And playing football, of course, is the one thing better than watching it.

14

Part of the excitement, own goals and breathing difficulties aside, was where the games were played. The fixture lists would read like a Rough Guide to Football: Goodison Park one week, Underhill the next; a game on a parks pitch in Solihull on Sunday afternoon and then one under floodlights at Wealdstone come the Wednesday night. Some of the ex-pros and better players would grumble about the state of a Jewson League playing surface in February. They were all Wembley as far as I was concerned. Mud's just mud, whatever the surroundings, if you spend most of every game on your arse in the stuff.

Everywhere, though, what made the thing work was people's endless enthusiasm – the one thing I had to offer, too: Villa Legend Johnny Dixon turning out at nearly 70 and sulking if he didn't get a full 90 minutes; Dean Houldsworth playing for us on a Sunday in between Saturday and Tuesday games for Brentford: a Class One ref like Alf Buksh happy to get grief from a crowd of 500 at a school playing field the day after he'd been slaughtered by 40,000 at a North London derby; office and ground staff showing up to work on their day off; sandwiches cut, the dressing-rooms cleaned and the pitch marked out. Nothing was too much trouble if there was a game of football in the offing.

That enthusiasm – selfless, passionate, obsessional – is the one thing, Laws Of The Game aside, that ties football together at every level at which it's played. People will do just about anything to be involved: in the Premiership, through to non-league and the amateur game beyond. Some buzz. The ground may be a palace or a cowshed, either way it's the pride of every soul that works there. The staff may number hundreds or just the very odd one: unpaid overtime goes without saying. Top of the Premiership or bottom of the Beezer Homes, someone's always ready to do the centre-forward a favour. Whether you support Arsenal or Rochdale or Bishop Auckland, however different the trappings, the football fan's routine of a little joy and much disappointment is the same wherever. It's the same passion, too – every football fan understands it – that drives the people who spend their lives making sure that next week's match-day happens, whether it's for 150 diehards in the middle of nowhere on a wet, windy Saturday or for watching millions at a televised Cup semi-final the following day.

Almost without exception, the people who work in football are fans before everything: fools for the game like the rest of us. Thanks to chance, or a sense of adventure, or stupidity or an unswerving ambition – all four together help – they've ended up devoting their working lives, as opposed to the cash and sleepless nights demanded of you and I, to That Bloody Football Team. Every fan dreams of playing for or working for – better still, being in full 'well, it's my ball' control of – the club they go and watch. What real life is like in that particular dreamland is what this book is all about.

* * *

'Unfortunately the media only picks up on the bad things that happen in football. There are 110 good things happening behind the scenes in every football club but it's not news.'

Glenn Hoddle, September 1994

One hundred and ten: interesting, to be able to come up with such a precise figure. In fact, Hoddle had at least one more Good Thing to add to the list at Chelsea a couple of weeks after the 1994/95 season ended. One of the genuinely great players of his generation – a World Footballer of the Year while still a teenager – Ruud Gullit arrived at Stamford Bridge in June on a free transfer from Sampdoria. After the spectacular success of the Klinsmania episode across London at White Hart Lane the previous season, this was like every Chelsea fan having a birthday on the same day. Fulham Broadway went gaga for Gullit overnight: a rush for season tickets, international media interest – the club shop ran out of 'L's in a morning, such was the demand to have a new hero's name emblazoned on the back of replica shirts.

Notwithstanding the player's age, doubts about the durability of at least one knee and a famously cavalier reputation, the signing of a pukka Dutch master was a coup to rank alongside Alan Sugar's Monte Carlo shipboard romance

16

with Jurgen Klinsmann the previous summer. Now – as then – the distributed quotes were all about the challenge of English football. Glenn Hoddle's reputation rather than newly visible director Matthew Harding's millions, it was stressed, had been the decisive factor in tying up the deal. All things being equal, of course, the Chelsea manager's pedigree as a player and his ambitions as a team-builder would make him an interesting proposition for anyone interested in playing the beautiful game. Ten or even five years ago, though, Pelé would have played for Peterborough before an international star of Gullit's stature would have taken a second look at England when deciding on his next career move.

Throughout the 1980s, Serie A, the Bundisliga and a handful of Spanish clubs were the clear market leaders in world football. Barcelona could boast almost as many season ticket-holders as the English First Division put together. Turin, Naples and then Milan vied for position as the Hollywood of soccer. The likes of Hamburg and Bayern Munich, though less spectacular, also had the political and financial clout to draw their playing staffs from anywhere in four continents. English football was, in economic terms at least, an also-ran. English club sides, Liverpool in particular, competed famously on the pitch with their European rivals. Off it, we struggled to keep the opposition in sight. The post-Heysel ban imposed on English clubs by UEFA just made things worse.

Insular, complacent and unimaginative, the national game had been in steady decline for 20 years, at least since the 1970 World Cup in Mexico. The problem, expressed in commercial terms, went back twice as long as that, to the end of the post-war boom in League attendances. By the mid-'80s, thanks to the efforts of everyone from Don Revie through to the English Hooligan Abroad, we'd been left standing while international football kicked on, as a game and as a business.

They say things have to get worse before they get better. Things couldn't have got much worse than they did in the late '80s. Football killed nearly 200 people at Heysel, Bradford and Hillsborough: not the game, of course, but the culture that had grown up around it, the old grounds, the hooligans and treating ordinary people like cattle. It's a shame on all of us that innocent people died before anyone thought to do something. Popplewell and Taylor gave football strong, bitter medicine: the game had to make the effort and foot the bill. As a result, though, thanks to CCTV, family enclosures, responsible crowd safety procedures, a massive programme of new building, the atmosphere inside English football grounds became safer and more relaxed within a couple of seasons.

Over the same period, the commercial exploitation of the game's massive appeal, which had begun in the early '70s with lotteries and enamel badges, began to take on a life of its own. While attendances continued along their steady downward trend, the archaic committee structures that had run football like so many old gentlemen's clubs died their natural death. The days of best malt in the boardroom and letting the rabble in on Saturday were long gone. Professional businessmen came in and started to run clubs along the lines of the companies whose profits had enabled this generation of entrepreneurs to buy themselves controlling interests up and down the country. The selling of football had begun.

The shadowy outline of football's future was already taking shape, come the new decade. There was a sense that the game had turned a corner, that things could slowly, steadily improve. Actually it turned out to be a pretty short fuse. Football, like England's horde of supporters at Italia '90, went fucking mental. There's a small library of books currently in print which have a bash at explaining why, covering pretty well everything from chaos theory through to secret conspiracy on a massive scale. Without doubt, two very different individuals played crucial roles in the explosion that's taken place. The impacts made by Paul Gascoigne and Rupert Murdoch were as significant as they were unforeseen.

In 1990 England flew off to the World Cup in Italy trying to rewrite a 20-year history of under-achievement. The last genuinely convincing national side had gone out to Mexico in 1970 as World Champions only to throw things away in the late stages of a quarter-final against West Germany. The class of Italia '90 turned in a shambling performance in their opening group game against Ireland. A 1–1 draw had critics assuming we'd taken a big first step towards an early, shamefaced return to Heathrow. Instead, the game was the start of an heroic and unlikely run to the semi-finals.

It was like watching someone learn to walk: England had, after all, been asleep for a couple of decades. The goals of Platt and Lineker, a player-instigated reshaping of the team pattern and a kind run of the ball helped see off the likes of Belgium and the suicidal Cameroon. The spark, though, was the coming of age of a remarkable and hitherto unreliable young talent, Paul Gascoigne, whose Bash Street Kid persona and outstanding technical ability combined to make him a talisman a whole nation could latch on to as the summer wore on. In the dramatic semi-final – you may remember it: we lost on penalties to Germany – Gascoigne's tears of disappointment and frustration, when a booking late in the game seemed set to deny him a World Cup final appearance, furnished Italia '90 with its most memorable image.

For the first time since 1966, the English public – as well as the game's long-suffering apologists – stopped what they were doing to watch and wonder. Here we were, making a mark on the game that had left us behind with black-and-white television and Labour Governments. Irrespective of the disappointments since, Bobby Robson's team – and Paul Gascoigne's tears – did for English football what the wingless wonders and an Irishman's shy smile had done in the mid-'60s. In Gascoigne, the game had found a star, like Best, you didn't have to know anything about football to recognise. And, suddenly, football itself was back in fashion.

Quite apart from his refreshing talents as a player, the cult of personality that grew up overnight around the young Gascoigne caught the spirit of the time. Gazza was bullish, iconoclastic and had an attention span lasting the 30 seconds of an average sound-byte. He could play football, all right; and he could play the fool, too, extravagantly well. Over the past ten years, Rupert Murdoch's *Sun* newspaper has cast itself in a similar role at the heart of the national culture. Ill-informed and xenophobic the journalism may be, but the *Sun* was – and remains – hugely influential and funny, too, in the same self-consciously outrageous vein as Gazza, the erstwhile clown prince of the paper's football pages. Gascoigne was a shot in the arm for everyone. For the *Sun*, Gazza was heaven-sent: he was one of Us, one of the boys, a little Englander who had it all and seemed genuinely not to give a toss.

The success of News International's British operation – in political as well as economic terms – helped underpin Murdoch's massively expensive move into the world's TV markets. Here, very early in the life of Sky TV, football was identified as an essential bridgehead in establishing an Empire of the Dish. As soon as Sky and the doomed – but football-friendly – BSB merged, Murdoch's foot-soldiers went shopping. It was easy: BSkyB got their 'whole new ball game' for £350 million and considered it money well spent. Football's coffers had never seen anything like it.

An élite of League clubs had been chaffing at the bit for some time. Developments like that which saw home clubs keep all their own gate receipts were very good news for the Liverpools, Arsenals and Manchester Uniteds of this world; evidence of the bigger clubs' desire to enjoy a larger proportion of what they perceived to be the fruits of their own labours. While the FA and the Football League fought a rearguard action, in line with their mandates, to channel spiralling profits at the top of the game down towards the grass roots, an ambitious minority lobbied remorselessly for greater control over the dividends to be gleaned from football's gilt-edged stocks – their own burgeoning big-city clubs. As it turned out, TV rights, a bone of contention worried over by the haves and have-nots for some time, only needed the arrival of a Murdoch on the scene to prove themselves the straw to break an evidently weary and outmoded camel's back.

BSkyB's millions are what made the Premier League work, as an idea and as a fact. Live football has been crucial in turning satellite TV into a viable commercial proposition. Almost overnight, English football – the Premier League at least – found itself swimming in serious money. The upswing in the game's popularity and a new-found and remarkable talent, at club level, for selling the product also helped to revitalise a long-moribund industry. With all but a handful of

Italian clubs staring the threat of bankruptcy in the face, English football could flex its economic muscle on the European stage for the first time. The ridiculous and unchecked spiralling of wages and transfer fees which has brought Serie A to its knees may eventually account, too, for the ambitions of many of our own leading clubs. For the time being, however, England is a glamorous option for the likes of Klinsmann and Gullit, not to mention a small army of lesser lights who have brought continental finesse to any club that can afford their wages. A couple of days after Gullit signed for Chelsea, the QPR chairman, Richard Thompson, did his best to boost his own season ticket sales by announcing his interest in bringing the world's greatest player, Roberto Baggio, to Loftus Road. It says a lot that such a preposterous claim was given serious consideration on several back pages. Domestic clubs can afford to be interested in anyone, and everyone is interested in our domestic game. Gascoigne's tears were instrumental in making football fashionable again. The ambitions of Rupert Murdoch have made it rich like never before.

* * *

'The growing pressure on clubs, players and managers has coincided with the start of the Premier League and the money at stake. Clubs in the Premiership are desperate to stay in it; those outside it are desperate to get a share of the spoils.'

Chris Waddle, May 1995

The unprecedented wealth washing around English football helped make the 1994/95 season a very strange one indeed. The Premiership is a gravy train, a seat at the big boys' table, constituted to afford its members access to both free money and the wherewithal to earn a lot more through their own efforts. Last season, as a grudging concession to the League's own manifesto promise to improve the quality of the game by pruning away some of its suffocating quantity, four clubs were due to take the drop into the Endsleigh League come the end of May. Despite the best efforts of the spin-doctors, the two-horse race for the title that developed between Blackburn Rovers and Manchester United never really captured the imagination. The scenes at Ewood Park the night after Rovers had become champions by losing at Anfield were a curiously private party laid on by a genial host, Jack Walker.

The Premiership's real drama as 1994/95 drew to a close sucked in half the competing teams in the division. Big clubs – Everton, Villa, Chelsea, Arsenal, Sheffield Wednesday – were white-faced well into the final month of the season. Because it meant losing out on a share of BSkyB's big pot and all that goes with it, the possibility of a place in the last four really did look like a 'whole new ball game'. For Ipswich, Leicester, Norwich and Crystal Palace going down meant being cast into football's equivalent of Outer Darkness. Never mind the broken hearts in the stands, the anguish in club boardrooms saw wailing and gnashing of teeth become a weekly ritual up and down the country.

Outside the top flight, too, the realities of life under football's new deal have begun to sink in. Thanks to the demands of new ground safety regulations, every club in the Football League and beyond has had to fund a capital investment programme very few were in any way prepared for. Despite the availability of Football Trust grants (which, belatedly, have now been made available to non-League clubs as well) the game's smaller fish are swimming against prevailing currents to survive. Money, now more than ever, is away upstream.

In some instances, a little investment and an effective administration can be enough. Five years ago, Carlisle United had drawn up plans to become League football's first part-time club. Last season, under Michael Knighton's chairmanship, United won the Third Division by the length of Hadrian's Wall with a fully professional playing staff intact. Elsewhere, local councils and regional businesses have been drawn into more or less ambitious ground redevelopment schemes – from Huddersfield's McAlpine Stadium through to the Bescot Stadium in Walsall – which have helped turn things round for the clubs involved, on and off the pitch. The likes of Gillingham and Exeter, though, continue to have a miserable time of it at every turn: models, perhaps, of what the future holds for the minnows of the English game.

During the course of the year, the idea of a second division for the Premiership began to do the rounds in public. It's obviously an attractive proposition for some of the bigger clubs languishing in the Football League, frustrated as the good times roll upstairs while they play host to teams who put a couple of hundred on the home attendance figures if you're lucky. It might also be a relatively painless way of bringing the number of the clubs in the current Premiership down to manageable proportions, with two divisions of high-flyers, say, of 16 teams each. More to the point, it would serve to further concentrate potential revenue at the top end of the industry. Restricting access to a proposed top two tiers of the football pyramid – to those who can compete not only on the pitch but in terms of gate receipts and commercial revenue as well – is seen by some as the only rational way forward. Many others, not surprisingly, see it as a death knell for the professional game at grassroots level. The exclusivity that makes the idea so attractive to some makes it unthinkable to a majority.

Of the 60-odd clubs in the current Football League, at least a third are beginning to think seriously about the prospect of a semi-professional future. Already they may have more in common with their counterparts in the Vauxhall Conference than with their wealthier peers. Their horizons are limited, too, not only by their teams' shortcomings but by the impossibility of real progress as commercial ventures. The show can only run as long as there's an audience ready to pay to come and see it.

Meanwhile, among the remainder – convinced of the possibility of a viable future – there's suddenly a desperate sense of urgency. Everyone's aware of which way the wind's blowing. As the richer clubs try to cut the dead wood away, widening the gap between themselves and the rest as each season passes, the rush to jump across and join them has become a stampede. For many, a high-risk strategy is the only option open to them: a bit like splashing money on a cab to the station when, for all you know, the train may be full up when you get there anyway. The feeling, though, is that any club left behind now may find the gulf unbridgeable within two or three years. Keeping your head above water will amount to just drowning slowly.

Anyone who's ever looked at their bank statement after going shopping on an empty stomach can recognise the contemporary transfer market as an appetite for prime cuts that has got completely out of hand. The price of a domestic player during 1994/95 spiralled to dizzy new heights and dragged football's wage bill along in its wake. Five years ago, we used to laugh at Italian transfer fees. Now we're paying them. There might only be a handful of takers for an Andy Cole or a Les Ferdinand, but every club in the Premiership is now solvent enough to speculate on players the market values at £2 million or £3 million. It's an extravagant game of brag, dangerously out of touch with the real value of what's being bought and sold.

Not surprisingly, the bullishness of the transfer market has already attracted the close attention of the Inland Revenue, as have the labyrinthine details of top professionals' contracts. Indeed, it was the taxman's interest which got The Bung rolling. It remains to be seen whether, in the long term, we can look forward to a genuinely thorough investigation into the corporate and individual liberties with the system which have long been taken, by way of routine perks, throughout the professional game. All concerned may be happy to settle, as many already have with Her Majesty's men, for something more along the lines of damage limitation: no names, no pack drill. The press, however, and therefore the football authorities, joined the hunt last season.

It says much about the game's importance in our daily lives, as well as everything about the credibility of our political masters, that while each new scandal surrounding a self-serving backbencher is greeted with a knowing, cynical shrug (inside the Commons and without), similar misdemeanours, as they emerged during the last football season – not just financial wrongdoings, but all the way down the scale to stories about players' use of recreational drugs – were grounds for eight months of soul-searching and finger-pointing on a national scale. It came as a shock, apparently, that backhanders and secret deals – not to mention cocaine – may be part of the fabric of our national game as they are of our political and business cultures.

The sorry drama of Paul Merson's private life and its shortcomings and the mystery surrounding some strange footage of Bruce Grobelaar shot in an hotel room by an erstwhile business partner are two stories which have perhaps already seen their best days on the back (and front) pages. Addiction, after all, is a very personal problem, unlikely to have the profound effect on football which the use of controlled substances has had on athletics for example. The Grobelaar/Segers/Fashanu scandal – finally, it seems on its way to court – remains bizarre and apparently exceptional rather than symptomatic of any more general malaise. The fall from grace of one of football's most successful managers, however, was played out like a Greek tragedy over the first seven months of 1995 and has every chance of affecting the game and its credibility for some time to come.

The scale of George Graham's achievements while manager of a club for which he had hitherto plainly had such admiration and respect, and Arsenal's own tradition – established over the course of 75 years at the top of the domestic game – as a bastion of stability and propriety, simply made the case all the more remarkable. The sacking of the man who had brought Arsenal so much success during eight years in charge was, of course, the harshest punishment that could have been settled on either party, not that much sympathy was felt for George Graham or the club under the circumstances. For a few weeks it seemed like a lot of closed doors in football were about to be prised open. Interestingly, though, the relative indifference which has succeeded the furious self-righteousness provoked in all quarters by What George Did would seem to corroborate Graham's own publicly expressed opinion: that his was a show trial, effective and high profile enough to calm the pack.

The exposure of the Arsenal manager's hand in the transfer till was supposed to be Exhibit A, only part of the first ever thorough investigation into what has long been tacitly recognised as commonplace malpractice. After their early season mauling at the hands of Tottenham's Alan Sugar, however, football's governing bodies are perhaps only too well aware that any attempt at root and branch examination of how clubs conduct their business affairs may simply land the game expensively, and embarrassingly, in court. It's reasonable to assume that any further de-bunging will be down to more dirty work by HM Inspector of Taxes or the gentlemen of the press. Greed, after all, whether on an individual or a corporate level, is always going to mean a few bob extra for the Revenue and a ready source of headlines for any editor who wants to dig a little.

* * *

'You're going to get your f***ing heads kicked in!'

Traditional

After a decade of relative calm, the other profound shock which in the 1994/95 season had in store was the re-emergence of violence in and around football grounds both here and abroad, where English teams were the visitors. It had seemed that improvements in crowd control and a genuine change of heart on the part of football supporters in general – fanzines and independent supporters' associations springing up, post-Heysel, in place of the crews of the '70s – had stemmed a tide that had disfigured and occasionally threatened to engulf the national game. As football came back into fashion, fighting seemed to be on the way out. Women and children returned to the game in numbers as CCTV and then the recommendations of the Taylor Report came on-line. By the early '90s, many people were enjoying live football who'd never seen trouble at a ground in their lives: aggro was the exception rather than the rule it had been for nearly 30 years.

Away from the cameras and the grounds, the problem rumbled on involving a committed and often politicised minority. However, they no longer drew in the hundreds of game hangers-on, who'd been happy to be seen giving it the big one on terraces all over the country since the early '60s. In

1994/95, though, the old malevolent tendency staged a very visible comeback. The violent scenes at Stamford Bridge after a Cup game against Millwall were like something out of old newsreel footage, so unfamiliar had such behaviour become to the majority of fans. Worse followed. Chelsea's progress to the semi-finals of the European Cup Winners' Cup attracted a small army of fellow travellers, many boasting their allegiance to far-right organisations, from all over the country. These away trips were by way of rehearsal for the main event at a disastrously unprepared Lansdowne Road in February. While from club to club those bent on using football as a battleground may number only dozens, when gathered together at the behest of fascist groups like Combat 18 they remain a minority who can pose a serious threat to football, as England's visit to Dublin showed. The televised pictures were a chilling remainder that the problem hasn't gone away. Terry Venables faces some very obvious difficulties preparing a team that will be ready to face the best in Europe next summer. The police, stewards and local authorities will have a job on their hands, too, if the hooligans make good their promises to disrupt Euro '96, here on our doorstep. A lot of hard work has gone into making football family-friendly. If the game's not to go backwards, Dublin – slack on the English side, naïve on the Irish – mustn't happen again. The biggest shock that night, perhaps, was how many people seemed to be taken by surprise.

Football violence, though perpetrated by a minority, thrives when the majority allow a nakedly aggressive atmosphere to develop unchecked. I was at a Wycombe versus Huddersfield match earlier this year when an away fan assaulted the Wycombe number three after the hapless player stumbled into the advertising boards at the Huddersfield end. It was a bizarre moment – completely out of context given the partisan but good-humoured atmosphere, despite an early sending-off – and plainly visible 50 yards away. The full-back caught a right hook as he pulled himself to his feet, then turned and walked away – as if he couldn't believe it had happened either. The Adams Park stewards moved in quickly and the spectator was escorted from the ground with a minimum of fuss. The game was memorable for two late goals that secured a home win. I wrote a match report and found I hadn't even mentioned the incident, so completely out of keeping was it with the match at which it had happened. One nutter, who could just as well have lost it, one suspects, at the local supermarket, doesn't really rate a mention.

When it's a case of Man Bites Dog, though, nutter or not, some kind of stir is inevitable. The colour of envy in football these days is red. Or sometimes green and yellow, or black, or, occasionally, blue: the confusion's part of the problem. Manchester United, season 1994/95's disappointments notwithstanding, are the team of the moment in English football. Not only have they enjoyed unparalleled on-field success, they have become the best-sold club in world football. As a business venture, United PLC leaves its nearest competitors, Arsenal and Newcastle, standing. Both aspects of United's success have given rise to a certain resentment among supporters of other teams: away from home, over the past couple of years particularly, an atmosphere of bitterness and confrontation has seemed to follow the club around. Occasionally, the behaviour of some of the team's players, and the unwillingness of management to criticise or recognise the implications of that behaviour, have helped to make the situation worse. Too often United games are an excuse for angry confrontation.

The atmosphere at Selhurst Park the night Eric Cantona launched his notorious assault on a particularly unsavoury Palace fan was typically poisonous, the potential for violence seething just below the surface, both between the players and up in the stands. Unlike the incident at Adams Park a couple of weeks before, Cantona's actions – shocking as they were – weren't out of keeping with the tenor of the evening's events. The supporter, after all, was the second person Cantona kicked that evening – he'd just been sent off for kicking Richard Shaw. Indeed, Mr Simmonds – unconvincingly portrayed as the 'victim' after the event – was only too ready to fight back. The pair probably deserved each other: both behaved shamefully. The murder of a Crystal Palace supporter before an FA Cup semi-final between the two teams three months later showed clearly that the ill-feeling which contributed so much to the original incident hadn't been addressed since. Nor had it come the replay, when Roy Keane was sent off for stamping on the Palace captain, Southgate.

Football spent much of the season in the dock. As well as Cantona's appearance before Croydon magistrates, Paul Elliott failed to set the envisaged legal precedents in his civil action against Dean Saunders over an incident during a game at Anfield which had finished the Chelsea player's career. After helping Everton to victory in the FA Cup final, Duncan Ferguson returned to Scotland and a custodial sentence as a result of an assault on an opposing player. The implication is that the game's own disciplinary measures – and its capacity to act as an arbiter in industrial disputes – no longer retain any real degree of credibility. The danger is that recourse to the courts, for whatever reason, puts football in the hands of people who know little and care less about the sport.

At present, whether the issue is crowd problems, player indiscipline or corrupt business practice, football's own contribution too often appears to be part of the problem rather than a part of any solution. The Football Association, sad to say, saw its already frail grip on the important issues weaken still further during 1994/95. The authorities invariably appear slow to react and feeble when they do so. Inevitable, when the events of each new week seemed always to catch Lancaster Gate completely unawares. Football's own inertia when dealing with any but the most parochial issues is the reason that government, the media and the courts have been the agents of change in the game over the years.

It's only too easy to blame everything on the FA. It should be remembered, however, that it's an organisation which simply isn't constituted to deal with the pace and scale of change within the modern game. The FA was established to look after the interests of a very popular sport in the late nineteenth century. It's perhaps asking too much that the same organisation be capable of controlling a burgeoning multi-million pound industry. The Association's structure is like those which existed within individual clubs 20 or 30 years ago. When things moved on, apparently, nobody thought to ring Lancaster Gate and let them know.

It's unfair – and not very constructive – to use the FA as a convenient scapegoat. It may be an easy target, but criticism of the Association has become too regular a routine for deflecting responsibility away from the vested interests within football – and in Parliament, the media and the legal profession, too – who prosper while Graham Kelly and his cohorts struggle under the sheer weight of everybody else's dirty washing. As the events of the troubled season of 1994/95 so clearly demonstrate, there's now an urgent need to apply some of the energy and expertise which has revitalised English club football in recent years to the potentially ruinous problems which face the game as a whole. Means must be found to identify, represent and rationally control the divergent interests tugging at the unity of the modern professional game.

At the moment, the supposedly central role of the FA is undermined by the organisation's lack of any real authority. The environment's unstable, leaving self-interested – and often shortsighted – parties free to pursue their own agendas without accepting any responsibility for the well-being of the game as a whole. In the long term, those who may profit now at the expense of football's lesser lights could come unstuck if their margins continue to be swallowed up in the spiral of transfer fees and wages. The lesson of the world's most successfully governed sports – American football, the NBA, the PGA tours – is that if the whole body's healthy, its constituent parts will prosper too.

Perhaps football's new-found riches have everybody too enthralled to think responsibly about the future beyond the next couple of seasons' profit column. It's to be hoped that alarm bells will start ringing soon. It's time the will was found to gather all those with any kind of investment in the game's future – not only chairmen and administrators, but the players, the managers and the customer, supporters, too – to consider seriously what kind of future that may be. Football's the beautiful game. It's also a very attractive product, unstable and dynamic enough to be exploited by those who care little for the best interests of the sport or those who work in it and watch it. Mesmerised by half-baked free-market philosophy, are we going to sell out to whoever puts most cash in the pot without considering why the cash is on offer or how best to use it to the game's advantage? There are a lot of clever people in the industry and a handful of wise ones. And a reassuring number of both who, besides good business sense and political *savoir faire*, set some store by the integrity of football as a whole. Too many, though, are on the periphery, either working exclusively in a particular field or at a particular club. Those people, covering every aspect of the industry – from top-line financial and commercial management through to youth and community development – need to be involved at the heart of things, in long-term planning and the execution of day-to-day practice. If football is to continue to prosper, it needs to develop a coherent perspective that draws people together rather than setting them apart. The first step, of course, must be to establish a sense of common purpose. Perhaps that's to be found in an appeal to football's lifeblood: passion for the game.

* * *

'It's all to do with how we get our kids to play.'
Gary Lineker, June 1995

Don't get me wrong. Football's in rude good health just now. It may be a good idea, though, to pause for breath while so much is going on, getting and spending. Amidst the TV deals, the sales of replica shirts, the big-name transfers, the takeover bids and the forest of headlines, there's every danger that the well could run dry. It's the game that makes the industry work. There's a real contradiction here: the industry, increasingly, is run by highly motivated professionals; the game, in many respects, remains in the hands of embattled amateurs. The time's come for the same attention to be brought to bear on securing football's future as is concentrated at present on realising its market potential. The problem is one that defines what has gone wrong with much of British industry in general: wealth that should be invested in research and long-term development is hived off to fund profit margins and provide shareholders with unrealistically generous short-term returns. Football, though, matters too much to too many people for that to be allowed to happen. Doesn't it?

The development of young players in this country is, perhaps, a model of what has gone wrong, and may offer a guide as to what needs to be done to put things right. The organisations ostensibly empowered to look after the interests of schoolboy football – the FA and, more particularly, the English Schools FA – are and have been run by amateurs and staffed by bureaucrats to a dangerous degree. The professional game will, by definition, be at the cutting edge of developments in coaching, theory and assessment. At the same time, the professionals will have their own specific interest in the production of talented youngsters which may not always be in the interests of youth football as a whole, a participation sport to be enjoyed by a majority of boys who have no pretensions to becoming involved in the professional game. On the continent – Dutch football, and this year's European Cup winners Ajax specifically, are obvious examples of the benefits – the game's governing bodies and the professionals involved in the industry long ago sat down and co-operated, to decide on policy and hammer out the practical details of how best to realise shared goals while still accommodating partisan interests.

In England, meanwhile, the two sides wasted at least 30 years on a policy of thinly disguised confrontation. Gifted youngsters played far too many games at too young an age as the ESFA's agenda for boys' football rolled on unchallenged. Professional clubs and professional coaches were seen as dangerous, threatening the interests of innocent young people – and, of course, the ESFA's own control over them. The professionals, for their part, pursued their own policies, often in direct contravention of regulations which, in some respects, were there to protect the interests of the boys involved. The services of young players were too often acquired by subterfuge: although involvement with professional clubs gave boys the coaching and experience that could offer them a future in the game, the fact that this was happening behind schools' backs undermined the boys' and football's integrity. Whatever the ethical and cultural issues raised – and problems like illegal payments to schoolboy players and the appalling narrowness of many young footballers' experience beyond the confines of the game remain to be addressed – the practical outcome was all too clear. Generations of young players have come into professional football who, because of playing too much and not training enough, were able to defend at corners and hit long balls into channels but struggled with basic technique. While slowly, belatedly, the problem is being faced up to, with the development of schools of excellence and the improvement of professional clubs' access to the best young players, the effects of decades of conflict between clubs and schools are still being felt, nowhere more keenly than at the level of the England team's preparations for the 1996 European Championships.

The pace of change remains sluggish. The game's governing bodies must accept – indeed encourage – professionals to do what they do best. Of course schoolboys should be able to have access to the best coaching and the best facilities, those available within professional clubs. Instead of trying to impede what is now the obvious way forward, those working outside club football can concentrate on the importance of their own contributions: schools will always be vital in uncovering and promoting young talent, in promoting the sport's relevance far beyond its professional manifestation; governing bodies will need to co-ordinate national policy that protects the interests of the boys themselves and of the game as a whole.

Schoolboy football is one instance which raises the relevant issues. A change of heart's needed at all levels and in all areas. The game's professionals must become central to running football as a whole. It's too complex and demands too much specialist knowledge and experience to be left in the hands of bureaucrats and a handful of club chairmen who've never played the game or watched it from the terraces. If those professionals can become working members of the football establishment, there's every chance of investing that establishment's broad perspective with the understanding, foresight and authority which, at the moment, it so plainly lacks.

It's supporters' passion for the game that has made a football industry possible, of course. The fans' role within the industry, though, beyond helping to fund it, is negligible to the point of complete invisibility. It's ironic that the people who, perhaps, should have the last word are seldom heard at all. Football's always done its best to keep its customers at arm's length: we're necessary but not altogether desirable. Everything possible's being done to make the game attractive to a new breed of corporate customer, who promises a higher spend-per-head and money in the bank before the season's even under way. But while ground improvements and stewarding arrangements are offered as evidence of a new deal for fans, the relationship between football and its ordinary and long-suffering supporters shows no sign of really changing very much. While clubs rushed to comply with all-seater legislation, the bulk of the Taylor Report's recommendations with regard to consulting, involving and empowering the game's customers have been studiously overlooked. A few forums and questionnaires, whose real function is to furnish clubs with mailing lists, are not really what Lord Justice Taylor had in mind. It's not only an appeal to natural justice: common sense tells you that supporters, loyal, passionate and articulate, must have more to offer football than the price of a match-day seat.

* * *

A fleeting moment, a hint of grace,
Brings back a feeling, a time, a place . . .
Gordon Jeffrey, from Men On The Terraces

To return to Glenn Hoddle's 110 good things: the problems roughly sketched here only matter because football itself matters so much. The complaints, the gloom, the anger only find their way into print and a million conversations a day because the good things in football make people care so much about it. Glenn Hoddle himself, of course, is one of those Good Things: the style and substance of a new kind of club manager – a generation of ex-players whose continued involvement in the game comes from their love of it rather than needing to make a living from it – may be an important part of a very bright future as regards how we play football in this country from now on.

In fact, the simplicity and accessibility of the sport aside, most of the Good Things in the game are the people working in it, and the values they represent: imagination, talent, honesty, endeavour, loyalty or, simply, the ability to tell a good story very well. The stories of the 90 people collected here come from all levels – and every corner – of English professional club football, outlining lives devoted to the game. Taken together, they may offer some insight into how the whole business works. Certainly it wouldn't work without them. It goes without saying, perhaps, that although the details and perspectives of the stories vary enormously, the single quality they all share is the one without which football couldn't function: a passion for the game.

It's All About Players

THE PROFESSIONAL FOOTBALLER

I do miss what it was like playing for the school when you could just shine and look good. Now, everything you do, you feel you've got to do it right because there's a contract at stake in a few months' time.

Ross Taylor

And it's all down to 90 minutes on a Saturday for you to prove yourself – to the club, your team-mates and the fans.

Cyrille Regis

Football's the most important thing in my life and I can't do anything to jeopardise that.

Chris Sutton

As far as I can see, the main enjoyment in football comes from playing the game.

Gary Mabbutt

Ross Taylor, second year trainee, Arsenal

Recent FA legislation means that boys don't have to make any formal commitment to a football club until they're 16 and sign YTS forms, the contemporary equivalent of an apprentice's contract. They'll spend two years as trainees, at which point the club involved may or may not offer them professional terms. Ross Taylor, a young full-back, played his schoolboy football in Southend, winning representative honours at district, county and international levels. He's a second-year trainee at Arsenal, a club famous for offering its young players every chance to come through into first-team football.

I grew up in Southend. I've always lived there and when I was young I got scouted by a few London clubs but ended up going to West Ham when I was 12 or 13. I trained there for a while and they offered me schoolboy terms. Arsenal came in for me quite late on. I came to Highbury and had a look around – I went to a few clubs, you know, to see the facilities and what the coaching was like – and it was on the basis of all that that I decided to sign for them. I talked the whole thing through with my dad and we both agreed. It's not been a bad move, as it's turned out! I signed YTS forms in 1992.

It's funny, you don't realise what a big decision it is you're making until after you actually sign. That comes from talking to people and working with the club once you're here. It was a bit of a shock when I started, all the chores. I didn't think I'd have to be doing all these cleaning jobs and all that! But it's been all right. You get bored with all the duties but you've got to do it, haven't you, if you want to become a footballer?

I used to come up on the train, which was hard work! Now, I drive up to the training ground to get there about 9.30 to do all our jobs, putting kit out, cones, bibs, balls, all that before anyone starts training. We start about 10.15, 10.30. The training's harder at the beginning of the week and eases off before games. But we do all the physical work and then games, five-a-sides. After training it's putting everything away again, load things up and, when it's your turn, take everything back to the ground. And then drive back to Southend. I used to be in digs but, now I've got the car, I'm back with my mum and dad.

I've had every injury going. Shin splints, hernia, the lot! You do worry about it a bit, but the physios here know what they're doing. Most important, they know straightaway if something's serious or not. Obviously, you want to be out there playing especially as you've only got one or two seasons to prove yourself. One lad my age came here and snapped his cruciate ligaments almost straightaway. He's only just come back so he's got half a season to show what he can do.

Pat Rice, the youth team manager, works on lots of different things because different people need help with different parts of their game. One day we'll do running if someone's short on fitness, another day we'll just work on technique. Me personally, I need to work on everything! Pat doesn't miss out on anything: you need to develop as a complete player.

For a game on Saturday, we kick off at 10.45 so we come into the club at nine. That means I have to get up earlier than in the week so I'm always knackered! I have to leave plenty of time to drive up from Southend so I'm usually here early. Then we all go up to the game together. Even if we have a game in Southend, I'd have to travel up to go back on the coach with everyone else for the game and then come back here again after to pick up my car.

I do miss what it was like playing for the school when you could just shine and look good. Now, everything you do, you feel you've got to do it right because there's a contract at stake in a few months' time. No one tells you off but you feel you're letting yourself down if you do things wrong. You still have a laugh, but it's a lot more serious. In a year's time, you could be on the dole. It means, as well, your relationship with other trainees is more acquaintances than friends. We have a laugh together, but the next fellow could end up taking your place, couldn't he?

I feel I'm doing okay. I hope I'll get a pro contract at the end of this season. There's nothing else I want to do but play football. I've set myself goals. At the end of my first year, I said I'd push for the reserves this season and I've played the last ten games. The target now is to hold on to that place, to be consistent. You know, you have dreams – lying in bed, thinking about playing for the first team, scoring goals in the Cup final – but there's some work to be done, isn't there? Like I said, I need to work on the lot!

Danny Granville, Cambridge United

Danny Granville grew up in North London. He's now a first-year professional at Cambridge United. Given the stature of the club, it's no surprise that Granville has already had the chance to prove himself in the first team, making appearances at left-back and in midfield during a difficult season in Division Two.

I started playing football about as young as you can get. I played for my local team, my school team. While I was at secondary school, I started training with Charlton. I was at Tottenham for a little while, too, and it was playing for them I got spotted by Cambridge who offered me a YTS place. Football's all I ever wanted to do, so that felt like quite a big step forward. I didn't do too well, my first year as a trainee. I found it hard, living away from home for the first time. The manager at the time – the first-team manager – didn't really take to me. He was very strong on discipline and, with being homesick and everything, I found that difficult at first. There were a few of us, though, who were living together at the hostel, all of us in the same boat, and you just come through it, you know: you're all together, all trying to make a living by playing football. It's funny, though, lads who don't make it – the ones who fall by the wayside – you're good mates with them but when they go, once they've finished with football, you never hear from them again. You never know if that might happen to you. You do your best in games but there could be something else, aside from football, that goes wrong, couldn't there?

Coming straight from school, all the chores hit me a bit hard! As well as training, you've got all the jobs like cleaning the pro's boots, keeping the dressing-rooms clean. If the first team was at home, we'd come down to the ground after we'd played our Youth Team game and work as ballboys. One time they even had us shovelling manure up at the training ground! I suppose you just get used to it after a while, in the same way your body gets used to the training. I think it was good, really. Especially with being away from home, I think I learnt a lot and grew up quite quickly.

By the second year of the YTS I was doing much better. I felt like I'd already learnt a lot, and I'm quite a confident person, anyway. You try hard in games and in training and you try not to do anything wrong off the field, too. They give you an idea of what's going to happen afterwards, but you have to finish your two years before you know for sure if they're going to take you on as a pro. I was managing all right on the money anyway: £29.50 the first year, £35 the second year. Coming straight from school, I'd never known any better!

I'd thought about it already so, when the club offered me professional terms, I accepted straightaway. I'd had to think about what I'd do either way, if I was offered a contract or not. I'd even got some digs sorted out for if I did turn pro and had to leave the YTS boys' hostel, and that's where I'm living now, with the family of a lad in Cambridge who's a YTS now.

Once you turn pro, a lot of things change. The money's better! There's a lot more pressure because you're playing against men for the first time instead of boys your own age. Training, reserve games: it's all a lot more physical and a much better standard, and you've got to start trying to match those standards. I was playing for the reserves and went out on loan for a couple of months to a non-League team, Saffron Walden. I really enjoyed that. I thought I did quite well and I was playing twice a week instead of once a fortnight like you do in the reserves.

I still enjoy training but there's a bit more pressure now, isn't there? It's my living now and so it has to be more serious as I get older. You have to learn about playing in front of a crowd, too. When I was at Saffron Walden, we played at Aldershot who had 2,000 or 3,000 people in. I made my debut as a sub here against Gillingham, for the first team, and there was the same kind of crowd.

The first game for the first team, I didn't know I was going to be involved until the last minute. I was nervous beforehand but once I came on, I just got on with it, you know. I think I did all right. I suppose I set myself goals. The next one is to get another contract here. Then, to get a few more games under my belt for the first team. Beyond that, I suppose you have to think about moving on to a bigger club at some point to make a name for yourself in the game. You know, you have to be positive. You'll never play for England if you don't think you can. But in football it's down to hard work. Whatever people get in the game, they have to work for, don't they? This is a good club, a friendly club, and they've got high hopes for the youth players coming through which makes it good for someone like me. It means I'm going to get a chance.

Lee Power, Bradford City

Although he grew up in South-east London, Lee Power came up through the youth system at Norwich, winning a first-team chance and international honours while still an apprentice. At ·21, he was transferred to Bradford City in 1993 for £200,000. Since then, Power has struggled with injury and illness. In season 1994/95 he was able to start just nine games, scoring five goals.

I think memories are what keeps you going in football because you want to make more of them. It's strange, while things are happening you can't take them in. A couple of seasons ago, I had a run in the first team at Norwich and scored seven goals in 11 games, our first season in Europe. While it was going on and I was scoring goals and getting all the publicity, I wasn't thinking about it: I was just happy, on a high. But I bought a tape of the season and since I've been at Bradford, if I've been depressed or feel I've lost my chance in the Premiership, I'll look at that and it makes me laugh. No one can take that away from me, can they? I may not have achieved as much as some people but at least, if I was to get run over or something tomorrow, I played 50 games in the Premier League. Millions of kids grow up wishing they could just play one and I've had the chance to play against some of the best players in the world. And if I play a season for Bradford and score 25 goals, it'll be the same: it'll be the season after I'll appreciate it, enjoying the memory.

As a kid, I never had any doubt that I was going to be a player. My last two years at school I drove my mum and dad mad, bunking off school. I was only a schoolboy at Norwich but I just knew I was going to be offered an apprenticeship. I thought I didn't need to bother going to school! I found out later that I only just scraped in as an apprentice but by then I was working hard. I was top scorer in the youth team and everything, and I broke into the first team at 18. The one thing I regret about that time was my attitude to money. I was getting first-team bonuses and spending it like a first-team player, going to the casino and all that. But when I came out of the team I wasn't on a first-team salary, of course, but I kept spending it like I was! I didn't really understand about money.

I suppose I started to run before I could walk. I was getting all the publicity, Jack Charlton said nice things about me and I played for the Irish under-21s at 17. I thought I had a God-given right to be in the first team and that meant I couldn't understand it when I wasn't. And, it's a thing with managers: they won't be straight with you about why. They'll lie to you rather than just say: *I think he's better than you.* Even if I think he's wrong, I can't argue with that, can I?

To tell you the truth, I always thought I'd leave Norwich. When you're a kid at a club, I don't think you get the same chance as a player that comes in from outside. I scored seven goals in 11 games, a better ratio than Mark Robbins, but as soon as Mark was fit he was back in the team. I thought the only way I was going to get on was by being sold. If a club pays money for you, they're going to want to play you. You've got a better chance. I was on loan to a few clubs who couldn't afford to buy me. I don't know what went on, really. I know Newcastle were interested. Norwich wanted too much money for me but then agreed to sell me, for less, to Bradford! I know at least one other club that would have paid the same money but Norwich wouldn't talk to them! Obviously, I couldn't say too much because I knew things which, according to regulations, I shouldn't have known. But I knew enough to realise I wasn't being told what was really going on.

To be fair, I've come up to Bradford now and everybody's been smashing. The chairman's been brilliant. When I first got here I was really ill with this virus that attacked my nervous system. I was in hospital for two weeks: I was shaking, out of breath, I couldn't do anything. That was after I'd played just two games. I'd scored both games and everything was flying, then the illness hit me. I couldn't play for two months but the club was brilliant. They've got me to see the specialists, the chairman was phoning up every day to see how I was. This may be a lower division, but I'm happy being at a smaller club where the people around actually seem to appreciate you. The club and the people make me happy I've moved here. As for the illness, the specialists told me it was stress-related. It's funny, I've never been someone who got bothered about things, even all the hassle with Norwich before I left. But I think I came here and it all caught up with me. They told me it's the kind of thing that's waiting to happen to you. I won't know for a while when I'm going to be all right.

It's a different world in the Second Division. I mean, at a Premiership club like Norwich you're spoilt, really. You can see the difference in all sorts of odd things: the cars in the car park, the amounts of money in card games on the away coach, the facilities at the training ground, having to wash your own training kit. But who knows? In a couple of years' time, Bradford could be in the Premiership and Norwich could have come in the opposite direction. That's football: everything could change. I've just got to get my head down here and see what happens. I'm only 22 now.

But what I said before about memories, I'll tell you one thing I'll always remember. You know how when you're a kid playing football, you always used to pretend to be someone? You know: *I'll be Kevin Keegan!* Well, the Sunday after my second full game for Norwich – we'd won 3–1 at QPR and I'd scored two – I'd read all the papers – they were full of it – and I was just dozing off. I'd left my window open and there were some kids playing football outside and I heard them going: *I'll be Power! No, I'll be Power! I want to be Power!* That's as big a buzz as I've ever had in football: not even playing, just listening to these kids pretending to be me.

Chris Sutton, Blackburn Rovers

Chris Sutton's father played football professionally for Norwich, Chester and Carlisle and continues to be a significant influence on Sutton junior's burgeoning career. In 1994, Sutton's £5 million transfer to Blackburn Rovers made him the English game's most expensive player until Andy Cole joined Manchester United. Sutton's partnership with Alan Shearer produced over 50 goals in their first season together, helping Blackburn to the Premiership title.

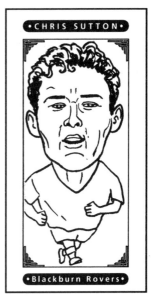

I was born in Nottingham but grew up in Norwich. I played football at school and for a local Sunday team, and then signed up for Norwich when I was 16. That was after they'd bombed me out when I was about 12! I'd been at the Centre of Excellence. They make a decision each year about who they think will be good enough to make it, and they bombed me out. But then, when they signed me at 16, lots of the boys they'd kept on at 12 they let go.

I always wanted to be a player. But wanting and doing are two different things, aren't they? I can still remember at school painting pictures of myself as a star footballer, you know, but I got very disillusioned when Norwich bombed me out. The thought that I wasn't good enough was terrible: I was gutted. I even turned to playing cricket! For a while I was better at that than football. I was still at school when Norwich came back to sign me as a YTS.

Those two years as a trainee are all the time you've got to prove yourself – which is harsh, isn't it? You're still very young. Personally, I was a late developer anyway. Getting in as a trainee, you've got to have luck. You may have trials over two or three days and you've got to play well on those particular days. Once you're in, though, it's not luck: you've got two years and you're either good enough or you're not. Even if you can't make it at that club, you may get an opportunity somewhere else if you're let go after the two years. That's what happened to David Platt, isn't it? He left Man United and went to Crewe.

My dad always had confidence in me and he's been brilliant over the years. He's the same with my little brother now. My dad looks deeper than football: he's into all this plyometrics. That's special training to build up both the fast and slow muscle fibres. He does it with my little brother: he's like Super Boy! He did some of it with me but didn't know so much about it all until the past couple of years. He's helped me a lot with my running though, to give me a base for my game.

The important thing for me was I always had my dad to talk to. He was always very fair. He was the PE teacher at my school and when I was playing for the school he used to crucify me! I don't think I ever played a good game, in his eyes anyway. I could score six goals but he'd be saying: *This wasn't right or that wasn't right.* It really helped me. I'd rather he was like that than a dad who was always saying: *Well done.* I go and watch my brother play now and all the dads see their boys as the be-all and end-all, even if they're useless. My dad's very honest and I couldn't change anything. He made sure I was never complacent. Even when I signed up at 16, I knew I was going to have to get my head down and work really hard. And I could always turn to him for advice – and still can. He's like my agent, even though he's not an expert on contracts and things like that. He'll talk to people and find things out. He still slaughters me after games if I'm not good enough, too!

The thing with my dad is he looks so deeply into everything. He helps me with training during the summer. If I've got an injury, he'll get all the books out about it, talk to specialists. And I really listen to him now, respect what he has to say. Of course, it wasn't always like that. When I joined Norwich I could have stayed at home but I moved into digs. It was just wanting to be independent, I suppose. I did go off the rails for a while there. For some reason, I've always been mates with lunatics and I almost got thrown out of the club at one point. But I hope I've learnt a few things over the years. Certainly, I've realised that football's the most important thing in my life and I can't do anything to jeopardise that. I still have a good time but I know I've got to give myself the chance to be at my best for football. Getting that balance is one thing me and dad don't always see eye to eye on. I think he's a bit too serious sometimes!

Looking back, it's so important what you do as a youngster. I can remember dad having me doing cross-countries and gym work at school which I just hated but it's paying off now. I'm still getting stronger and quicker and a lot of that's down to all that work. He worked with me on my left foot, too, which still isn't as strong as it could be, but it's better. You should see my brother, though: completely two-footed, which is great.

I'm glad I was at Norwich, too. A lot of the big clubs, you don't get the same chance. I got into the first team as a second-year trainee and there have been lots of lads like me at Carrow Road who had that opportunity. The thing is to make yourself a regular: to get past that stage of being in for a couple of games and then back to the reserves. A regular place in the first team gives an incredible boost to your confidence. And that's when opportunities like a move to Blackburn come up, isn't it? But when clubs are looking at you, and you know it, you've got to shut that out of your mind and work on the game. Nobody signs you on the strength of one or two good performances. Whatever club you're at that's the essential thing, isn't it? You've got to work to be consistent, to never get complacent. And now all the training as a kid's paying off. It's when you're young – slogging up and down sand dunes at Lowestoft with dad – that you can really maximise your potential. The last couple of years, it's all started to click.

Cyrille Regis, Wycombe Wanderers

Ask any of his managers – Ron Atkinson, say, or John Sillett – to name their model professional and there's a good chance Cyrille Regis will be the first player that comes to mind. Now at Wycombe at the tail-end of a memorable career with West Brom, Coventry, Aston Villa, Wolves and England, Regis remains as enthusiastic about the game – and the job – as he's ever been. His route into the game and the challenges he faced as a young player have left him with an attitude to football that's able to marry a sense of romance with hard-nosed pragmatism.

Being born in French Guyana, I didn't have a football background. When I came here, at primary school in Kensal Rise, I used to play but I wasn't outstanding. Then I went to secondary school, Cardinal Hinsley, and when I tried out for the school team I couldn't make it. I was a right-winger then. It wasn't till I was about 13 that I crept into the first team. I would say I was a late developer. I just loved playing football: you know, my parents used to go crazy because I'd wear out a new pair of shoes in a week! But, looking back on it, I never really had any aspirations to become a footballer, maybe because there weren't really any role models. I mean, I remember Clyde Best – and Pele, of course – but black players were very rare in England. What motivated me – and does to this day – was just the love of playing. I still remember, as some of the best times of my life, just putting jackets down for goals and playing in the street with a load of your mates.

Anyway, I progressed through school and youth club teams – I played with Mike and Steve Gatting for Oxford and

Kilburn youth club – and I played for the borough. Mid-'70s, I was playing for Rider Brent Valley, Sunday mornings in Regents Park – we used to change in the back of a works van – when I met a man called John Sullivan who was at Molesey Football Club. He asked me to go down there – I was 16 – and I played a couple of games, and the next season I signed a contract: £5 a week. He used to sidle up to you and slip it into your pocket: I thought it was great! I was an electrician and I was only earning £15 to £20 at work!

I scored quite a lot of goals for Molesey and some bigger non-League clubs came in for me, but I told them I was under contract. Eventually, Hayes wanted me and told me I couldn't be under contract at 16! So, the fellow had been lying to me, really, and I just walked out of Molesey. My first season at Hayes I scored 24 goals and pro clubs started sniffing around but no one was ready to put money down.

By the time I was 19, I'd done all my exams and was a fully qualified B-grade electrician. I thought I was too late for pro football and, anyway, I was getting £30 or £40 a week, plus bonuses, at Hayes and I had a good job. You still didn't see any black players in League football. I thought: *It's all right. I'm enjoying what I'm doing.* But that was when Ronnie Allen, chief scout at West Brom, came down and said they wanted to buy me! I signed in May 1977.

The firm I was working for said they'd keep a job open for me in case things didn't work out. I packed my bags and went up there – at 19, it was a bit daunting – and I was frightened, really. But as you know, things worked out! It's interesting, though: it could all have been different. WBA weren't sure about me: Ronnie Allen actually bought me with £5,000 of his own money, to be repaid if I was successful!

Once I got there, though, it all happened very quickly. Even so, it took time to get used to: physically, it was a strain switching to full time and mentally, too – playing in front of thousands of people when you're used to a couple of hundred! But it was a fabulous side and that helped. It's easier for a young player coming in if the team's successful and there are some experienced players: we had Laurie Cunningham, Bryan Robson, John Wile, Derek Statham, Ally

Brown. It was a fantastic side. I think it helped me, too, that I hadn't played youth football. I'd been playing against men since I was 16, getting knocked about, learning the tricks. It's a big jump for kids, having to start playing against the likes of me now!

Looking back, it was quite radical, that team. There were some black players around – Luther Blissett, Viv Anderson, Ricky Hill, Garth Crooks – but mostly in the lower divisions. West Brom were First Division and we had three: me, Laurie and Brendan Batson. We used to get some flak, big time! You know, I can remember, say, the whole of the Shed going: *Nigger! Nigger! Lick my boots!* Monkey chants, throwing bananas, the whole works. You're not thinking about yourself as a pioneer or a role model, are you? You're just trying to deal with it and, from that, you do develop an inner strength and learn to turn pressure to your own advantage. I'm lucky that I've never come across serious racism in the teams, the players, I've played with. To be honest, now, the anti-racist campaigns coming in are really good but they're 15 years too late. Most teams now have black players and that's what's changed things. You'll still get isolated incidents but when I started it was racist chanting, 10,000 people at a time!

The full-time game brings a lot of new things to deal with: money, fame, the media, public criticism. It's still fun, but it's a different kind of fun. There's a pressure to perform. You're aware that there's a spiral – loss of form, out of the team, loss of fitness, no new contract – it can take just a couple of years to slip out of the game. All it needs is for the wrong person to be running the club, for your confidence to go, and you're into that spiral. You can only feel secure, that you've made it, when you can look back on ten or 15 years as a pro. I would say that when you become a real pro is when you have to dig in and pull yourself through when times are bad. And it's all down to 90 minutes on a Saturday for you to prove yourself – to the club, your team-mates and the fans.

Anders Limpar, Everton

Anders Limpar has played top-flight football all over Europe during the past seven years. Limpar joined Arsenal in 1990 and was an integral part of the team that lost just once in winning the First Division championship in 1991. After moving to Everton in 1994 Limpar was outstanding in his new team's successful FA Cup run. He has been capped 52 times by Sweden.

There are no professional players in Sweden. We are all amateurs so my ambition was always to play abroad, professionally: for the money, yes, but also for the experience. I began at six years old and I played in the Swedish Third Division when I was 15. My first year we went up, so I played in the Second Division when I was 16. I moved to a team in Gothenburg a little while later and played for the first time in the Swedish Premiership when I was 20. Like all players in Sweden, I had a job at the same time – I was a salesman in a sports shop – and trained every evening after work.

I became a professional player in Switzerland, where I played for Young Boys for a year before I moved to Italy and joined Cremonese. It was quite hard, after five or six years with an ordinary job, to know what to do with my spare time! I was in a foreign country and didn't know the language at first. It was a culture shock, really: you have to meet new people, make new friends and learn a new language while playing really good football at the top level. You have to really concentrate hard to learn the language. At first, that's the most important thing. I was lucky that, as a Scandinavian, German is very like Swedish – the same grammar – and it was quite easy to learn. It took six months to get to where I could speak properly and understand. Then you can put the schoolbooks away and concentrate completely on football.

Obviously, from the start I had big ambitions. I'd always wanted to play in the big leagues in Italy or England or Germany, with the best players. When I joined Young Boys, though, I was simply trying to improve my game. I was very happy there. I wasn't thinking of it as a stepping-stone to bigger things. But after six or eight months I realised I could be something in Switzerland and then take another step, which I did when I moved to Italy.

Just as I'd mastered the language and began to feel comfortable in Berne, I had to leave the friends we'd made and go off to somewhere else to try and make new friends and learn another language. Italian was much more difficult to learn! The way of life is completely different to the one we know in England, Switzerland or Sweden. It's like starting all over again, except for the football: training is the same everywhere. You have different styles of play in different countries but the training is the same. You play five-a-sides, you work on skills, you work on defending, you do lots of running. How well you fit in depends on your own level of skill. The basic training is the same everywhere, even if some managers have different ideas about the detail of what you work on.

The move to Italy was one I had to make. It was an easy choice. I had the chance to play against the best players in the world: Maradona, van Basten, Gullit, the lot. Economically, too, Italy is a great place to be if you are 23, 24 years old. But I wanted to play for a big club and win things. When Arsenal came in for me, I wanted to move not because I would earn more money but because it was another step up. Arsenal were a far bigger club than Cremonese, just as Cremonese had been a bigger club than Young Boys. Unfortunately, Cremonese were relegated, too, and I was keen to keep my place in the Swedish national team. The move to Arsenal was an obvious choice for me to want to make.

English is our second language in Sweden, so that

wasn't a problem, but I did have to learn a different way of seeing things here. I was very well taken care of in Switzerland, and even better in Italy: the clubs helped me find a house and everything. It wasn't so easy in that way in England even though everything else was better because I spoke the language already. I think it should be a club's business, though, to help a player settle in quickly. When I arrived in England, I was in a hotel for a long time and eventually had to ask Alan Smith to help me out with estate agents! It was the same when I came to Everton.

I found it physically very demanding here. I would have to agree with the English players who say they play too many games. Look at the rest of the world: they have one league and one cup. Look at someone like Paul Ince: he'll play in the League, two cups, the European Cup, internationals and friendlies – that will be towards 100 games in a year. Now, no normal person can do that! I know that the big clubs are trying to make as much money as they can, but two cup competitions is too much. If you just took out the Coca-Cola Cup, took those eight or ten games out of the season, it would make a hell of a difference. The best players here are as good as the best players in Europe. There are one or two continental players, like Romario, who have a little something extra but players at Manchester United, Liverpool, Newcastle are as good as their counterparts in Italy, in technical terms. The game itself here is very physical, too, and very quick and very hard. I think the players here are good enough to play that way but they would be fresher if they didn't do it so often!

Pat Nevin, Tranmere Rovers

Since the splintering of the old Football League and Football Association structures, the Professional Footballers Association has emerged as one of the few organisations within the game with a constituency broad enough to represent the interests of professional football at every level. Pat Nevin's 24 Scottish caps have been won during a playing career at Clyde, Chelsea, Everton and, most recently, Tranmere Rovers. He was elected chairman of the players' union in 1993.

With football – and the union – I've never really planned anything, but things have just seemed to move forward to me. I was actually a Celtic schoolboy. I was a mad Celtic supporter and still am but when I was 16 they said I was too small. I chucked football then and there and carried on with my education. A while later, a fellow who'd seen me play boys' club football asked me to come along and play for his under-17 team in a game against Clyde reserves. It turned out to be against Clyde first team but I didn't know this and, being totally relaxed about football at this stage, I just thought I'd go out and have a laugh. And I did. I'd scored a couple of goals – I was playing central midfield – and turned to my mate and said: *If I beat four men and score, will you give me a fiver? Well, give me the ball, then!* And I won my bet! As we were coming off the pitch, the Clyde manager's gone: *Come here, I want a word with you!*

Clyde signed me immediately. That was part time and it suited me perfectly because I was doing a degree course at the time – a BA in commerce at Glasgow Tech. I played for Clyde for two years. A few clubs, Chelsea in particular, wanted to sign me but I said: *No, thanks. I don't want to be a footballer.* I was having a great time being a student, going to watch bands and all that, and earning a few quid from playing. It had never entered my mind to be a footballer. Even as a schoolboy, I never thought I'd be good enough so I'd never tried to be one.

Eventually, I got asked to go out to Mexico with the Scottish Under-19s. Chelsea came in for me again at the same time. I took a two-year sabbatical from college and came down. It went so well I never went back. All the time I've been playing, at the end of every year, I've thought: *Do I want to carry on? Yeah, it's fun. I'll carry on!* I've never really thought about it as building a career. Football's been good to me. It was a similar story with the PFA. It's usually the man who picks the short straw who becomes the union rep! I'd been quite interested at Chelsea but we already had someone. Adrian Heath was the rep at Everton and he was leaving. He said: *Will you do it?* I said: *Well, I don't know, maybe.* He said: *That's the most positive reaction I've ever had!* So I started doing it. Basically, the job's about liaising between the union and the members. But I got interested in some ideas I thought were for the wider good of football: I got this idea for a poster – Merseyside Against Racism, featuring players from each of the clubs up here – that ended up in youth clubs and so on trying to do something about the problem. I talked to the PFA about a national poster campaign using the same sort of idea. For whatever reason, it never got off the ground – I still think it's a good idea! – but, as a result, Gordon Taylor (the PFA chief executive) got in touch with me and said he wanted me to come on the management committee of the union.

While I was on the management committee, there was the possibility of a players' strike over the Sky TV money. We decided to ballot the Premier League players, even though I wasn't sure what would happen. I considered the membership to be politically very conservative. The result changed my attitude to football completely: 94 per cent voted in favour of strike action. The Electoral Reform Society, who conducted the ballot, said it was the biggest percentage in favour of action they had ever come across. That really struck a chord with me. It was the moment that made me really happy to work for the union when I realised how aware players were of what the PFA tries to do. People may think of top players as very selfish people, but there they were prepared to take a very great risk, for the most part on behalf of their comrades in the lower leagues.

A year later, Brian Marwood was standing down as PFA chairman and Gordon Taylor said: *Are you going to be chairman, then?* And before I'd answered, he said: *You are!* Well, I agreed to be nominated and was voted in. That was two years ago.

It's a really interesting job. It's fortunate I've got some grounding in economics and accounts because it involves quite a lot of that, being a trustee of the pension scheme and so on. I see the job as acting as spokesman for the management committee, being able to put forward the union's policy from the player's viewpoint. I don't see it as a position of power at all: I see myself as a spokesperson on behalf of the players and the game in general. And I think what power the union has as an organisation we always try and use in the most positive way: for our members, of course, but also for football as a whole, whether it's funding educational programmes for youth trainees or establishing the Football in the Community scheme nationwide.

Gary Mabbutt, MBE, Tottenham Hotspur

Gary Mabbutt joined Spurs from Bristol Rovers as a 19-year-old. He's been club captain at White Hart Lane for the past eight years and led the team to victory in the FA Cup in 1991. Mabbutt has represented England at full international level 16 times. He's currently a member of the PFA's management committee.

I captained the England Youth team once and was captain of the under-21s a few times but I'd never been a club captain. In 1987, after the Cup final, my contract was up and I was approached by several clubs – Arsenal, Liverpool, Man United, Atletico Madrid. I decided, though, that I'd already had five great years at Spurs and thought we had great things to go on to, so I decided to sign for the club again. I was happy here and saw no reason to turn my back on that. Within two or three months, David Platt made me captain and I've survived since then through Terry Venables, Peter Shreeves, Doug Livermore, Ray Clemence, Ossie Ardiles and now Gerry Francis!

You look at some of the great names who've been captain at Spurs and it's a great honour to have. Obviously there are good and bad times. Back in 1993/94, when we were having a rough time on the pitch and in the boardroom, the pressure was on all the time from the media and from supporters, wanting to know why things had gone wrong and how we were going to put things right. When things are going well, it's the other end of the scale: everyone wants to talk to you about how great everything is! And, of course, the ultimate for me was winning the FA Cup at Wembley. It was an incredible feeling being the person to go up those steps, lift the Cup and show it to the fans.

The actual responsibilities of being captain are mostly to

do with being a spokesman for the club and the players. You're the person who's approached for charity functions, hospital visits, that kind of thing. I do my captain's page in the programme: I talk to someone who goes off and writes it up and then checks it with me. That's something I try to take a positive line with. And, on the pitch, the captain's role is mainly to make sure the manager's instructions are carried out. If you have to change things during a game, you change them as you see them – and take the stick if they don't work out! Of course, the most important job is tossing the coin!

It's nothing like the responsibility you have as a cricket captain where you're involved in picking the team and deciding how things are done. As a football captain you're not involved in that, although you may be asked for your opinion if the club are thinking of buying or selling a player, or even for an opinion on the manager's plans. But it's certainly not for me to say: *I want to play this formation.*

We only train for two, two-and-a-half hours a day, so you do have the time for all these other things, as club captain. It's not exactly a full-time job but it's certainly a responsibility I enjoy having. I never set out to be a captain. As a kid, you just set out to be a footballer, don't you? But to be asked to do that job, at this level, is brilliant. To play for Tottenham and to end as captain is the stuff that dreams are made of, really.

I don't know exactly what the quality is that makes a captain. Most captains are the same kind of characters. For a player who's highly strung and liable to fly off the handle, perhaps captain isn't the best position to be in! Especially as you're having to play a mediator's role, at times, between the referee and your players. My biggest job when Paul Gascoigne was here was trying to keep Paul and the referee apart! I do know that I actually enjoy the extra responsibility. You take in your stride and get on with it.

I've been at Spurs for 13 years now. Testimonials used to be a regular thing but it's quite rare now for players to stay with one club for ten years. I suppose big transfer and signing-on fees may have something to do with it. With me, it's not simply a case of being loyal – although I am loyal and really do love the club – it's that I've enjoyed my time here. If

I'd had a problem or been unhappy over the years, I'm sure I'd have moved on and, likewise, if the club hadn't been happy with me, they'd have moved me on. It's a personal thing. I haven't stayed just out of loyalty. I've had a very happy – and successful – time at Spurs.

When you get to a certain age, people start referring to you as a 'veteran' or a 'seasoned campaigner'. Those phrases do start putting ideas in your mind! In life terms, early thirties, you're still a young person. I look at players who are 36, 37, 38 and are still doing the business at the top level. You want to think you can do the same. I'm convinced that if you start to think about things too early, you lose that edge you need to stay at the top as a footballer. As far as I can see, the main enjoyment in football comes from playing the game. Of course, I've thought I'd like to stay in the game when I finish – in management, the media or administration – but I'm 33 now and looking forward to playing another three or four years! My aim is to stay as a player as long as I can, to get the most enjoyment I can from playing the game.

Ian Alexander, Bristol Rovers

Ian Alexander grew up in Glasgow where he played junior football for Rangers, only to be released at 16. Thinking he'd missed out on a career in the game, Alexander began an apprenticeship as a signwriter and played amateur football. At 19 he was offered a pro contract by Emlyn Hughes at Rochdale and life for Ian and his young family was turned on its head: the opportunity was too good to turn down. He moved on to Motherwell and Morton before following manager Willie McLean out to Larnica in Cyprus. Since returning to the UK, Alexander has

played under Bobby Gould, Gerry Francis, Malcolm Allison, Martin Dobson, Dennis Rofe and John Ward in ten years at Bristol Rovers.

For me, I look at each contract – say, two years – and I just concentrate on that, go in and train and just base myself on those two years. I think it's harder for the women: they don't know if they're coming or going. My wife just said: *Wherever you're going we'll go.* Pack our bags and off we went. But, you know, it's like when we first moved down here, she said: *Nobody knows me, everybody knows you. You could murder me and bury me in the back garden and nobody would know!* Pat was just left in the house by herself, basically. The players go off training – we meet people – it's got to be hard for the wives. At least we're settled now. I've been at Rovers for ten years and there's no way I'm going to move on now.

When I came back from Cyprus, I put together a standard letter. I wrote to all the clubs saying I was back in the country. The wife typed it all up and sent them off. I think three clubs came back and Rovers were one of them. I came down: Bobby Gould was the manager then and he offered me a year's contract. And I've been here ever since.

The first year I started in the first team but after Christmas I was in and out. Then Bobby Gould went off to Wimbledon and he took John Scales up there. Gerry Francis came in and was looking for a full-back. I was playing right-wing but he dropped me back and I've stayed there. Getting to know the new position was like going back to basics: learning to stay on your feet, covering your centre-back. It took some work. But I didn't think I was going anywhere as a winger and I didn't want to leave, so I buckled down. I'd had enough of moving: I thought it was time we settled. The kids were coming up to school age and we didn't want them to have to be changing schools. And the club, even though it wasn't settled – playing down at Bath, training at Keynsham, the offices were somewhere else – people were very friendly: people like Ray Kendall who'd been there for years. It was the first time, really, I'd been at a club and though: *I don't want to move.*

About 18 months ago, I had trouble with a groin strain and went into hospital for a hernia operation. When I got back training, I still felt it wasn't right. I went to see a couple of specialists and I've been told I've got arthritis in the hip: the hernia was just a symptom of that. Over the years I'd not had much trouble with injury. Before this, I'd played almost every game for eight seasons. It does put a dampener on things, but I suppose every player goes through it. It's very frustrating. The two specialists have advised me to pack in playing. I'll just have to see our chairman to work out what's going to happen next.

There's got to be life after football, hasn't there? I've had a good innings. I played over 300 games for Rovers. I'm 32 now: I've had a good ten, 12 years. I suppose it would be harder if I was younger. What I've got to think about now, of course, is how I'm going to pay the mortgage. I've had a couple of enquiries about managing non-League, so I hope there's things in the pipeline. But I'd never really thought about it before: you just think you'll go on playing for ever! My biggest regret now is that I never finished my apprenticeship as a signwriter. I think, perhaps, the PFA could do more to make sure youngsters have something else to fall back on if things don't work out. They'll put money there now which is brilliant, for courses and that, but I think they could get more involved and push the kids more. The afternoon I was told I had to pack it in I couldn't really take it in. I'm lucky, Pat's quite brainy! She works for a building society and I think, with the money I'll get from the League and the PFA, we've worked out what we'll do. Whether it'll be in football or not, though, I don't really know.

Brian Hughes, Gloucester City

•BRIAN HUGHES•

JEWSON

•Gloucester City•

Brian Hughes grew up in Hampshire and played 150 League games for Swindon and Torquay United. Since 1983, Hughes has been playing non-League football for Cheltenham Town and – for the past five years – for Gloucester City in the Beazer Homes Premier League. He runs his own glass and glazing business and is currently City's player/coach at the age of 34.

When I went to secondary school, I went to a school that didn't play much football. It was all rugby and cricket. I kept playing local football at weekends even though I didn't think I was anything out of the ordinary as a player, never won any kind of representative honours. I was 15 and playing in a league with a lot of Wiltshire teams. Swindon's youth team manager, John Trollope, was at one of our games to watch someone in the other team. We won and he ended up asking me and another lad in my team if we wanted to come to Swindon as apprentices. I'd never really thought seriously about football as a career until that came along. The school I was at was a grammar school geared very much towards exams, but when Swindon offered me the apprenticeship, I thought: *Yes, I'll have a go at that!* It wasn't something I'd grown up as a kid wanting to do, but as soon as he asked me I wanted to have a go. I thought at 15 I had nothing to lose. It all happened so quickly, I was chuffed to bits and I had a great time at Swindon. I was there for seven years.

A lot of people don't. but I really enjoyed my time as an apprentice. It meant living away from home for the first time: I stayed in a hostel run by Paul Rideout's mum and dad. I'd never even been to Swindon, even though it wasn't that far away. I think what I really enjoyed about it was something that I think's missing from the game now. A little while ago, I was at a Conference game and ran into Bobby Smith, who'd been the manager at Swindon when I was a boy. I found myself calling him *'Boss'!* Just out of respect for the fellow and what he stood for. Sixteen- and 17-year-olds now think they know it all, don't they? Want to be in the first team straightaway! When I was an apprentice we were in total awe of the first team! I used to have six or seven pros whose boots I had to keep clean. Teenagers now don't want to know about all that! There's less respect for experience in football today, I think.

I loved that time. In many ways I enjoyed it more than when I turned pro and started to play for the first team. There seemed no pressure on us then. We'd play youth team games and reserve games, turn up at the Arsenals and the Chelseas and play on their pitches. It was dreaming for two years. At the end of that they decide whether you're going to stay or go, and you turn pro. Then it gets serious. Before that, it's just dreaming: *This is great. I can't believe this!* And, of course, being around the club – watching them beat Arsenal in the League Cup in front of a packed crowd – you get the spark and ambition comes. Even so, it was never the end of the world for me. If they'd not taken me on after the two years, I knew I could still walk away a better player and a wiser man. I was chuffed to bits, though, when they said: *Yes!*

Once you turn pro, the game's your living, isn't it? The competitiveness comes in and it's every man for himself: if there's half a dozen midfield players at the club you need to make sure you're one that's playing so you can pay your mortgage. I had three or four years as a pro with Swindon at what wasn't a good time for the club. I was 18 and single. I think my first pay packet was £110 and that seemed like a lot of money to me! I enjoyed myself, you know. But a new manager came in and he bombed me out – me and half a dozen other lads who'd come through the youth team – the summer I bought my first house and got married!

Fortunately, Torquay were interested and I ended up signing for them. I say 'fortunately': actually it was a disaster. It was ragged-arse Rovers! The first day of pre-season training, there were only eight players! The first League matches, the manager was getting players in from Western League teams to make up the numbers, you know. Needless to say, we didn't win a game for three months. And then the manager injured one of the younger players out at the training ground during a five-a-side game. It was a really ugly incident. He knocked the lad out and broke his jaw. It just destroyed the thing for me. I knew I'd made a mistake as soon as I got to Torquay, but after what happened I just became totally disillusioned. It wasn't easy, either, with a wife and a mortgage, trying to survive on £130 a week.

I started looking for other things, not really knowing if I wanted to stay in football or not. I was at a mate's wedding and ran into three or four lads I'd known from my Swindon days who were playing non-League with Cheltenham. They'd dropped straight out into non-League football and had jobs which, with their football money, meant they were earning a lot more than I was at Torquay as a pro. I ended up joining Cheltenham and can honestly say I've enjoyed the last ten years more than I did my five or six years as a pro.

I managed to set up my own business, which has made money and moved in the right direction. I've enjoyed the social side of non-League, playing without the pressures of the professional game. I've got a good life now and there's so much more to football at this level than people imagine. You still play to win, of course. It's very competitive. But you can't mope and worry about failure like you do as a pro. Maybe if I'd been single, I'd have taken £130 a week – I'm not money orientated – and stayed at Torquay hoping to go on to better things. But with a wife and kids, you're not thinking of yourself and lack of money becomes a pressure. Maybe I could have pushed myself more but I've no regrets at all. There's a sense of comradeship here that I don't think exists in the professional game where everyone has to be out for themselves. Football's something I can really enjoy.

Best Seats

OWNERS, CHAIRMEN AND DIRECTORS

All I ever wanted was to be part of the club. It's me. It's my life.
Bill Kenwright

The job's an almighty challenge, and it's a job I love doing.
Robert Chase

Whatever one may say, whether you're the owner or the chairman of a club, you're only a custodian for that club.
David Russe

Only those clubs which are financially viable can afford to compete.
Owen Oyston

Bill Kenwright, Director, Everton

Bill Kenwright has been hugely successful as one of the country's most prolific theatre impresarios. The drama that really counts for Kenwright, however, is played out on Saturday afternoons at Goodison Park: he's been a director of Everton since 1981. The 1994/95 season was a particularly good show: Kenwright watched his team beat Manchester United in the FA Cup final in May.

I was the very first young lad to be taken on in a soap opera to appeal to girls in the audience. This was, what, 26 or 27 years ago? Before I joined *Coronation Street*, everyone in soap operas seemed to be old! I was a very shy lad – very ambitious but shy. I'll never forget, my first day, Pat Phoenix said to me: *Listen, son. You're a good-looking boy and you're not going to be prepared for what's going to hit you. Make sure you keep your feet on the ground.* I thought: *What's she talking about?* But on the Friday of the week my first episodes went out, I travelled home on the train and I was mobbed! I couldn't believe it. I'd achieved a celebrity status overnight.

Of course, I was still watching Everton from the terraces like I always had. I remember queuing all night for a ticket for the 1968 Cup final. Fellow behind me said: *You're Bill Kenwright, aren't you? Out of* Coronation Street? *What are you doing queuing up? Why don't you just phone up the club?* But I just didn't want to know about all that. I was happy standing on the terraces. Well, eventually, there was a night match I couldn't get into – against Swindon, I think – and I've phoned them up. I got down to Goodison and went up to the door that said 'Directors'. I didn't know what to do. I was used to swearing at football! But I really enjoyed it and decided I liked these people.

Anyway, I got to know the secretary, Jim Greenwood, who's become my closest friend in football, and it became a regular thing, sitting up there. I'm really uncomfortable, though, about just taking from people, so I asked if there was anything I could do in return. By this time I was producing shows so, whenever the lads came down to London, I'd sort out tickets for the theatre or whatever. I just got involved with the club on any level I could.

When I was with Koo Stark, one evening she said we were going out with her best friends. I thought: *Here we go! A dreary evening out with some chinless wonders!* Well, we got to the restaurant and I was introduced to Barbara Dein who apologised for her husband being late: he was off watching Arsenal reserves, wasn't he! Well, David arrived and we were introduced. I said: *How was Rixy?* He looked at me and I said: *Graham Rix was back from injury tonight, wasn't he?* Well, from that moment on, we were inseparable, weren't we? I remember listening to him talking about what he was trying to do, talking about the Premier League years before it happened. We became very close friends and it was David who suggested I should try and get on the board at Everton.

I was based down in London, of course, and so I didn't really consider it seriously. But I got a phone call from a London club who knew I was into football and wondered if I'd be interested in putting a bit of money in and becoming a director. I went to meet them but I thought: *What am I doing? If this lot were playing in my back garden, I'd draw the curtains! I'm only interested in Everton.* I eventually wrote a couple of lines to the chairman, Phillip Carter: *I know you'll not want me, but if a vacancy ever did come up, etcetera!* I thought no more about it.

A while later, I was out in Los Angeles for the film of *Stepping Out* with Liza Minelli. I was hot out there at the time: *Stepping Out, Are You Lonesome Tonight?* Now, all I'd ever wanted to do was be involved in movies and I decided it was the right time to give it a shot, even though it would mean moving to LA for a large part of each year. I came back to England and I was in the office explaining what I was going to do when the phone rang. Phillip Carter wanted to know if

I'd be at the Millwall game on Saturday and could he see me beforehand. Seven minutes to three, I was in his office. *There's a vacancy and we'd like to invite you to join the board at Everton. We know you'll need time to think about it.* As he finished speaking, I can still remember hearing the *Z-Cars* theme filtering through from the PA system outside. I just started crying! I said: *I don't have to think about it!* Los Angeles and all that went straight out the window and that was how I became a director. I was sat with my dad and looked down towards the boys' pen that I used to bunk into when I was a kid. I just can't describe the feeling to you: a dream come true.

It's not a sleeping board at Everton. Every director has a specific duty. When I joined, we were just starting up a Football in the Community programme and I took that on. It's my job to make sure Everton's involved with under-privileged kids, dealing with areas with drug problems, working on anti-racist campaigns. Football to me is about community, so it's an area I love working in: getting the name of Everton across, making Everton mean something to people whether they come to watch games at Goodison or not. As football gets bigger and bigger, I think our job as directors is to enhance that, yes, but also to make sure that the club stays in touch with its roots, with people like I was once – bunking into the ground as a kid!

I'm up at Everton so often everybody knows me on the London to Liverpool train! It takes up that much time that Goodison Park's become my home. I mean, it always was but now even more so: it's where I feel good, where I feel I belong. Whenever people had talked about buying football clubs, I'd said: *You can't. You could buy Goodison Park but you couldn't buy Everton, what Everton means.* Well, a couple of years ago, there was a board meeting and someone announced that an offer had been made to buy the club. We were in financial trouble and it was proposed we should meet this person. Now I'm usually the sort who only wakes up at board meetings to hear the manager's report, but I couldn't believe this. The alternative, it turned out, was for me to go to meet the Moores family with a view to buying Everton myself!

The Moores were fantastic. They said they'd been waiting for me, that I was the one their father would have wanted, the one Evertonians wanted. It was there in front of me. Can you imagine what that meant? I was introduced to a consortium – great guys, Evertonians, who wanted what I wanted for the club – and, although I'm someone who's used to doing things on his own, I agreed to go ahead. On 21 December 1993 the contract arrived. I'd bought Everton Football Club.

From there on, it's history: we were gazumped. Peter Johnson arrived on the scene and from a state of total euphoria – a dream of taking Everton into the next century – it all started going wrong. The team started losing games, everyone began getting restless with all the boardroom controversies. It was breaking people's hearts – mine, too – and I started to feel responsible. Every time Tony Cottee missed a goal, I thought it was my fault. I couldn't sleep. I couldn't work. For five months my whole life turned round trying to sort things out. And we were sucked into a relegation battle. It was killing me and it was killing Everton. Eventually I sat down with Peter Johnson, even though he wasn't an Evertonian, to try and work things out the best way for the club and, incredibly, it was me in the end who talked people round for him. We did the deal just a couple of days before the Wimbledon game which we had to win to stay up.

We announced it on the Saturday morning so the fans would know things were settled and that I was going to be around. I didn't sleep a wink the Friday night: were we about to go down for the first time in my lifetime? I brought my whole family up on the train. I couldn't eat. We got to the ground about 1.30 and there was none of that buzz you get on a match-day. Thousands of people queueing up to get in, afraid to even look at each other. Twelve thousand were locked out. And the roar when we kicked off I've never heard anything like.

Seven minutes in, we've given away a penalty. It's the worst thing that could have happened. I've looked around and, everywhere, people were in tears, so angry and upset. After 20 minutes, an own goal for 2–0. People went mental, started walking out. I'd lost it completely. I would have caught the 3.45 back to London if I could have without anyone noticing! At half-time we were back to 2–1 but I really didn't think we were going to do it. Phillip Carter got me sat back down and then Barry Horne equalised. I was running around like a madman trying to get the other scores. And then Graham Stuart got the winner. I've never experienced anything like it in my life. I was stood on my seat in the directors' box. I was gone! When the final whistle went, they thrust me down to the front. Eighteen thousand people were singing: *There's only one Bill Kenwright!* I had Johnny Moore's scarf round me. I didn't know where I was.

The next day I went out on to Hampstead Heath and cried for three hours. I said: *Never again.* My business went to pieces for those five months. My life went to pieces. That's the other side of being a director. If you're not prepared to suffer like that, to feel that responsible, don't be a director. There are directors in football who are in it for the beer. But all I've ever wanted was to be part of the club. It's me. It's my life. Everton are my team. And if I ever lose that passion, I'll move on.

Robert Chase, Chairman, Norwich City

With a population of around 125,000, Norwich is a city that's always struggled to fund top-flight football. The Carrow Road club has traditionally been forced to sell its most visible assets. Chris Sutton's £5 million move to Blackburn was the latest, just before the 1994/95 season started. Amidst ugly scenes at the ground, Norwich were relegated in May 1995. Robert Chase, in his eighth season as chairman at Carrow Road, took much of the blame from unhappy fans.

•ROBERT CHASE•

•Norwich City•

My father was secretary of a village football club in Caister-on-Sea, just north of Great Yarmouth. In fact, my father-in-law played in goal for the same team! My dad was a real football fan, dead keen on the game, and from the age of seven he took me to Carrow Road whenever he could. When I was about nine I had my own little football team. We used to play in the Den – a low playing field between two big banks. I remember it was quite revolutionary when we became the first team to have actual goals: empty five-gallon oil cans for goal posts! Later on, we even got some white painted posts with a wooden crossbar.

I was never successful at school – I don't think I ever got out of the bottom half of the table! – and I left at 15 and went to start work on a building site. I was very fortunate. I was involved in the heyday, when land prices were rocketing and opportunities were there. When I was about 23, I bought 12 acres of land: that was the turning point. I built over 100 bungalows and I was lucky: the market was rising. And, in those days, to make £25,000 was to make a lot of money!

My first seat at Carrow Road was in the small enclosure in front of the Main Stand: concrete steps with two by nine pieces of timber screwed to the top. Then Norwich put seats in the South Stand and I bought two season tickets. I'd only sat there for a year when David Stringer, who was playing for Norwich then and lived in Yarmouth, happened to say to me that someone had died and there were two seats available in the Main Stand. We moved across and had two seats in B block, second row back, and I thought I'd really arrived!

By the time we built the River End Stand my company had really progressed and I bought the first box – right in the centre, number ten. David Stringer had become youth team coach and, when he took the boys abroad for tournaments, the club couldn't afford to send them so my company sponsored the trips. I think because of that I was invited to become one of 25 honorary vice-presidents, which led to me meeting the chairman, Sir Arthur South, and the directors and the manager.

Like everything in life, it was a question of opportunity. There was a financial crisis at Norwich and they had a rights issue which wasn't taken up at all. This was ten years ago. And I was asked if I would make the football club a loan. I refused, but said I'd be delighted to buy a block of shares. I was offered 25,000, which was more than the existing issued share capital. The chairman made the offer at 11.30 in the morning and we completed the transaction the same day. I can remember my wife saying, when I was making the arrangements to draw the money from the bank: *Are we really in a position to give away £25,000?* She thought we'd never see it again: a good judge of football, really!

It was only a few days later, in the gents toilet at Nottingham Forest of all places, Sir Arthur came in. We were standing, washing our hands and, looking in the mirror, Sir Arthur said: *How would you like to join the board at Norwich, Robert?*

I was put in charge of players' contracts – the biggest single expense at a football club – which was a challenge I really enjoyed, establishing the principle that you can't spend more than you earn. It wasn't very long – 18 months – before Sir Arthur stood down and I became chairman. Of course, we were still in financial trouble and in my first week we sold Dave Watson to Everton and Chris Woods to Rangers and all the headlines were about relegation and disaster – but that same year we won the Second Division and got promotion!

The job's an almighty challenge, and it's a job I love doing. I had three tasks when I took over as chairman. First, Norwich must never hit a financial crisis again: well, we've turned a negative situation round and now have about £15 million worth of fixed assets. We've improved the ground, the facilities at Carrow Road, and we're developing a new training complex out on the Southern Bypass. And the third objective is to now go on and win something. You have to get the finances and the facilities right and then commit the same amount of effort, the same amount of funds, to winning a major trophy at Carrow Road. I know the fans might like us to remortgage everything and really go for it, but what's the point of winning a trophy and then going bankrupt? You have to get the structure of the business and the fabric of the ground right first. Despite the flak I get, I'm going to stick to my three steps!

David Russe, Chairman, Bristol City FC

David Russe grew up in Knowle, a Bristol City heartland, watching from the Ashton Gate terraces as a six-year-old. A successful industrialist, initially in stone restoration and quarrying and, more recently, in property, Russe had been a season ticket-holder for several years when, in 1982, the club faced insolvency. He became a major shareholder in Bristol City FC 1982 PLC and served as a director until 1985, when work commitments forced his resignation. Eight years later, another crisis saw him back in the boardroom at Ashton Gate. Things may have to get worse before they get better: City were relegated to Division Two in May 1995.

In 1993 the club was under investigation by the FA over certain misdemeanours, which led to one director resigning, and at an extraordinary general meeting that November a new board was elected on the strength of a five-year business plan. We made it clear from the outset that there was no chance of a Jack Walker-type individual coming here, but we promised we would look carefully at reducing the wage bill at Ashton Gate. The ultimate goal was, and is, Premiership football within five years.

Of course, you don't really know the lady until you've married the lady. We have to rely on a strong youth policy: we can't compete in a transfer market where a lad like Chris Sutton, not even a full international, is costing £5 million. We're refurbishing the stadium: the cost of the new Carling Atyeo Stand, all told, was about £1.8 million. The Football Trust has been magnificent – we're hoping to receive around £900,000 – but that still leaves us to finance the rest on crowds much lower than in other parts of the country. Down here, we don't get the six or seven local derbies every season that boost gates in the Midlands, say. And, of course, we no longer share away gate receipts. In the past, too, we haven't given commercial activities the attention they deserve and we need to address that. Attracting two new sponsors, Bass and Auto Windscreens, has been a good start.

The job takes anything between 12 and 50 hours a week, depending on the circumstances. Each director has been given a clear area of responsibility, be it catering, the stadium or commercial activities. We've also engaged a general manager who's responsible for the day-to-day running of the club. My job is to monitor and try to make sure that every part works smoothly, and to have a very clear interface, a working relationship, with our manager, which is something crucial to the running of any club.

Whatever one may say, whether you're the owner or the chairman of a club, you're only a custodian for that club. The club's bigger than any one individual. It's what you can achieve during your time there that you may be remembered by. But you know how it is: when things are going well, its Ours, when it suddenly goes wrong it's Bloody Yours!

I would say we're slightly ahead of the schedule we set ourselves. You don't buy canaries unless you've got a cage to put them in, and that's why we've started with ground refurbishment. We've now got a Premiership stadium. But, of course, I realise that whatever work you do behind the scenes, whatever the infrastructure you establish, everything depends on what you achieve on the park. A city the size of Bristol should have Premiership football. Because I can see this great gap emerging between an élite of big clubs and the rest, if we don't achieve that quantum leap within the next five years I have my doubts as to whether we ever will.

When I went along to that extraordinary general meeting I wasn't expecting to be made chairman of Bristol City. It wasn't till after we won and our plan had been accepted, the other directors asked me to take up the position. I thought about it for a long time: it was a great honour and not something to be done lightly. I said then I would review the situation in two years. Nothing's forever in life and if someone was more committed and energetic I would step aside and let the next person take it on. The club's the thing. An awful lot will depend on what happens in the next few months. I would hope we'll be able to look back on the years of office and see we've made substantial improvements at Bristol City. Surely, no one would be able to argue with that.

Owen Oyston, Owner and Chairman, Blackpool FC

Blackpool's finest days in the 1950s were, and feel like, a lifetime ago. I can remember visiting Bloomfield 20 years ago for a League Cup-tie. The club was heading nowhere at full tilt. The rain poured down on to open terraces, Arsenal nicked a draw with a dodgy goal and nobody seemed much to care: not the players, not the fans – and certainly not the town. More recently, local-boy-made-good, Owen Oyston – certainly the north-west's most visible entrepreneur – has put his toe in the water. Oyston bought Blackpool in 1986.

•OWEN OYSTON•

•Blackpool•

I came into football for emotional reasons. Blackpool's my town. When my parents moved down from the north-east, they bought a boarding house 300 yards from the ground. I watched Matthews and Mortenson as a boy. The town gave me my start in business and when the club was in financial difficulties I saw it as my chance to put something back into Blackpool: something good for me and good for the town.

At first, I simply became the owner. Eventually, I recognised how complicated football was – and how expensive! It took me two million pounds to discover this! – I began to take a closer interest. The worst year was 1990 when

78

the family had to put in £800,000 to keep the club afloat. The next year, we thought, was a triumph because we reduced the losses to £397,000! The year after that we were down to £7,000 and last year we actually made a profit of £108,000.

We've managed to turn it round. We've done this, first, by improving the commercial side of the club. Secondly, we've invested heavily in the youth policy. I know the fans prefer us not to sell our best players, but if you're in the old Fourth Division, as we were, there's no way you can hang on to someone like Trevor Sinclair. It's better to negotiate a decent price rather than losing out at a tribunal when his contract's up. It's worked well for us and we believe that's the way the future lies.

We've also got the detailed planning through for a new stadium development. The old ground was nearing the end of its life: we're now putting together the finance and detail for a completely new site. The beautiful thing about it is that although football's been the rationale, the driving force, behind the scheme, most of the money's coming from outside football: the stadium has a closing roof so we can use it for shows, exhibitions, conferences and concerts. It's a duplicate with a difference of the Skydome in Toronto. We're looking at it as a project that will generate revenue that will one day help to get us into the Premiership. With a fair wind, we'll be there sooner rather than later.

The new stadium should be ready in two or three years. But I don't want to rush, I've been involved with Blackpool now for over eight years, and having lost or spent or invested – whichever word you want to use ! – over three-and-a-half million pounds, I want to make sure it's a viable proposition. I've got no problem admitting I want to make profit from the club: if I didn't, there'd be no future for it. Only those clubs which are financially viable and profitable can afford to compete in the major leagues.

Once you get into the Premier League, of course, the economics change and start working for you. Now, there's talk about a second division of the Premiership. But, unless they leave the door open to the other divisions, that would be the kiss of death for football. There's a few people out there who want to become exclusive. I don't think that's in the interests of the industry or the public. It has to be stopped. The dream has to be there or clubs will waste away.

Football's the toughest game I've ever been in and Blackpool's taken its toll! Obviously, I'm at every game. I spend every Wednesday and sometimes Thursday at the club. I'm on the phone every day of the week. I'm in London all this week for meetings about the new development.

The game has an irrational, magic spell. It's frightening how it can control you! At first, you don't know what's happening but football takes you over – your will goes – and you find intelligent, rational business people making ridiculous decisions in football! The passion draws you in, the will to win and the desire to see your town up there and successful. You know, it's a great, great feeling when you win!

Alan Parry, Director, Wycombe Wanderers

Anyone who's watched Alan Parry play charity football for the TV Commentators will readily describe his enthusiasm for the game as ferocious. Parry's career as a sports broadcaster for BBC Radio, BBC TV and, more recently, ITV have established him as a hugely well-respected voice in football. Since 1989, Wycombe Wanderers have put both Parry's enthusiasm and his standing in the game to good use behind the scenes at Adams Park. Season 1994/95 saw Wycombe consolidate their position, finishing sixth in Division Two. However, manager Martin O'Neill departed for Norwich City in June 1995.

• ALAN PARRY •

• Wycombe Wanderers •

I was born and brought up in Liverpool. I used to watch Liverpool when they were in the old Second Division – I first went in 1958. They were my first love, back when it was difficult supporting them in the early 1960s, while Everton were the big club on Merseyside. The involvement with Wycombe came later, after I'd had to move south with my job.

In 1975, when Wycombe were in the Isthmian League, they got through to the third round of the Cup, to play Middlesbrough, who were top of the old First Division and had a really good side: Graeme Souness, David Armstrong . . . Jack Charlton was manager. It was a big day for non-League clubs: Wimbledon, who were in the Southern League, played Burnley the same afternoon. I was working for BBC Radio and went to cover the Wycombe game. This was at the old ground, Loakes Park, with its sloping pitch: Jack Charlton said it was like the north face of the Eiger!

Anyway, it was a 0–0 draw and Wycombe could have won it. They were really unlucky. I remember the draw for the next round taking place at five o'clock that afternoon, as it did in those days, with everyone in the boardroom gathered round to listen. They were really hospitable. Wycombe lost the replay 1–0, a last-minute goal, but later that season they asked me to speak at their annual dinner. That was when I started getting to know people at the club a little.

I was living half an hour away and began taking my son to midweek games. I liked the atmosphere, everyone was friendly. I suppose what accelerated my involvement was that, when I moved from BBC to ITV in 1984, it was to do athletics, not football. For the first time in my career I had Saturdays and Wednesdays off. I used to watch Liverpool when I could, but started getting more involved with Wycombe. I was playing for the TV Commentators charity football team and the Wycombe manager at the time, Mike Keen, said I could come and train on Thursday nights with the lads. I got to know the players, helped the club with a bit of press and publicity.

Wycombe were very old-fashioned, run by a committee. But to take the next step forward, they knew they had to get a more professional set-up behind the scenes. A new chairman and two new directors came in and I was asked if I'd like to get involved on the board. I had to stand for election, do a speech to the shareholders. I'd never done anything like it before, but even though I'd worked for TV and radio I got quite nervous! But I got in, and the six years since have just been fantastic.

I like to think I've made my contribution. I thought there were enough people on the board who knew about business. I told them I wouldn't understand finances and balance sheets. But I'm a fan and I understand what fans want: a winning team. And that's my policy – to help fans to get what they want in terms of success and the facilities and fair treatment that supporters deserve. Obviously, my press background helped us raise the club's profile and develop commercially, attracting some of the money that's definitely out there in the Thames Valley area.

The most important thing I've contributed, I think, was attracting Martin O'Neill to the club. I'd known Martin for years, since he was a player, and got on well with him: he was sparky, humorous, intelligent. He was working for Save and Prosper and managing the likes of Gainsborough Trinity in his spare time. I was always telling him he could do better than that – in those days, because he hadn't gone straight into management when he finished, I think he lacked confidence in his own ability. Anyway, I put Martin forward for the Wycombe job some years back, before I was on the board, and he didn't get it. Then, five years ago, they were interviewing again, by which time I'd lost touch a bit with Martin. Norwich were playing Liverpool the afternoon of the interviews and I'd gone to the game, to watch Liverpool really, and I ran into Martin, in the gents of all places. We talked about the job and he was really keen, but when I phoned the chairman he said they'd appointed someone. As it turned out, though, the following day the fellow pulled out and I brought Martin down to meet them and he was offered the job on the spot.

Since then a lot's happened incredibly quickly. Martin's second season we went to Wembley in the FA Trophy. The next season, we lost the Conference and promotion on the last day of the season: talk about heart-breaking, losing it on goal difference even though we won our last game on a beautiful sunny day in front of a big crowd – it was the worst feeling! But then, the next year, we went to Wembley again and won promotion. At which point, I think I did my bit in helping convince Martin to stay with us when he was offered the Forest job!

I suppose my job on the board is a bit vaguer than anybody else's. We've got a financial director, a guy who looks after the ground, liaising with the police and stewards and so on, another who's a catering and hospitality expert. All the others have specific areas of responsibility. I suppose mine would be vaguely called public relations: from introducing Martin to Cyrille Regis after Graham Taylor released him, through to lobbying the Beeb to get our Cup game against West Ham on to Match of the Day. At board meetings, I look on in bewilderment most of the time, but I do have a lot of contacts and a gut-feeling, too, for the supporters' point of view which means, I hope, I can be useful in my way! I'll try to break down barriers – and build bridges – between the supporters, the staff, the players and the board and I think that's useful enough to offset the fact I can't make a contribution from a business point of view.

John Gibson, Chairman, Gateshead

John Gibson first started writing about football for the Newcastle *Evening Chronicle* nearly 35 years ago. He's been covering his boyhood heroes, Newcastle United, for the past 30. In 1992, Gibson became involved with the non-League side across the Tyne, Gateshead. Under his chairmanship they've pushed for promotion from the Conference for the first time since leaving the League in 1960.

•JOHN GIBSON•

•Gateshead•

Having been a journalist for 30 years in football, mostly covering Newcastle United, for the past three seasons I've been chairman of the local Conference side, Gateshead. Even though I'd been on the 'inside' of football, it's totally different when you go into the boardroom. A lot of people think that directors spend their time turning up late to games and drinking gin and tonic. What I've found is that I spend most of every week being a nursemaid to players with private problems which nobody knows about but which are enormously important within the club. Affairs like Cantona, Merson and so on are the public face of it, I suppose. Dealing with problems week to week gives you a completely different insight. It's hilarious, really: as a journalist, it's my job to get stories on Newcastle United; as chairman of Gateshead, it's my job to stop the local paper getting the same kind of stories about us!

I sort of slid into it, initially. A local Italian restaurateur wanted to put cash into Gateshead and take over as chairman. He had problems with the language and with understanding how English football works. Because I'd been the original contact, putting him touch with the Gateshead board, he asked me to go along as his adviser. Well, the fellow dropped out but within about six months I went from adviser to director, director to vice-chairman and then I bought the club, bought 61 per cent of the shares in the club. It had never been my intention but I must say that if you're a journalist, telling clubs what they should be doing, you ought to have the guts to try it for yourself.

It's gone well, too, but you've got to have the courage to do it. And never mind covering World Cups and top-level football as a journalist, this is the biggest challenge I've ever taken on. It's hard work, too. I work at the paper seven till five and then spend four or five hours over at Gateshead every evening. But it's a drug, it really is. And I'm lucky I've got close personal friends from my work as a journalist, people like Frank Clark, Malcolm Macdonald, David Macreery, whom I can go to for help and advice.

To go back to how I got involved with football in the first place: I was born and bred in the West End of Newcastle and was always a United fan. Probably because I knew I had no talent, I never wanted to play football. I always wanted to write. I was brought up by my grandparents and my granddad used to make me scrapbooks out of that shiny brown wrapping paper so that I could write match reports and get autographs from the likes of Jackie Milburn and Joe Harvey.

I got a start in journalism at ground level with the *Hexham Courant*. Reporting on Hexham's GPO's games on the local pitch was the highlight of my week. I joined the *Evening Chronicle* as a cub sports reporter and my first job was to cover Gateshead who had just lost their League status in 1960. I got very close to the club back then, the two managers, Jack Fairbrother and Bobby Mitchell, who'd both played for Newcastle in the 1950s Cup finals, and a then-unknown coach who's been a good pal ever since, Lawrie McMenemy.

I went on from there to Fleet Street and worked for the old *Sun* newspaper and the Sunday *People*, doing match reports and features on sport. I thought that was going to be my life but then the *Evening Chronicle* came back to me in 1966 and said: *Come home and cover Newcastle United*. It was the only job I'd have left London for, the chance to follow my club.

It was a great time. We won the Fairs Cup in 1969, got to FA and League Cup finals and had four successive years of European competition: one of the great periods in United history. The players used to joke that if they wanted to know the team they had to read the *Chronicle* because Joe Harvey, the manager, told me before he told them! For me, it was the dream job. And the relationship between writers and players was different then. You could establish real friendships with people like Supermac. People's private lives stayed private and the word 'trust' meant something, which is no longer true unfortunately.

I would have been happy standing on the terraces for the rest of my life but I was given the opportunity to write about my club. It's a careful line to draw between the head and the heart, being careful not to gloss over things or over-react to situations because I'm a fan. There are times, though, when you've got to stand up and be counted. There was a period in the 1980s when Newcastle sold Waddle, Beardsley and Gascoigne, all of whom were Geordies, and you could see the club was going nowhere. The team was relegated and John Hall, who was a box-holder at St James Park, challenged the board. We talked about it at the paper and decided to run a campaign to get John Hall in at United. At the time, he didn't own a share and we were risking our paper's long-term relationship with the club. It was heavy going. It took four years to happen and then, of course, when he did get in we thought: *What if it doesn't work? The finger will be pointing at us!* In fact, it's been glorious. He's gone in, bought the whole club, brought Keegan in and the club's taken off in the way the fans wanted – and I wanted – all along.

It's been a dream career. Perhaps I haven't exploited it as I might have for cash, but I've done it for love. I'm a fan with a typewriter, although I hope I write more considered pieces than a fan would, perhaps. My ambitions now are with Gateshead. If I could get Gateshead back into the Football League, that would just be fantastic. I could die happy then!

Boss

THE MANAGER

I know I'm good at my job.

John King

People used to say I was too nice to be a manager but I think that's been forgotten about now.

John Ward

I've always looked for enthusiasm in people, in players: everything else will fall into place.

Ron Atkinson

I'm like any fan: I'll do anything for football.

Barry Fry

Ron Atkinson, Manager, Coventry City

In a 20-year career in football management Ron Atkinson's record stands comparison with the very best. He has enjoyed successful spells at Kettering Town, Cambridge United, West Bromwich Albion, Manchester United, Atletico Madrid, Sheffield Wednesday and Aston Villa, with whom he won the Coca-Cola Cup in 1994. His association with the club for whom he had played as a youngster ended in November of the same year. Atkinson was appointed manager of Coventry City in March 1995.

While I was a player at Oxford, I'd always been involved on the coaching side, with the University, the Polytechnic and with local amateur teams. In those days it was great to go on coaching courses. When I was in my early twenties, we used to go to Lilleshall for a couple of weeks in the summer and be involved with all the top coaches in the game. There was none of these six-week holidays in America then – a lot of players had to get jobs during the close season. The courses were stimulating and a lot of fun, mixing with other professionals, enjoying the crack. And a lot of good came out of those courses although these days the coaching's become less inventive and more functional, I think, and a lot of the enjoyment's gone out of them.

Having said all that, in my last six years at Oxford I was involved with the commercial world, working for a builders merchants, one of the biggest in southern England. My intention when I finished playing was to go into the sales management side of that company. All within the space of a month, I was offered three or four jobs in coaching or management: Reading, Crewe, Bournemouth. And a fellow called John Nash asked me if I'd be interested in taking over as player-manager of Kettering Town. My initial reaction was no, but I went to see him – out of politeness as much as anything – and by the time I left his office he'd pretty well convinced me I should give the thing a go.

It was a case of his firing my enthusiasm. It's a love for the game. At Oxford, we used to get a carload together and drive off to see a match in London or the Midlands. I don't think there's so much of that now. One player I do know who has great enthusiasm is Chris Waddle. I see him at games all over the place and it makes me think he'll end up in management at some point. I look at football like a hobby. It's not work. I've had a real job and I know which I prefer! I don't understand some players now who look on football as a necessary chore. I've always looked for enthusiasm in people, in players: everything else will fall into place.

And the same's true of clubs. When I went to Cambridge, even though the club was second bottom in the Fourth Division, the place was bright, clean, you felt people there really wanted things to happen. On the other side, when I went back to West Brom after leaving Man United I couldn't believe what had happened. When I'd left five years before, we'd had a great team – Statham, Robson, Regis, Cunningham – and finished third in the League. Now, they were bottom of the Second. I don't know what had gone on but you could feel that apathy had got a real grip on the place.

For good or bad, things often just seem to happen in football. When I first went to West Brom, I'd been offered the Watford job but, for one reason or another, it hadn't gone through. Graham Taylor had been offered the job at West Brom but similar circumstances meant that hadn't happened either and he became manager at Watford instead. Ten years later, I had a spell in Spain. I'd taken Atletico Madrid from second bottom to second top of the Spanish League. I came back here one midweek to sort out some domestic business and got a phone call to say: *Don't bother coming back.* Jesus Gil, the president – Mad Max I used to call him – had decided to sack me. I've still got absolutely no idea what had gone on back in Madrid. Something happened and I was out of a job!

The most satisfying thing in management is when you

see your team actually play to the level you imagine they're capable of. In 20 years in management, I can only remember it happening a half dozen times: you're sat in the stand and wishing the players would do this and then do that – and everything you're wishing, they do. West Brom winning at Arsenal one Boxing Day morning, Manchester beating Barcelona – Maradona, Shuster, all of them – 3–0 at Old Trafford. I can actually remember the games when that's happened or, in the case of a Sheffield Wednesday game against West Ham, just the first 45 minutes of a match in which we ended up struggling to get a draw!

But losing is awful. Honestly, without a shadow of a doubt, it's the worst thing there is. Sometimes you can put your hands up and say: *It wasn't our day.* But a bad performance – a game Villa lost at Coventry two years ago still rankles with me; I still lose sleep over it! I've always gone out expecting to win every game, so ten victories will never make up for a single defeat like that. Victory never compensates for losing. I absolutely hate it!

John King, Manager, Tranmere Rovers

Season 1994/95 saw Tranmere Rovers knocking on the door of promotion to the Premiership for the third successive season. John King is now in his 15th year as manager of the Birkenhead club, Mersey-side's perennial poor relation. A tough wing-half, King played in all four divisions. Promotion would have meant he could achieve the same as a manager.

•JOHN KING•

•Tranmere Rovers•

My first job as a manager was with Tranmere. I was here for seven years and people were starting to refer to me as the 'long-serving

manager' when there were changes in the boardroom and I
got the sack. There were contractual wrangles so, to start with,
I just stayed out of football altogether. The trouble is, if you're
not involved, people forget about you. So I started working
with Northwich Victoria, in the Northern Premier League.

We had a brilliant time. The first season, we went to
Wembley in the FA Trophy. We lost, but I remember saying to
the players afterwards: *Get your heads up. I hate being a loser but
we'll go in and have a drink with them. We're good enough to come
back next year*. We went back the next season and the season
after that. We had a great side that regularly beat League
teams in the FA Cup. It was part time but the players worked
really hard. I used to get them in for extra sessions during
the day – this being Liverpool, a lot of them were
unemployed – and I even negotiated a bit of extra
floodlighting so we could train until ten in the evening instead
of nine! Eventually, I got the sack for being too successful: I
was looking to make Northwich a League side and the club
didn't want that.

I worked with Vic Hallom, whom I'd had as a player, as
assistant manager at Rochdale. Again, we did really well. We
were third in the division when I got the sack this time! A new
chairman came in and decided the club couldn't afford two
men to look after the team. I ended up at Caernarvon in North
Wales and created a really good side there: we beat Stockport
in the Cup and York and Barnsley away from home. It was
then that Peter Johnson and Frank Corge came in at Tranmere,
with the club on the point of going out of the League, and
asked me to come back.

I turned them down at first but, when I realised that they
really meant business, I met them and agreed a three-year
contract. I was left with 15 games to keep Tranmere in the old
Fourth Division, which we managed on the last day of the
season. I was glad of those experiences in non-League where
you'd had to do everything: it was the same at Tranmere – I
was manager, coach, trainer, everything. The club was in a
bad state financially and all they could afford to give me was
a sponge man! But that was the start of a new era for
Tranmere. We've been at it nearly eight years, and it's been a

slow continual process but it's been a success. I really think this team can go into the Premiership.

As we've become more successful, the job's got bigger and bigger. I'm not doing everything like I was to start with. You need to be able to step back and survey the situation, so I've learnt to delegate. I've got a really good backroom staff now. No one's more important than anybody else. They're a group of really good ex-players, most of whom have been captains in teams I've managed and know the way I work. The team spirit we have, me and those boys, which transmits itself to the players, is the reason we've had the success we have. We've a youth policy here that's second to none. But when we bring kids through I don't want to have to sell them to make money; but you have to be in the Premiership to be in that position. We have to get our gates up to 15,000 rather than 8,000 or 9,000. My dream is to get the club to where we can survive on gate receipts and what have you, instead of having to sell players.

Of course, they always say that it's when you get into the top division that your problems really start. You've got to stay there. I know I can do that. It's a challenge: the objective I've always had – even when we were bottom of the League – has been to put Tranmere up alongside Liverpool and Everton. Even if we can't be a luxury liner with all the trimmings like them, we might be a pocket battleship that could sink them both! I won't rest till I achieve that. And I will.

You've got to know your job, you've got to be able to motivate, you've got to be able to bounce back from disappointment and you've got to be lucky, to succeed. I'm very lucky that I knew the great man, Bill Shankly, very well. I spent a lot of time with him and learnt a lot. When I first started in management – I was 34 – he rang me up one night and said: *Young man, I've been asked who I think is the best young manager in the game and my finger's pointing at you.* The great man singled me out and, if I ever feel a bit low, I can think back to that conversation. That's always meant so much to me. And it's made me believe in myself. I know I'm good at my job. I know I can manage in the Premier League.

Barry Fry, Manager, Birmingham City

•BARRY FRY•

•Birmingham City•

Barry Fry continued playing non-League football for several years after doctors advised him that blood clots in his thigh meant he should stop. More recently, and more famously, heart specialists have told him to avoid the excitement of a career in football management. His first season in charge at Birmingham City saw the club drop into the Second Division and the manager, somehow, firmly established as a home-town hero. It's possible Fry's apparently haphazard approach to the job will see him come unstuck faced with the challenge of running a big club. Conversely, there's every chance that David Sullivan, Birmingham City's new owner, has found the man to bring top-flight football to St Andrews for the first time in 30 years. Despite persistent rumours of his imminent departure, Fry guided City to the Division Two title in season 1994/95.

I started off at Man United – I was a Busby Babe, you know! – went to Bolton, then to Luton and then out of the League with Gravesend and Northfleet. I was 25, 26 when Dick Graham brought me to Orient. One particular game – I wasn't in the team – our sponge man didn't turn up. Now, I'm like any fan: I'll do anything for football. So I go: *I'll do the sponge job!* They said: *What do you know about all that? Fuck all,* I said, *but I'll do it!* So Dick's gone: *Alright!* I'm there, running on to the pitch, saying: *Get up, you silly bastard – I don't know what I'm doing!* But we won. And he's a very superstitious fellow, Dick Graham, and I ended up being sponge man for the next six games, because we didn't lose. It was better than watching from the stand, I suppose.

After that, every now and again, Dick would ring up and

say: *Look, I'm going to be late, can you take training?* Well, I didn't have a clue! But I liked it. I couldn't get a game – as a player, I was the great has-been that never was – so I loved bawling and shouting at other players.

After I left Orient I was playing non-League: Romford, Bedford, Stevenage and, finally, Dunstable, where the manager left and they offered me the job of player-manager. We'd been bottom of the League for eight years, so I thought there was only one way to go: up. I took the job and we still finished bottom that season! But in the summer I sort of got to grips with it and my first full season as manager we got promotion and scored 105 League goals. I really enjoyed it. I loved it then and I love it now, 20 years later.

And I'll tell you what: I still love those non-League people. I've been involved at that level most of my life and that lads there give their all: go to work at seven in the morning, finish at five, come over to training, train – they're very dedicated people. You compare that to a club like this where you get players who are looked after, get more money than they're worth, but don't give you the same commitment.

Pre-season's vital for me. It's like building a house: you've got to get the foundations right. So for six weeks you've got to work fucking hard! Train together, live together, eat and drink together: you learn about players, about who you can rely on. My thing is getting a team spirit. We had it at Barnet for years – if you're not getting paid and they're repossessing your car, you need to have team spirit to get through that! If we've got spirit, I always believe my eleven can beat your eleven, whoever you are.

I've made my career, really, by getting players nobody else wanted and getting them to believe that they are the bollocks. Getting them to believe in themselves. That's why when I was at Southend and we got £2.2 million for Stan Collymore and the chairman, Vic Jobson, said I could have half of that to spend on quality players, I told him to put 450 grand into a training ground, then get a few players for £50,000 or £75,000, and we'd make our own.

Why did I come to Birmingham? Well, look, when I left Southend we were third in the League and Division One top scorers and for a game against Leicester, who were fourth, 6,000 people turned up. My second game here, we were at home to West Bromwich Albion and got 28,500, even though we were bottom of Division One. David Sullivan's shown a real commitment here, spent money even when we were struggling. The potential here is enormous. If I can do here what I did at Barnet or Southend, you won't be able to get into the place. The expectations are higher – you get more stick: the club's done nothing for 118 years and I was getting blamed for that a week after I got here! – but I love the fans here because they're so passionate. They stop you in the street – pull up in the street, hold up all the traffic: *Beep! beep! beep! Shut up, I'm a Blues fan!* – and want to talk to you for half an hour. It's incredible the way they feel. At Barnet there were a few like that, and at Southend, but here there's bloody thousands of them. And I want to do it for them. This could be another Newcastle, you know.

John Ward, Manager, Bristol Rovers

While you could never describe the Bristol Rovers job as a fashionable one, the club's had its fair share of big-name managers over the past few years: Bobby Gould, Malcolm Allison, Gerry Francis. A high public profile isn't one of the obvious qualities in John Ward. Ward played for his home-town club, Lincoln City for eight years before moving on to Watford and Grimsby. In his second season as manager at Rovers, the virtues of stability, honest hard work and attacking football took the club to the Division Two play-off final at Wembley where 30,000 supporters saw them lose 2–1 to Huddersfield.

A lot of my career's been connected with Graham Taylor! We played in the same team at Lincoln and then I played for him when he became manager. He took me to Watford as a player, then back as a coach there and at Aston Villa. When I was out of work for a while – between losing my job at Villa, when Peter White came in, and becoming manager at York City – Graham was the England manager and I helped out with the under-21s and England 'B'.

I always wanted to be a manager. I was very interested in the technical side, reading about coaching and so on. While I was a player, I got involved with the Lincoln and District Coaching Association: I got roped into being the secretary – there were only four members so it was hard to say no! But we got a lot of things going, got the membership up to 40. I took my coaching badge in 1978. I tried to prepare for coaching and management where, perhaps, most players don't really think about the future until the dreaded 30th birthday comes round. I had the support, too. A fellow named Bert Locksley, who'd done everything at Lincoln – player, manager, physio – really backed me up and encouraged me. I try and do the same now with players here. If they're interested in coaching, I'll get them involved with our centres of excellence. It's trying to pass the thing on, I suppose.

It's a big jump from coaching to management. I was lucky, working with Graham, because he was very keen on delegation and sharing the workload. I got experience then of everything, really, apart from negotiating players' contracts. I ran Watford's centre of excellence, which introduce me to the schoolboy side of the game. Bertie Mee was there at the time and taught me a lot about scouting and how to organise a network. At Villa, I had 18 months when I was responsible for dealing with the Midlands press. Graham used to let me organise pre-season tournaments and so on: let me make all my mistakes! I learnt an awful lot from him about how to run a club and I'm grateful for that.

The big difference is that while you're an assistant or a coach, you're always working off somebody. Going into management, you're suddenly the person everybody wants to work off. Every time there's a knock on a door, there's a decision you have to make. I wouldn't say it's a pressure. It's a responsibility and I'm happy to have a go at that. It's what I always wanted to do and I think I've toughened up over the years. People used to say I was too nice to be a manager but I think that's been forgotten about now!

During the time I spent at Aston Villa, it seemed you could explain things to players and they'd happen. When I became manager at York, I found that I needed to get out on the training pitch and show them. So my whole basis now is to get on the pitch as much as I can – every day, if possible, whatever the demands of work in the office may be. What supporters want, above everything, is a good team to come and watch. So I'm out there with the players three or four hours a day, and then talking to them and to the coaching staff, preparing for the next match and going to see games. It took me 14, 15 months to get a team together that was my team, playing the way I wanted to play.

Just recently we played down at Swansea City. We were on an unbeaten run but didn't start the game well and, after half an hour, our captain was sent off. We got to half-time at 0–0 and I'd thought about how we were going to cope, being down to ten men. I knew how I wanted to organise things and asked the players if they were willing to put in the extra work to cover. I promised them I wouldn't make decisions that could let them lose 4–0 or 5–0 by losing our shape. We went out and finished 0–0, nearly nicked it. We had about 1,000 supporters there from Bristol and the response for a couple of minutes at the end of the game, of the players and the supporters – the effort everyone had put in together – was superb. It was only a 0–0 draw, but we all felt we'd really achieved something together. I came in afterwards thinking I'd got it right, the players had worked hard and they'd got it right, and that the fans had respected and appreciated that. In the dressing-room that night there was a real feeling of mutual respect between myself and the players. I think, as a manager, that's got to be the best feeling there is.

Dario Gradi, Manager, Crewe Alexandra

Dario Gradi played for England as an amateur and moved into coaching, first with the FA as a regional officer and, then, with Dave Sexton as reserve-team manager at Chelsea. After 12 years with Crewe, Gradi is now football's longest-serving boss. The team reached the Division Two play-offs in season 1994/95, while the sales of Ashley Ward to Norwich and Francis Tierney to Liverpool raised over £1 million to help secure the club's economic future.

When I first heard about the Crewe job I was working for Frank Clark as youth team coach at Orient. I quite fancied it. I remembered it as a fairly decent pitch, not too far north and, the main thing: they'd always been bottom! I wanted to make an impact somewhere. I thought that if I could get Crewe out of the bottom half of the Fourth Division everybody would think I was brilliant!

At the time, I didn't apply for it. We had some good kids at Orient, I was enjoying it and felt tied up there. By the time Crewe were looking again, though, I'd been made redundant. I applied but they said they'd offered it to someone else. I started at Crystal Palace with their kids on the Whit Monday. By the Wednesday it had become clear I wasn't going to be able to work with the manager, Alan Mullery. The Friday, Crewe phoned to say the fellow had turned the job down and was I still interested? I came up and they offered it me on the Monday!

My attitude then was that I'd be here for a year. But by the end of that first year, I found I'd started something I enjoyed. The beauty of the job was that you were starting from rock bottom. They'd got nine players. One of them was any good! He was a goalscorer, which was an asset. Other than that, there was nowhere to train, no footballs, no kit, poxy premises, no money: nothing. It was a question of going round and getting free transfers, people I knew.

We had a good spirit, though. They could see I was having a go. There was a fellow called Bob Scott here, a big scouser, mate of Bruce Grobelaar: an extrovert-plus, he was. He was captain and people had said to me: *You'll have to get rid of Bob. He's the king, runs the show – you'll never have any authority while he's here.* I said: *What do you mean? We need about a dozen of those here, don't we?* Anyway, the first day of pre-season training I only had ten or eleven of them. I'd got some new kit, bought cheap off Adidas and Le Coq Sportif, and some balls. I'd arranged with a school to train on their premises, got some portable goals. There was a mini-bus outside: I'd done a deal with the local garage who also agreed to lend the Player of the Week a top-of-the-range Renault till the next home game! This Bob Scott's gone: *Hold on! Hold on! I've been transferred, haven't I? Things like this don't happen at Crewe!* It was terrific, really. We were in it together and things went well: we finished about halfway, I think.

We started getting some good players in: Geoff Thomas, David Platt, John Pemberton. And I'd promised the directors the team wouldn't be full of arthritics, that we'd bring a bit of life and enthusiasm to the place. The local junior league, the Lads and Dads they call it, is quite strong and I wanted to get them down here, as much as spectators as anything. I organised a seven-a-side competition on the pitch here and was impressed. I took about a dozen of them, under-13s, and worked with them during the summer. One or two of them were playing for a bloke called Barry Burrell who was connected to Manchester City and didn't want them down here. In the end, I got Barry on the staff here and he really started the youth system at Crewe. I was his 'assistant' to start with! We've taken it on since Barry left, since the first good young ones started coming through: Steve Walters, Rob Jones. For a while I did it all on my own but that killed me: evenings, weekends. Now, I oversee it and work particularly with the under-14s because that's the vital stage, when boys are moving into competitive adult-type football. A club like this has to have a youth system and this is a good area for young players:

we've got 17-year-olds, 18-year-olds pushing into the first team, others down at Lilleshall. We look after our boys here and we've never lost one to a big club coming in and offering the parents money: they know they'll get a chance here. They know where they stand with me, too: by the time they come through, we'll have had all our battles! It's a matter of trust.

I've had offers from bigger clubs and maybe another job will come along that seems right for me but, until then, why should I go somewhere I won't enjoy as much as Crewe? I've got the excitement of managing the first team. As the manager, I don't have to ask permission to do things. I can coach the way I want. And then there's the pleasure of days like yesterday: a seven-a-side tournament for under-tens with four of our young players taking a team each as player-manager. Like a club within a club. Everybody has a great time: no big-heads, no superstars. Whatever frustration there may be in the team being held back by having to sell our best players, I accept it has to be like that, that there isn't any money, and get my consolation in watching the young kids develop.

Gary Johnson, Manager, Cambridge United

Gary Johnson was the 'fans' choice' to take over as manager when Cambridge United and John Beck parted company in 1992. By the time Johnson got his opportunity in the summer of 1993, the club had slipped into the Second Division. Although Cambridge had an amazing run in the spring of 1994 which almost saw them to the play-offs, things haven't been easy. Indeed, at the end of 1994/95, with United doomed to relegation, Johnson was fired by the Cambridge board. He'll start next season as manager of Conference side, Kettering Town.

•GARY JOHNSON•

•Cambridge United•

It's unbelievable how different people's attitude to you is depending on whether you've won or lost. Not just your supporters. I mean, the cleaner that comes in; the person up the corner shop; the bloke at the garage. Even the other kids at my boy's school. He's 12 but, fortunately, he's a 32-year-old midget so he can handle it. You can lose five on the trot and the minute you win it all changes. And the same the other way round. Of course, we're up and down and so I'm getting it both ways every bloody week!

I was a pro at Watford and then got transferred to a club in Sweden. When I came back, I met a bloke called Kit Carson who was running soccer schools – before anyone knew about them, they were the first – and asked me if I'd get involved setting them up. I'm a Londoner and I'd never thought to live up here but Kit sold me his house in Newmarket cheap and I found I loved it.

I was player-manager at Newmarket Town and running the schools when Chris Turner got the manager's job here at Cambridge. He got me down here doing a bit of coaching, took me under his wing really, and asked me to become reserve team manager. I was running my own business – the soccer schools – so Cambridge were getting away with paying me £40 a week. I brought a couple of players in – John Taylor and Richard Wilkins – who did well and I think the club got a bit embarrassed about my wages. So they've said: *The good news is we're going to pay you £100 a week. The bad news is you're going to have to be commercial manager as well!*

After Chris Turner left, John Beck came in as manager and made me his assistant. I even got a bit more money! And whatever you think about Beck's system we reached some heady heights – promotions, Cup runs. We took a bunch of free transfers and made Cambridge famous, you know, with the cold showers and all that. Towards the end, though, I thought John was going too far down the road: no football, just kick it out. And I didn't want to coach like that. Gary Peters came in but the club didn't want to lose me so I took over the youth set-up. I got Paul Ashworth involved on youth development and we ran that for two years until John got the sack. I was made caretaker manager, Ian Atkins came in, we got relegated and I was back as the boss.

We'd never had any real continuity here and we're trying to get that now. Obviously, having done all the different jobs I know how all the different parts of the club run and everybody knows me. I'm giving first-team debuts now to players I had here as kids five years ago when I was youth team manager. I've seen them all the way through. You can develop an affinity with everyone at a club this size – the stewards, the supporters, everybody. We are all in it together.

The other side of that is the finances. Cambridge isn't a football town and we've only got around 3,000 really regular supporters. At the start of last season we were losing something like £15,000 a week. I can't afford an assistant manager, we've cut out almost all our overnight away stops. I've got a player I can't put in my team because if he plays another game we'll have to pay the club we bought him from another £20,000! We've got to be a selling club. We have to bring on our kids, get players in for next to nothing and let people go – Dion Dublin, Liam Daish, Steve Claridge – as soon as the price is right.

Of course, the thing is, as manager you've also got to get the results. I'm looking to get this club on to a sounder footing: we brought in £1½ million on transfers last season and I gave a dozen lads first-team debuts who, in two or three years' time, will turn things around, I'm sure. The thing is, as youth team manager, as long as I'm producing kids I've got all the time in the world. Now I'm manager, it's not like that. I've got to be winning games at the same time, haven't I? For the club and for me personally in my career, you've got to have success before anyone knows who you are. But even an Alex Ferguson has had a bad time before it comes good.

John Radford, Manager, Bishops Stortford

John Radford was a fixture in the Arsenal team that won the UEFA Cup in 1970 and the League and Cup double in 1971. After moving on to West Ham and Blackburn, his career as a professional player came to an end in 1980. Since then, he's been involved at Bishops Stortford in the Diadora League for most of the past 15 years, taking them back into the Premier Division of that League in 1994.

•JOHN RADFORD•

•Bishops Stortford•

My involvement with Bishops Stortford goes back quite a while. It was around 1979 I packed up with Blackburn. I had a friend in the licensed trade and, after I phoned him to say I'd had enough of playing football, he looked around and found me a pub, the Greyhound in Thaxted, Essex. My wife Engel and I came down and had a look: a nice little country pub. We took it.

Within a couple of weeks of moving in there, I had a knock on the door from the manager of Bishops Stortford. I'd never heard of them but he'd heard I'd got the pub and over he came. It was funny: he brought the vice-chairman and a couple of the other committee-men. They'd all sit there drinking of an afternoon, trying to impress me on the drinking side, I think! I said I wanted to rest – I had a few problems with my back – and I did nothing for at least three months.

He kept pestering me, the manager, and eventually I decided to go and have a look, at least to do a bit of training, you know. It was towards the end of the season by then, so I just played a couple of games in the reserves for them. Anyway, the summer came and went. They got a new manager, a fellow called Trevor Harvey, and he came to see me: *John, just come down and see how things go.* That was

1980/81. I warned him not to expect me to play every game. I thought that maybe 20 games in a season would be about my lot.

We were playing in the equivalent to the League we won season before last, Division One of the Diadora. The season got under way and it turned into a battle between our local rivals, Billericay, and ourselves. We'd also started off in the preliminary rounds of the FA Trophy which is the biggest knockout competition you can win outside the pro game. We got to the quarter-finals and it was getting exciting! We were getting 3,000 and 4,000 people here and I was playing every game. I couldn't believe I'd kept going! It wasn't until a month or so before the end of the season I started to struggle, at which point I'd just play on the Saturday and rest during the week. I ended up playing about 65 games!

It was fantastic. Even in non-League terms, the lads were just ordinary players. Top wage was about £30 a week and I was the same! We beat Sutton in the final of the FA Trophy at Wembley and we won the League. Exactly ten years after doing the double with Arsenal, I did the same thing at non-League level. I played most of the games the following season, too, when we managed to stay in the next League up, the Premier Division. In fact, the club stayed there the next eight or nine years, until we got relegated three years ago.

Anyway, my third season I started doing some coaching and I took over as coach the year after that, when we had a great run in the FA Cup. We beat Reading in the first round, Slough in the second. I'd had the TV cameras come down to the pub and everything and they were in our dressing-room after we won at Slough, for the third round draw. We got Middlesbrough away. Malcolm Allison was their manager, Cyril Knowles was coach. We've gone up on the Friday night and stayed in a hotel. About 11.30, after the players had gone to bed, someone told me Chubby Brown was on at a wedding reception at the hotel, so we got all the lads out of bed to come down to listen and have a few beers. We were 2–0 down at half-time, just scared of them really. We knew we had nothing to lose and second half we went and had a go at them. We got it back to 2–2 and missed an open goal in the last few seconds!

No one had been expecting a replay so we just had four days to get this place ready. We had 6,000-odd people in here but Middlesbrough won 2–1. The round after next, Middlesbrough drew the Arsenal. That would have been a dream! But it was a great time anyway.

The pub was just ticking over really and I was getting a bit restless. I got in touch with Jim Smith, who was managing QPR, to ask if there were any jobs around he knew about. He said they were after a reserve team manager and I thought: *Well, if I don't have a go now, I never will.* I did that for a couple of years but the travelling and the nights out watching games and scouting were hard. And then the manager's job came up here. They'd made a bit of money selling some land and offered me a full-time job – having run the pub, I could look after the bar, too. I talked to Jim Smith about it. He'd managed non-League Boston and he said: *It's great but you'll end up doing everything yourself.* And he was right: that's exactly what's happened! But I've been here ever since.

The people who run clubs like Bishops Stortford are basically just working people, ordinary people who do what they can for the love of the club. Obviously, things have changed. It's no longer run by committee. The club's now a limited company. But the directors are still ordinary people. They can't pull £10,000 out of their pocket, so the club has to pay for itself. That makes it inevitable that I end up doing all sorts of things to keep it ticking over behind the scenes: looking after the kit, organising medical supplies, laying out the boardroom on match-day. The directors do what they can but a lot of what goes on behind the scenes, they think the fairies do it! I'm the manager but I'm the cleaner, the kitman, the barman and the groundsman too! I've just got one person here with me, Chris, who works full-time hours for part-time money. People like her are worth a million pounds to a club like this. I've got nothing written down to say what I have to do or don't. I think it just comes down to: if I see a thing needs doing, then I'll do it. That's why they call me the 'general' manager!

The Boot Room

COACHES, PHYSIOS, KITMEN, SCOUTS AND YOUTH DEVELOPMENT STAFF

I love football and I've been in the game 30 years now. And I think I understand it.

Jim Walker

I'll tell you what the best thing is: the buzz you get on match-days.

Terry McDermott

The way a mother looks after a baby, that's how you have to look after players.

Ken Barry

The great satisfaction of the job is being able to develop a love of the game in every kid you work with.

Kit Carson

Terry McDermott, Assistant Manager, Newcastle United

After a hugely memorable career, during the course of which he won every honour in the game at the heart of Liverpool's 1980s side, Terry McDermott's involvement with the game was a regular Sunday kick-about with Emlyn Hughes' Charity XI. Management wasn't part of McDermott's plans but he's now in his fourth full season as Kevin Keegan's number two at Newcastle United, continuing the transformation at St James Park which is already one of the modern game's most stirring success stories.

I never really had any aspirations to get into the coaching or management side of football. All I ever wanted to do was play. As for what would happen afterwards, I never really gave it a thought. I mean, I used to love playing charity football: meet up on a Saturday night, have a drink, play on Sunday half-pissed and go home. That was me: I loved it. No pressure, have a laugh with the lads. I'd never wanted to get involved on this side of things. I'd never tried to.

When I finished playing professionally, I had a mate who had a catering company. He'd always said when I finished I should come and be part of this company, you know, doing outside catering. And that's what I did. I put a bit of money towards it and I enjoyed that. I travelled round the country – big air shows and things like that – where we had food outlets set up, checking that everybody had what they needed. It was very different from what I was used to, wasn't too time consuming. I mean I was lucky: I didn't really need to work. I had a pension I could survive on comfortably. But I wanted to do something.

Well, as it turned out, the catering business was running

down, going bust. After I finished with it, I used to go and train at Liverpool. Dave Johnson and me would go out to the training ground most mornings, do our weights, have a run, you know, general fitness, before the players came down. We'd often still be there when they arrived and, knowing most of them, we'd stop for a chat. I'd sometimes go for a run with Graeme Souness. We'd run round and he'd tell me stories about what was going on at the club. People might think I had ulterior motives but, to be honest, I just liked the gossip. I loved that life, doing what I wanted with the rest of the day: playing golf, snooker, having a pint. But you do get bored doing the same thing – like Kevin got bored playing golf all the time, in Marbella.

Anyway, Kevin got the Newcastle job. I was astounded. I knew he was like me and hadn't had any intention of getting back into football. Now, I used to talk to Micky Quinn up there a lot: we both like the horses. I've phoned the training ground one morning to speak to Micky. The physio's said: *Hang on, Terry. Someone wants to have a word with you.* So, Kevin came on, asked what I was doing and then said he wanted to give me a ring later.

I thought he probably wanted to ask me about a player or something. Anyway, that night he didn't ring and I didn't want to wait around for a phone call, so off I went, training, the next morning. I was chatting to Ronnie Moran and Roy Evans about Kevin getting the job. When I told them about the phone call, they said: *Oh, there's a job there for you!* I go for my run with Graeme and he said the same. He even said that Liverpool had been thinking about offering me a job, too. So, one minute I'm playing snooker and the next I'm supposed to be involved with two of the biggest clubs in the country!

Anyway, Kevin phoned and asked me to come up and help him: *Of course I will!* He said it was just for three months, to get Newcastle out of trouble. I was up there the next day. And we kept them up by the skin of our teeth. It was just going to be those three months and I loved it. End of the season, that was it. We went our separate ways. Of course, Newcastle now wanted Kevin to stay on. But after a month or so of talking, he phoned me up from Marbella to say it wasn't going to happen. I said: *No problem.* I'd had three great months, loved every minute of it. I just thought I'd get back on with my life. So, I've told everyone it wasn't going to come off and then, two days later, Kevin's phoned and said: *We're going back, pal! We're going to change that club round!* Back we went and signed three-year contracts.

The most important thing I do is to try and take as much pressure off Kevin as I can. Any manager at a big club needs that. I call myself The Buffer. Any problems, I try and take them away from Kevin, like Bob Paisley used to do for Bill Shankly; phone calls, the scouting network, tickets, the press, anything I can get involved with. Out at the training ground, we've got Derek Fazackerly does all the fitness work and warm-ups, Arthur Cox is here now, too. Kevin knows what he wants but he'll have a little chat with all of us to see what we think. That's what Kevin's great at: listening to other people, communicating with people.

I'll tell you what the best thing is: the buzz you get on match-day. One thing's for sure: being a player is an absolute doddle! Sitting on the touchline, look: I didn't go grey, I went straight to white! I love the matches, the atmosphere when you go out to kick around with the players before a game. The hardest thing is not being able to do anything about what's happening in a game, if you've been a player yourself. The ups and downs during a game, it's terrible. I understand why managers get old before their time! But at least we don't rant and rave on our bench. I do my bit before a game, go round and try and lift individual players. With all of it, I'm doing something I love doing but if it finished, well, I'm like Kevin, financially secure. And I think that rubs off. It's not so intense: you've not got to win or you're out of a job. We can have a joke, have a laugh with the players, don't pile pressure on them. We can enjoy it, can't we?

Gary Phillips, Assistant Manager, Barnet

Gary Phillips returned to Barnet in 1989 after spells at Watford, Brighton, Birmingham, West Brom, Brentford and Reading. As well as being the team's first-choice goalkeeper, Phillips has worked behind a desk at the club for several seasons, too. 1995 was his testimonial year at Underhill.

I'm now officially the assistant manager. But I've had a few other titles! When Barry Fry first brought me here from Reading, I was the groundsman. Barnet were semi-professional then, in the Alliance Premier League, but I came on full-time money so, to justify that with the rest of the lads who just trained two evenings a week, I was groundsman as well. When I first came, on the Christmas Eve, Barry got nicked: he was rolling the pitch, driving up and down it in his car! He used to get us to train with a roller too, rolling the pitch – or the mudflat as it was then. When the club went full time I was able to jack in the groundsman job. Then, when the shit hit the fan here in 1993, and we had to get rid of all our players, I was put in the position of caretaker-manager and then full-time manager. Ray Clemence arrived in January '94 and, at first, I was team manager and he was general manager. This season I've become assistant manager. Of course, all the time I've been playing too. Except last Saturday: Ray gave me the big E! *Sub (not used): Phillips.* Yes, I'll just have to get over that. I'm only 33: I've still got a few months left as a goalkeeper!

I'll tell you about a week when I am in the team! On the Monday I'll get in about 9.30, go straight to the training ground and deal with any phone calls. Ray rolls up about 10.30 and we start training. If we've any problems, we can sort those out in the changing-room then. Monday afternoon, we'll usually find a game somewhere. The previous Thursday, we'll have looked through all the fixtures: League, non-League, reserves, everything. So Monday afternoon I might be covering a reserve game at Highbury. That evening, I might be at a Stevenage game in the Conference.

If we've got a game Tuesday evening, we'll come in for an hour in the morning just to loosen up, play a bit of five-a-side and have a bath. Then I'd go home and have a sleep in the afternoon, before getting to the ground a couple of hours before the game to prepare myself and play. During the afternoon I completely change: kick the cat, sleep and just concentrate on the game as a player.

Wednesday, the lads will have the day off but I'll be in here quite early. I handle all the letters from kids asking for trials. Even though it's usually a Dear John letter, I like to make sure we do reply to everyone. Even if it's bad news, you give them enough respect to recognise that they've made contact. I think that's important so I suppose I've lumbered myself with the job, but it's something I don't mind doing. In the afternoon I might cover another reserve game somewhere then, if we've got a reserve game, I'll be in charge. I enjoy that: it's my team and I organise it as the manager. It's good fun because you've got the kids playing for the reserves as well and you can watch them progress without the pressure for results you've got with the first team.

Thursday we'll train quite hard after the players' day off. We'll have watched the opposition so that we can work on tactics for Saturday's game, which is an interesting session. In the afternoon, myself, Ray and the other coaching staff – Terry Bullivant and Terry Gibson – go through all the fixtures for the following week and work out which games we're going to cover, and talk about players we might be interested in. I'll then phone round our scouts to tell them which games we want them to go to and who we want them to see. I try and get Thursday evening as my one night off.

If we're away on the Saturday – we were at Darlington last week – we left at ten in the morning on Friday, trained up there in the afternoon, played on the Saturday and I got home at 11.30 Saturday night after the game. Then, unless there's a game to go to, I'll usually have Sunday off. You can see there's not a lot of spare time in a week! Sometimes it's a pain but, you know, as a player you finish at 12.30, and what do you do? Off down the golf course for the afternoon? That gets boring. It's why it's easy to step out of line, too: I can remember, when I was playing, I used to go out on the razzle in the afternoon with some of the boys just because I was bored stiff. Now, I just don't get the chance to do that!

It's hard work and I enjoy it but playing, for me, is still the point of everything and if I get dropped, like I was this week, it hurts like hell! The position I'm in, I can't afford to be seen moping about, can I? At least with all the other stuff I've got something to occupy my mind but my priority is just to get back in the team.

The most difficult thing about the job is being stuck in between being one of the lads and being part of the management. It's something I knew I was letting myself in for and I've just got to work at it. When I'm out there playing, I've got to be one of the lads. Just because I'm assistant manager, it doesn't mean that if I let a goal in it's not my fault! The difficult part is the point where you have to cut yourself off from all the banter and look at things from another point of view. It wasn't the same when I was manager: that was such a unique situation because everybody knew we were all in the shit together. I had the final word on things as the manager but it was just a great time, everybody giving everything they had not just for themselves but for me and the club. The buck stops at Ray's door now and, of course, that takes a weight off my shoulders, giving me the chance to concentrate on my game as a player. And I think it's gelled now. I'm still learning – there's a lot I can learn from Ray Clemence.

The club's my second home. Barnet have done a lot for me and I hope I've put something back. It's special down here with the fans. On the social side, we've still got a non-League attitude: the players and the supporters aren't separate. If you asked anyone who's played for Barnet over the years, they'll tell you there's a bit of a buzz about being here. The ground's awful and we've had every problem under the sun but the place is a bit special. Obviously, we all want to go on to bigger and better things but I know I come into work in the morning and I'm really happy that I'm here.

Geoff Sweeney, Coach, Bristol City

Geoff Sweeney started his professional playing career in the Scottish Second Division before an eleven-year spell with Bristol City, which ended with the financial crisis that led to the club's restructuring in 1982. He has been working on the Ashton Gate coaching staff, on a non-contract basis, since early 1993.

Well, my day starts at 4.30 in the morning. I'll get myself up, have a quick cup of tea and then off to the post office. I work at Portishead, about eight miles from home. I've got a little Honda 90, gets me there in about 15 minutes and I work, sorting and delivering mail, through until about 9.30 when I have a meal break. Second delivery comes down about ten and I'll go out and do that. When I get back the gaffer's usually pretty good about letting me go if everything's done back at the office. I make my way down to the training ground, which is at St George's in Bristol. By that time the lads have already got there and done their warm-up. What I do varies according to what the manager wants. With Clive Whitehead, I'm in charge of fitness at the club and we both work on youth development, too. One day I might work out some runs for the first team, the next I might be with Leroy Rosenior, working with the reserves. Another day I might be with the youth team. We'll usually stop for lunch about one o'clock. Three afternoons a week we take the kids in the gym, working to build them up physically. The other afternoons we may work on technique with anyone who needs it. That takes us through till about 4.30 and that's my day nearly done.

My wife died about two years ago so, after work, I have to go home and assess the shopping: I've two boys, one of whom lives at home, and I've got to make sure the pantry's full for him! There's the household chores: hoovering, washing, ironing, gardening. I'll usually get to bed about ten o'clock. And then it's up again at 4.30 the next morning. That's a full day but it's good to be busy. It wasn't a nice experience, losing my wife, and the club have been very good. They've taken me on to help them out and kept me occupied at a bad time in my life. Everybody at the club's been good for me and I appreciate that. Working at the club, I try to put a wee bit back in.

I was born and played junior football in Scotland. I ended up at Glasgow Celtic – that's a long time ago, they won the European Cup while I was a boy there! – but it was Greenock Morton signed me. I played for them for about five years until Bristol City bought me in May 1971. It was a good time. There were two or three of us more experienced players and the rest were lads out of the youth programme. That team played together for about five years and we won promotion to the old First Division in 1975. It was an eye-opener, a real thrill, to play at that level: Highbury, Anfield, Old Trafford. We did all right up until our last year in that division – 1980 – when crowds started to drop, the club couldn't afford to strengthen the team, the youth programme wasn't producing. We got into a downward spiral: losing money and selling our best players, people like Chris Garland and Tom Ritchie. The club ended up owing more than its assets.

In 1982, after a Cup-tie against Villa, seven of the lads got letters to come in on the Monday. They were told the club was in debt and were asked to tear up their contracts – First Division contracts, of course, City having been relegated only two seasons before – which the club couldn't afford. I got a phone call on the Monday morning – I remember I was out washing my car – and I was told to come down, too. When I got there, the lads were saying I was going to be made manager – Bob Houghton was about to leave to work in

America – but it turned out I was in the same boat as the others, they'd just forgotten to call me down with them after the Villa game. I thought it was a wind-up. I just couldn't take it in. I said: *How long have we got to decide?* The finance guy said: *Now. The club hasn't got the time.* In the end, we had three days. None of us had known the club was in such a bad state. We got the PFA down who managed to put things off for a while, but in the end there was no alternative. If we didn't back down, Bristol City would go to the wall. It wasn't a nice experience. One or two of the lads were threatened by supporters. It was a big story: the Ashton Gate Eight. In the end we settled for 20p in the pound, I think it was, the club carried on and new directors came in.

I was 37 then and it was a bit of a blow. I'd thought I had the 18 months left on my contract to sort myself out but then, suddenly, I had to start thinking about alternative employment. I found it hard to accept I wouldn't be playing football. I still find that hard and I'm nearly 50 now! After 17 years as a professional footballer, I found it very difficult to adjust to life outside the game. I played non-League, had a job with Securicor, a job at a printing factory: I couldn't adjust. I went up to Walsall for a couple of years as assistant manager before coming back here and getting the job at the post office in a department run by Tom Ritchie whom I played with at City.

It was Jimmy Lumsden got me involved here again. When he was manager, he asked me to do a bit of scouting for him. I'd watched games at Ashton Gate when I could and still had an affinity with the club in spite of what had happened in 1982. I'm glad that City survived – for the supporters, because they're the club after all. From scouting I started getting involved with coaching the under-16s, which I'm still doing. When Russell Osman came in as manager, he asked Clive Whitehead and myself to help him. We kept them up that first season and I've been involved ever since. There's so much players need these days that we didn't as players: pace, first touch, quick feet and quick awareness. That's what Clive and I are working on now.

Jim Walker, Physiotherapist, Aston Villa

•JIM WALKER•

•Aston Villa•

Aston Villa's training facility at Bodymoor Heath is built, literally and metaphorically, around Jim Walker's treatment room. Walker will work on an injured player or stand, watching quietly, while half the first team crash through or hang about after training. The Villa physio describes himself as 'football daft'. His patience and a dry sense of humour help him stay in charge when things get raucous. Graham Taylor, Ron Atkinson and, now, Brian Little have all benefited from Walker's quiet, professional approach to his job.

When I was a player – I started at Derby County – I was always interested in injuries! Not because I got a lot of them but I was always last out of the bath after the game and I used to chat to the physio, Gordon Guthrie, who's still there now, that's 20 years later. I always thought, while I was a player, that it was something I'd be interested in doing. When I actually finished playing in 1981 – because of an Achilles tendon injury – I'd already done the FA treatment of injuries course. I went straight into a job. Well, out to a job – in Kuwait with Dave Mackay – for two years, where I worked as a physio but did some coaching, too.

It's a case of being in the right place at the right time, I suppose. Dave was coming back after two years and I got a call from Blackburn Rovers asking if I fancied being physio there. And after two years at Blackburn, Graham Taylor asked me to come to Aston Villa. I've been here eight years now. I love Birmingham and I love this club. I'd be happy to finish my working days at Villa.

The FA's treatment of injuries course is over three years. You do two weeks each summer at Lilleshall but there's a lot of work during the year to prepare you for those two weeks. It's a bit like doing the full coaching badge. In fact, at the time, you didn't need the qualification but now you can't be a physio without it. I can't say the studying came very natural to me but, as a player, I had the advantage of finishing work at two o'clock so I could go home and get the books out! Even after a game: like most players I wouldn't be able to sleep so I'd get started on homework! I'd have liked to have done the chartered physiotherapy course but I played most of my football in the old Third Division where you only really earned enough to get by day to day. When I finished playing I was offered a place on the chartered course at Salford, but with a wife and family I just couldn't afford it, really. Especially as I had a job to go to.

I think I made the right choice going into this side. I love football and I've been in the game nearly 30 years now. And I think I understand it. But it's funny: as a physio you watch it from a different angle. I'll have the manager and coach next to me during a match and they'll be really uptight for the 90 minutes. Obviously, I'll want the team to do well but I'll see the game differently. Not better, but from a more detached point of view.

I think the two most important things in the job are common sense and caring for people. You know, when it comes down to it, there are doctors to diagnose problems – although you can do more as you get experience – you just have to go out there and listen to the player. If he's hurt and can't move something you shouldn't try to either! You just get him off. And, of course, a lot of the knocks you've had yourself as a player and you know what it feels like. I think it makes a difference looking after people properly: going with them to hospital, for X-rays, that sort of thing. One other thing that's important is confidence. Players need you to be in command of the situation, don't they?

Obviously, psychology's a big part of the job, too. You see players at their lowest ebb, of course, sat in here injured watching their mates out playing. You know bodies mend but it often seems like it's never going to happen. I think, again, having played myself helps me understand how they're feeling: I can be positive, set goals for them. At least I can say that every day they're in here they're going to be a little better. I can remember parents of young players in here saying we don't mind if he can't play football again, just get him to walk properly. Eighteen weeks later they're playing again and they forget how worried they were! You get to know players in those situations in a way not many other people ever will.

Danny Thomas, Physiotherapist, West Bromwich Albion

After his transfer from Coventry City, Danny Thomas became a fixture at full-back in Spurs' stylish side of the mid-'80s. At 26, playing against QPR, Thomas was the victim of a tackle of such ferocity and malevolence that he might easily have been crippled forever: certainly, Gavin Maguire's lunge deserved its X-certificate on Match of the Day that evening. Thomas, however, spent very little time feeling sorry for himself. Indeed, the end of one career that achieved a lot has pushed him into another that promises to be even more fulfilling. Danny was appointed physiotherapist at West Brom in 1992.

After the operation to rebuild my knee, I had a seven-month spell at a rehabilitation centre down in Surrey, run by the Combined Services. The physios there were really good – not just with me but everyone who passed through – and really seemed to enjoy their work. When you've had a job where it's never a problem to get up in the morning and go into work, you don't want to spend the rest of your life in a job you don't enjoy. My experience there turned me on to physiotherapy.

The rehab centre took me away from football for a bit.

When you're a player you tend to live in your own little world, mixing with other players. You ask a player's wife and she'll tell you that sometimes you can't get through to him he's so focused on his form, or his fitness. Those seven months showed me a bit about other ways to live, another perspective.

I went back into hospital to have scar tissues cut away to try and improve the knee's flexibility: if I could get past 90 degrees the rest would have happened naturally. Well, I've come round after the operation and my leg's on one of those CPM machines which bend your leg for you. It looked to me as if it was bending about 100 degrees and I thought everything was going to be okay. Unfortunately, that turned out just to be because of the angle I was lying at. The surgeon came round and said he'd not been able to remove more scar tissue without damaging and destabilising the knee. He said it was better to settle for a knee that worked fully but within 90 degrees than an unstable one. Either way it meant my career was over. And, believe it or not, that night I told my wife I was going to become a physio.

I talked to John Sheridan, the Spurs physio, and Mike Varney, his predecessor, got an interview and a place at college. At the time I wanted to get away from football completely because I thought I'd be bitter. I was still at an age when I could and should have been playing. I thought to stay around the football environment would be a bad thing for me. Of course, it hasn't turned out like that.

The physiotherapy course was three years. And qualifying was the most satisfying moment in my life, from a work point of view – far more satisfying than anything I'd achieved in football, although I achieved a lot in a short career: international caps, the UEFA Cup at Tottenham, Young Player of the Year while I was at Coventry. Qualifying was more satisfying because I wasn't a natural student. I mean, I was born able to run faster than the next man, I had ability without even trying. At college I had to really dig deep.

Once I'd qualified I waited for the right job to come up: I knew where I wanted to work and the area – out-patient physio – I wanted to concentrate on. When I started at the hospital in Rotherham, there was a lot of publicity but I realised it was important to me to be known as a physio not an ex-footballer.

My wife and I split up while I was training but I still saw the kids every weekend. They'd moved back to the Midlands where my wife was from. I was wondering how I was going to be able to see them regularly – this was after a year or so at the hospital – when the offer to work here came up. Ossie Ardiles was manager. We're old friends – he'd actually asked me to go up to Newcastle United the year before – and, although I wasn't sure about going back into football, I didn't know what the hospital jobs were like in the Midlands either, so I took a chance on West Brom.

It was funny. After the ultra-professionalism of the health service, being back in a dressing-room, with all the mickey-taking, was like coming home. With the long working hours and responsibilities it's not like being a player, though! I've been here a couple of seasons – and I'm close to my family – but I want to be good at what I'm doing and that means more study. I'm doing an MA at the moment and, long-term, I see my future back in the health service and private practice. I enjoy it here and I love football, but family life is the centre of my life and, ideally, I want to be in an environment where I can spend more time with my kids while they still want to spend time with me!

Ken Barry, Kit Manager, Millwall

Ken Barry is the first to make the comparison between his army background and the qualities he brings to his job as kit manager at Millwall: high standards of cleanliness and personal appearance, the ability to establish routines and a willingness to work until the job's done. Football, especially the dressing-room, is another all-male environment. Barry's very much in charge of what he's doing, quietly spoken as he may be, and very much at home. He's looked after the Lions' kit for nearly seven years.

I was working as a schoolboy scout for Millwall, you know, in my spare time. I'd been doing that for four or five years. When John Docherty became manager at the club, he offered me the job of kit manager. I accepted and I've been doing that full time ever since. I was in the army for nine years and when I came out I was going from job to job: a couple of years here, a couple there. It was mainly long-distance lorry driving, which meant I had my weekends free and I could go round looking at players. The scouting was my first involvement with pro football since I was a lad. I actually had a trial with Millwall when I was 16, although I was a Charlton fan when I was a boy – I was at the Valley in 1947 when they had 74,000 for the Arsenal game – and I still look for their results.

I played football, representing the army, for nine years, which I understand is some kind of record. It was quite a good standard, too. A lot of players came in to do their national service which meant I played with people like Bobby Tambling, who went on to play for Chelsea and England. In a way, I'm sorry I ever came out of the army. I was a staff-sergeant and if I'd stayed in I'd have retired on a nice pension by now! I lost a few mates in the army. I saw my best friend killed in Aden a little while before I came out and I found it very hard to settle outside. I ran Sunday junior teams – some of my boys came through as pros at Millwall – and that was very satisfying. If I saw really good boys, I'd get them down here. When the full-time job came up I jumped at the chance.

I work seven days a week. It's hard work but it's very rewarding. In the time I've been here, I've worked for four managers: John Doc, Bob Pearson, Bruce Rioch and, now, Mick McCarthy. As I understand it, it's very rare for a kit manager to be sacked. When a manager leaves a club, usually the assistant and perhaps other staff go too. But the kit man usually stays.

The way a mother looks after a baby, that's how you have to look after players, their kit and everything! I've always said that if a youngster's good enough at age 12, he'll be picked up by a scout, his mum or his dad'll take him to every game. At 14 he might sign forms, his parents still think he's the best thing since sliced bread. At 16 he signs YTS. He's told where to report, how to get there. They don't have to think for themselves. Unfortunately, a lot of the players go through life like that! It's like, if I'm outside working on my car, they can't believe it's possible to service your own car! They've always been able to just chuck it in the garage, where people like me have to do it for ourselves!

So, with the kit, you have to get to know all their different ways. A lot of players have got their little superstitions: how you've got to lay their kit out, who wants long sleeves, who wants short, where their pads go. They've got their rituals: some you mustn't talk to before a game, others you've got to talk to! It's unbelievable some of the things.

If you look at a week: we had a game Sunday. So, after the game I collect up all the kit and supervise the apprentices, cleaning up the dressing-rooms. Monday, I'll wash the kits – first team, youth team and under-18s from Saturday and schoolboys from the Sunday. In between that I do the dressing-rooms again – you could have the YTS boys in there for ten hours and you'd still have to go over them again! Pack up clean kit, bring it down to the training ground and pick up dirty kit from here – staff and reserves. This morning the

124

washing machine's gone wrong so I've dived in there and fixed it. Cleaned yesterday's kit. Take delivery of medical supplies and bring them down to the training ground, here, then take dirty kit back. We've got a game tomorrow, so have the reserves and under-18s, so that's a full day through to 11.30 at night, doing kit, dressing-rooms, all the refreshments for us and the visitors. Thursday, all those kits will want washing and I'll pack up the skips to travel away on Friday. I'll pack up the reserves' and youths' kits for their games down here while we're up at Tranmere. And then, back in on Sunday to do all the washing again. That's how it is: week in, week out. It's the sort of job that if you didn't like it, you'd say: *No way!* And you have to be a single person. A wife would never put up with it: you'd never see her!

There's a personal satisfaction when the team runs out and the kit looks good, when people say how the kit always looks new. But the only real satisfaction at a football club comes with success, on the pitch, with good crowds, the club making a little money. And it's rewarding to be working here when that happens.

Ray Kendall, Kit Manager, Bristol Rovers

Ray Kendall grew up in Stapleton Road, a couple of miles from Bristol Rovers' old ground at Eastville. Sixty-six this year, Kendall followed the Blues as a boy and was involved behind the scenes by the time he turned 20. The club's present situation – playing home matches at Bath City's Twerton ground, while training and administration are based several miles north at Keynsham and reserve and youth fixtures use another site again, east of Bristol – makes the job of being Rovers' kit manager a little complicated, to say the least.

On a normal day I'll leave home about 7.30. I live in Bristol, about nine miles from the training ground. I call in at the Crest Hotel to pick up some bags of ice – we haven't got a machine here and there's no running water. Then I come back into Bristol and up to the local launderette in Queens Road to pick up the kit I'd left from the previous day. We're here in the portakabins and I can't do the washing: I have to take it in each afternoon for a service wash. I'll get out here around 8.30 and put all the kit out on hangers. The pros take their kit home but I do it for all the YTS boys and staff. The YTS boys come in about nine to do all their chores, the players go out to train. I then sit down to try and work out where we are with different match kits: bag some up for washing and repack the clean sets. It all needs to be organised.

For every game – and all our games are 'away' games, of course – I'm travelling with over 2,000 items: studs, laces, tie-ups, insoles, bags, a TV, telephones, ice. On Saturdays, for games at Bath, I make sandwiches at home for the boardroom and the match officials, load the van up here, go down to Twerton Park and set out the dressing-room. Then I go up and set up a bar for the directors upstairs, organise refreshments for half-time in the dressing-room. The YTS boys will help me load up again after the game. I take the dirty kit up to the launderette, pick up a clean one and drop it back here to the training ground in Keynsham. Saturday's a long day!

How it happened for me was, one afternoon in 1949 I was watching Gloucestershire play Somerset at the County Cricket ground in Bristol. I was sat alongside a fellow called Ron Moules, a lovely man who turned out to be Bristol Rovers' assistant secretary, although I didn't know that at the time. We sat talking and struck up a friendship, and he asked me what I did on a Saturday in the winter. Well, I used to play football on the Downs: not much of a player, to be honest, but I used to enjoy it. He asked if I'd come down and help them out.

That first season, 1949/50, I started taking school tours: 40 or 50 boys, showing them around the place. I was a steward for a while, then I went on the lottery. I was chairman of the lottery when it started and for 19 years. I was chairman of the

True Blue social club and did the public address system, both for 19 years too. The 19 years was because all that time I was working at the tobacco factory at Hartcliffe. Sixteen years ago, the price of cigarettes went up 12p and I was made redundant. The Rovers chairman said to me: *You're going nowhere! Come and work for us full time.* And I started then as kit man.

I've been doing things in the boardroom for about 25 years, one way or another. I was up there the afternoon we had to quit Eastville. Things started going downhill after the South Stand fire: the market was on – it was a Sunday afternoon – so the fire engines couldn't get in and the stand went up like a box of matches. That was just before I started full time. Anyway, the crunch came when the stadium company was considering a new lease for Rovers. We owed money and Tesco came in wanting some of the site and we ended up moving out and just playing at Eastville on Saturdays. Then, one afternoon, we were all in the boardroom having a whale of a time – I think we'd just beaten Mansfield 3-0 or 4-0 – when the chief executive came in and said we had to be out by six. He turned up with this big furniture lorry and we literally emptied the boardroom: cup, saucers, shelving, carpet. And that was it. Such a sad time. And then we negotiated Twerton Park.

It's all right at Twerton but there's only 1,100 seats. It's not enough revenue, is it? We've tried to move to so many sites: Hanbrook, Filton, out by the Parkway, Mangotsfield, Severnside. The council just keeps turning us down. You can imagine, it would be a dream for me: having a cupboard I could lock to leave all my things in! But we carry on. We're down here in these five portakabins and I still enjoy every minutes of it. This is a real family club, we're all in it together. It's a huge part of my life: the comradeship of all the people you've known over the years. I've just had a testimonial season. There's no way I want to pack it in now, no way.

Allen Batsford, Youth Development Officer, Millwall

Allen Batsford was spotted playing junior football for a club called Chase in Middlesex by the legendary Arsenal manager, Tom Whittaker. It was the start of a 50-year career in the game. As youth development officer at Millwall, Batsford now works in an environment profoundly different from the youth scene that he grew up in. Now in his 60s, he appears to have kept up with changing circumstances. Manager Mick Macarthy, has reaped the benefit: Roberts, Dolby, Beard, Savage and Thatcher are all ex-YTS boys who've made their mark in the first

team over the past three or four years. Another, Mark Kennedy, cost Liverpool £2 million in March 1995. During the course of a working life that's not been without its disappointments, Batsford's learnt the virtues of patience without sacrificing his excitement at the prospect of a new boy making good.

I signed amateur forms for Arsenal when I was 14 and then went pro at 17. I was there from 1949 to 1955. I left Highbury and went down to Folkestone, Ramsgate, Margate, a lot of little non-League clubs. I couldn't see how I was going to get in the Arsenal first team and I had a mate who was already playing at Folkestone. Their manager came up and signed me. I think you always need someone to talk to. I could have done with someone then to take me aside and say: *You can do better than that.* But I was on my own, really. It's one thing I hope our young lads have now: even if they're going elsewhere, it's my job, I think, to advise them, to help them. We didn't have that then and I went down to Folkestone.

I started coaching at Feltham and we were quite

successful, got into the Surrey senior league, and after a couple of years the Walton and Hersham job came up. I went there as manager and was there for nine years. It was a very happy time: we won the Amateur Cup at Wembley, had a couple of good Cup runs and the club was a real family – good players, too: Dave Bassett came to me from Hayes where he was kicking everything that moved and getting sent off every week. I took a chance on him, made him captain and things took off for him from there.

Time came, though, when the club had run its course. We'd done what we could and things were starting to change at board level. I read in the paper that the Wimbledon job was available. I just picked the phone up and got straight through to the chairman. They were Southern League, semi-pro, which was a step up for me. I was so keen to get the job I took a pay cut and didn't ask about players till after I'd started. Well, it turned out they only had six! They'd had a big clear-out when the old manager went. When I asked about money for new ones, they told me I could only pay £15 a week. In the end, they backed me and I brought five lads from Walton, including Dave Bassett. We started with about 14 players – no reserves, no youth team. The club was broke. We lost our first game at Nuneaton and then went 26 unbeaten, including an FA Cup run when we beat Burnley 1–0 up there – they were third in the First Division – and then drew Leeds away – Bremner, Giles, Lorimer, all of them. It was great: we ran and ran, shut them down and got a 0–0 draw. We played the replay at Palace, about three weeks later for various reasons. About 44,000 in the crowd and we lost to an own goal by Dave Bassett! It was a great time for the club. We won the Southern League three years running, too, and that got us into the Football League.

Once we went up we struggled a bit: we were still part time, the club had no income, really, and not everyone involved was pulling together. It was a new thing for everybody but a new board had come in by then under Ron Noades and I felt isolated, really, and under a lot of pressure. It got to me, to be honest, and one day I just blew my top. Went out to the training ground and told the lads: *I'm finished.*

I shouldn't have done it, really. Again, I could have done with someone taking me to one side but that was it.

I did a bit of scouting for QPR. I'd packed my job in and gone full time at Wimbledon, so I needed the work. I went to Hillingdon for 18 months. Then Wealdstone, where we turned things round after a bad start. We were rolling along, fourth in what is now the Conference. I went down the High Street to bank the week's money and got a really bad pain in the chest: it turned out I had to have a triple bypass. By the time I got back, they were ready to sack me! I was out of a job again.

For a few years I worked with Dave Bassett at Wimbledon, then Watford and Sheffield United, until the job here came up, first as chief scout, then on the youth development side. And it's a seven-day-a-week job this! Talking to parents, organising coaching, the centres of excellence, games for the different age levels, running a scouting network, inviting kids in, doing the admin for the YTS boys, their lodgings, looking at players. But you can't get away with less. It's a great job and Millwall are super: I thoroughly enjoy it. Sometimes I'll get a hankering for management, but then I think: *Hang on, I'm 63 now and I know all that goes with it – I'm better off here.*

Kit Carson, Youth Development Officer, Peterborough United

Norwich City's unlikely success over the past decade was, in large part, the result of bringing on young, home-developed players like Tim Sherwood, Ruel Fox, Chris Sutton and Robert Ullathorne. Kit Carson was the youth development officer who saw those and a dozen other youngsters through into the professional game at Carrow Road. When Carson joined Peterborough

United three years ago, of 36 associate schoolboys at Norwich at the time, 34 asked if they could join him at London Road.

I come from a football-mad family and I've always been in love with the game, but was never really good enough to play it. I went to university in Hull and while I was there I qualified as a coach. I got a job teaching economics down in Bedford. It was a rugby school, so I formed a football club in the school, thinking I could put my ideas about the game into practice.

I always remember, as a boy, meeting Albert Quixall, the Sheffield Wednesday and Man United player – a genius, a real Stan Bowles type – and him saying how football could be dramatically different if everyone could learn to make a friend of the ball. English football's always had this battle between individual skill and systems, I think, and I had this idea that if you could produce really skilled players and then organise them, you'd be able to change things for the better.

Anyway, I'd made a team with the kids at the school and, rather than being intent on winning, we just tried to be brilliant, to look brilliant! We never won any leagues – won a few cups – but people would say: *What a cracking little team!* I realised quite quickly I was more interested in that team than I was in teaching economics.

When I was about 24, I set up a football school. I wrote to people and asked if they'd come and do some coaching. This was in the mid-'70s, before soccer schools were happening. Although we didn't have premises I got people like Steve Heighway, Brian Hall, Bryan Hamilton and Dai Davies to come and work with the kids wherever I was running a course. My first-ever school was in Liverpool for 40 youngsters: 180 kids turned up! Well, we managed somehow. It was a roaring success and we never looked back. The schools became the PGL soccer schools and I used to pull the most talented boys out to make up a national PGL team, with their own school, who we used to play against teams at pro clubs.

As a result of all that, Norwich City offered me a full-time job. I tried to establish a policy there of finding boys when they were quite young, developing their skill and

131

abolishing the need to win anything. We worked hard at it at Norwich and built up a system based on skill rather than winning, at least up to ages 15 and 16 when the aggression and hardness of competition needs to come into their game.

Today, nothing that I'm saying sounds new but back in the '70s the FA banned my schools and tried to stop FA coaches working on them. They were furious somebody was doing something they should have done 20 years before. They didn't know how to do it themselves and were completely opposed, in those days, to the idea of professional players working with kids. But I loved all that, taking on the establishment! I used to take PGL kids over to Ajax in Holland to train with their boys. Leo Beenhaker, the Ajax coach, used to have hysterics about how backward attitudes were over here. Coaches all over Europe used to say to me that the English set-up would get nowhere until they let the professional clubs work with the youngsters. There are lots of good people in education doing great stuff with kids and with clubs, but the Schools FA still has far too much power. We've got to move forward.

You can never spot the ones who'll make it. Chris Sutton is the classic example. He was with us at Norwich but, under-14, we just didn't think he was going to be good enough. At 16 he scraped in as a trainee and then, after a year in the youth team with Lee Power, he never looked back. You know the future internationals are there in your teams but you can't tell who they are! I suppose if you could, I'd be out of job!

Apart from the thrill of seeing boys you've worked with make it, knowing you've had something to do with their success, the great satisfaction of the job is being able to develop a love of the game in every kid you work with. Although most of your boys aren't going to make it, almost all of them go on into the world loving football. And that's my greatest pleasure, passing that on, whatever those youngsters end up doing with their lives, inside football or not.

Paul Ashworth, Youth Development Officer, Cambridge United

Paul Ashworth has been bringing on school-age footballers at Cambridge United for nearly four years. He founded his own company, Pass Soccer Schools, as an 18-year-old. Still only 25, Ashworth is the youngest youth development officer in the country. The importance of his role at a club like Cambridge is reflected in the proportion of last year's youth team – six players – who made first-team debuts last season.

My involvement with football started through Kit Carson, who's now youth development officer at Peterborough. He used to have a company called PGL which ran soccer schools. Kids from those schools used to go all over the world: I went to America when I was 13, Sweden, Denmark, playing in different tournaments. I knew at 16, though, that I wasn't going to be good enough to make it as a player. I remember Kit ran a weekend, a Careers Weekend he called it, where he got all the boys in and asked then what they wanted to do. The idea was that he'd advise or help you in any way he could if you wanted to go off to university or whatever. Like any eleven-year-old or 12-year-old, I'd thought that I was going to be a pro, but by this state I knew I wasn't strong enough. At 16 most kids would know in their hearts whether or not they're good enough. The difficult thing is admitting it. Well, when I said this to Kit, he said: *Thank God! I didn't want to have to tell you!* Anyway, when he asked me what I wanted to do instead, I told him I wanted to do what he was doing. That was natural: a lot of my boys have said the same to me. Kit said: *Great! Why don't you come with me to Finland with my under-12s?*

I went off with them the following summer and I loved it. From then on, I didn't want to do anything else. I was 16, remember, and here were these kids who were ready to run through brick walls for you. You could tell them how to do things on the pitch: it wasn't the power, it was the pleasure of seeing things work for them. I knew it was what I wanted to do.

I was still at school that summer. When I went to see the careers officer and told him I wanted to be a football coach he just smiled and patted me on the back: *What else do you want to do?* I knew myself that at 16 I'd no chance of being a coach, so I went off to college for two years in Kings Lynn. That meant moving away from home for the first time which was a good experience. I did two A-levels and a sports course which was an A-level equivalent.

At the end of my first year, me and a mate decided we'd run little soccer schools in the holiday. His didn't really get off the ground, but I went back to my village just outside Norwich and got 38 kids to come along. I went round local schools explaining what I was doing, hired premises, put posters up everywhere, photocopied my own booking forms. It cost the kids just £19 for the week's coaching. Ronnie Brooks, Norwich's ex-chief scout, came down and helped with the coaching and Ian Crook came and presented the trophies. It really took off. I even made about £400 which, for a 17-year-old, seemed like a lot of money!

I finished my A-levels and got a place at Liverpool Polytechnic but I decided to defer that for a year and have a go at running soccer schools. If it didn't work out I'd have the place at Poly to fall back on. I produced a little brochure and ran about five soccer schools, earning enough to live on while I lived at home. I selected a representative side from those five schools and took them to Belgium for an under-ten tournament. The parents came along too and that was a really great trip. We even finished runners-up! I just loved having that kind of responsibility for the first time.

The following year I went into partnership with a fellow named Tony Williams – who now works with Kit Carson at Peterborough – and we ran 24 soccer schools during that year, all over Britain. We put together representative sides from under-tens to under-14s which, after a couple of years, were good standard. A couple of lads started being taken on as schoolboys at pro clubs, here at Cambridge, at Leyton Orient, and I began to realise that the whole process was working!

A fellow named Neville Proctor, who was chief scout with Cambridge, introduced me to the then manager, John Beck, with a view to bringing my school set-up into the club. Cambridge had nothing organised with the younger age groups, you see. John Beck was all for it. I met Gary Johnson, who was then the youth team manager, too. I came in part time but kept running my schools which now had the connection with Cambridge United. I got on very well with Gary and it was he who pushed to get me here full time. That was three years ago. The soccer schools are still going. I have someone who runs them full time – about 60 schools a year which are open to anybody of any standard. I concentrate on the representative sides which are, in effect, Cambridge United sides. I've now got a network of scouts, too, who recommend players whom we'll get involved with the representative teams and the Cambridge set-up even though they've had nothing to do with the soccer schools.

The kids have got talent. That's why they've found their way to you. My job is to get the best out of them and a lot of that is psychological, dealing with their backgrounds, giving them confidence. That's why I still run a lot of trips. A lot of their development as people can happen in those situations and so a lot of my time goes into organising them, raising funds and so on. It's worth it, too, because it's often the kids with difficult backgrounds or personal problems who are the ones who've really got a chance of making it as players. And even for the boys who don't go on to be footballers, the trips are experiences they'll remember for the rest of their lives.

Graham Rix, Youth Team Coach, Chelsea

During the 1970s and 1980s, Graham Rix enjoyed a hugely successful playing career with Arsenal. In 1993, at 37, Rix was appointed youth team coach at Chelsea by new manager and ex-England team-mate Glenn Hoddle. Late in 1994, injuries and UEFA's 'foreigners' rule led to the youth team coach making first-team appearances during Chelsea's European Cup Winners Cup run.

I'll be perfectly honest. My last year out in France with Caen and my year in Scotland at Dundee, I was always on the lookout for a manager's job or a job as a player-coach somewhere. I wanted to carry on playing but I left Dundee not knowing what I was going to do. Glenn Hoddle got the manager's job here in 1993. We've been great mates for 20 years and, two days after starting work at Chelsea, he phoned me and offered me the youth team job. I thought about it: *A three-year deal whereas, if I carried on playing, it would be a year here and a year there.* The money wasn't great but I knew Glenn and wanted to work for him, so I agreed.

I've come in not needing the job but wanting to do it: wanting to work for someone I trust and admire, and to have the chance to work with – to influence – lads of 15, 16, 17. At 23 or 24, players have got all their bad habits but with the kids it's different. And they can't believe it: with mel it's all football, football, football – skills and touch. I've come to the job straight from being a players, so working out pre-season training, I thought: *What did I enjoy most as a player? Playing!* So that's what we did. Hard work, but with the ball.

When I say skills, I don't mean standing around flicking the ball up and catching it on the back of your neck. I'll work on simple activities: a 20-yard pass, say, on to your mate's chest; he flicks it up, catches it on his foot and then does the same for you. I'm still able to show them exactly what I want. And then they have to do that 20 out of 20 times. Then 30 out of 30. I ask them: *Why do you need to be able to do this?* Because it's the FA Cup final, there's a minute to go and you get the ball. There's a lad free, there, and you've got to pick him out. It's got to be played perfectly: that's when you need it. At some point in your career – you could be playing for Barcelona, you could be playing for the King's Head – you're going to need it. And at that moment, you'll know exactly what to do and know you can do it.

I remember years ago saying to my wife that I'd like to be a youth team coach. Then, as time went by and I got to my mid-30s, I started thinking: *No. I should go higher than that.* But I'll tell you: now I'm in this job, I'm glad I didn't get some of the manager's jobs I applied for. That's really hard. If you've not got the money to spend, coaching and enthusiasm will only take you so far. If your players are no good, you're no good. I've seen what the pressure can do to people like Glenn or Liam Brady. If my lads lost on a Saturday I don't like it but it's not splattered all over the papers. My job here isn't to win the Youth Cup or the South East Counties League, it's to try and produce lads at 18, 19 – two or three at a time – who understand the game and can fit into the first team. That's what Glenn wants from me, too.

I've got no coaching qualifications. Neither has Glenn. People have said to me: *Why don't you go off and do your badge?* But I don't agree with a lot of the FA's methods and, anyway, I think they should be teaching people how to coach not what to coach. I won't go off and pretend to agree with it all for two weeks: that just helps them carry on doing things the wrong way. I'm lucky that I do know how to explain things to people, so when I got this job what I had to do was sit down and work out what I thought a player needed at top-class level. You've got to be fit – if you're not fit at 16 you never will be. You've got to understand the game – that comes from experience. You've got to be able to pass and control the ball, which is what I spend most of the time doing with my boys: learning to control the ball, already knowing what you're going to do with it, able to do what you want to do.

It's good that I know what it's like to come through a youth system, leaving home at 16. It's happening to my lads now and it's a difficult time: you're homesick, you're growing up, feeling a lot of pressures for the first time. It's hard work, too, and I can relate to how they're feeling. They're important years, 16 to 19.

I can't remember ever working so hard in my life! After the first couple of months of my first season here, I was drawn, haggard: I was knackered! I'd been a player for 20 years: coming in at ten, putting on your kit and boots that someone else had cleaned for you, going out and kicking a ball around for a couple of hours before you came in, slung your dirty kit in a corner, showered and went home. Four days a week, Wednesday off: I'd had that for 20 years. Now, I've got to be in here with my lads while they're cleaning the first team's boots, haven't I? It's a nightmare. I never see the missus! I never see her! Things actually got difficult between us for a while because of it, after 17 years being happily married. I was never at home and, when I was, all I wanted to do was plonk in front of the telly, have a drink and unwind. People had warned me but I thought: *No, four great kids, a great wife, I'll have no problems*. But I did. Gill and I sat down and talked about it and she understands this is a stage I need to go through if I'm going to end up managing Arsenal! But it's hard. It hit me like a brick wall, I'll tell you. I think I'm getting used to it now, but this is the hardest I've ever worked in my life and the wages are the lowest I've earned in the last 20 years! I must really want to do it, mustn't I? I love it! I really enjoy it.

Gwyn Williams, Chief Scout, Chelsea

Since he started work at Stamford Bridge nearly 16 years ago, Gwyn Williams has been youth development officer, assistant chief scout, youth team coach, reserve team manager and first team coach. He has been Chelsea's chief scout since Glenn Hoddle took over at Stamford Bridge in 1993.

I remember my first day at work here: Chelsea 2 Preston North End 0. Clive Walker and Ian Britton scored to take us to about halfway up the Second Division. Geoff Hurst was manager and Bobby Gould was his assistant. I'd been a deputy headmaster at a big comprehensive school in West London. I was a pastoral deputy which meant, basically, I had to oversee the welfare of all the kids with problems and their families. They gradually took all my PE work – the work I enjoyed – away from me. Because I could handle the kids with problems, I got them all and I started to become very disillusioned. When Geoff Hurst took over as manager at Chelsea, he sacked everybody and advertised all their posts in the *Daily Telegraph*. I applied for every job! And I ended up with the job at the bottom of the list: youth development officer. That was Saturday, 2 December 1979, and I've been here ever since.

At the moment, I'm chief scout but I'm also overseeing youth development because our officer, Dave Collier, was seriously ill last year. Quite early on here, I worked with a lot of very good young players, some of whom – like Graeme Le Saux and Gareth Hall – signed for us, some of whom – like Paul Merson, Vinny Samways and Martin Keown – didn't. Dennis Wise I've known since he was 13 and tried to get him here then. By the time Southampton let him go at 17, we had a very strong youth team and couldn't promise him anything. Four years later we had to pay £1.6 million for him. Mind you, we could probably double that money now. It can be a funny old job, trying to bring kids on!

The sooner we can streamline the whole business, the better it'll be for the game. We need to take the cream of ten-year-olds – the top two per cent – and give them the time and attention – train three evenings a week and play small-sided games at weekends – so that at 15 we and they will really know if they've got a future. This wouldn't just help the clubs it would help the kids, too, giving them the chance to develop with other boys of the same standard. At the moment, the Schools FA still has a very strong hold on the game at grassroots level. My daughter's a swimmer, she swims for a club as well as her school. If there's a clash, she swims for her club. With football it's the other way round: school commitments come first. We've got plenty of good players in this country. We need to spend more time with them when they're young, working on their basic technique – touch, control and awareness – rather than them playing several games a week for school, representative and Sunday sides.

My attitude is that if you've a good relationship with your kids they won't leave. There's a lot of fear at clubs, of losing a ten-year-old who might become a good pro somewhere else, but I've always felt that if you look after the kids and their parents they won't want to leave you. All right, one or two might imagine the grass will be greener somewhere else, or another club might give the parents money to get the boy: that's always gone on in football, perhaps it always will. Basically, all clubs are in it together, aren't they? The important thing is to raise the general standard, whether it's at Man United, who've a successful youth policy because they've paid attention to it and have the facilities and financial resources, or at Crewe, where they succeed just by hard work. Those are the standards every club should be striving for.

Potentially we can achieve more now: we know more about diet, physiology, the science of sport. But it still comes down to hard work: the boys who'll succeed are the boys who want to succeed. There may not be as much talent out there as there used to be but the network for finding it is much stronger now. I've got a lad here now at under-13 level who's already been at 20 different League clubs. If a boy's good, clubs get to hear about it! Mind you, a good 13-year-old doesn't necessarily make a pro. You can't really tell if they've got the desire until they're about 15. So few players have the ability of a George Best but players like Roy Keane or David Platt can be successful because they have that desire and are prepared to work hard.

Coming back to me, I wanted to be a player. I was at Leyton Orient as a boy but wasn't taken on. I didn't really know what to do so, at 18, I left North Wales and came to London University to do a degree in Physical Education. I stayed in London to teach and played semi-professional football, amateur football as it was then: Walton and Hersham, Kingstonian, Hayes, Southall, Wembley, Maidenhead, Wimbledon before they joined the League, training Tuesday and Thursday evenings and playing on a Saturday. I became a head of department in PE but football was always my specialist sport. The promotion to deputy head came very early and I thought it was where I wanted to go: I wanted to be a headmaster. But, as I said, 18 months later I was thinking: *I don't need this job!* The 12 years of teaching were invaluable, though, coming to work here: whatever age they are, whatever they're doing, kids need discipline and they need handling. Young players are no different and my experience made that side of the job straightforward for me.

At the time, my family weren't in favour of the move. As a teacher I was in a job for life, whereas the general rule in football is: last in, first out! You can imagine, when Geoff Hurst got the sack a few months after I arrived, I started scurrying around, phoning up schools about the possibility of work. But when John Neal came in and, on Ken Bates' instructions, cut back on staff by making youth development and youth team manager one post, I was fortunate enough to keep the job. Even though I've been here a long time, you're never secure, are you? Glenn could call me in tomorrow and say: *Sorry, Gwyn, you're not my cup of tea.* Or he could get a job elsewhere and a new man might come in and say the same. But that's football. For my part, I've loved the club since I first came here and have been happy to stay. I've the satisfaction now of looking at half a dozen of the first team whom I've known since they were 12 or 13. I've still got all my desire: for the job I do here.

Ron Howard, Chief Scout, Millwall

Ron Howard has been involved with football for nearly 50 years as a player, coach, referee and scout. He was 40, though, before his love of the game became the basis for a career in football. It sounds like a fan's dream: Howard will watch half a dozen games a week throughout the season. It's a job, though, that comes with its fair share of paperwork as well as the responsibility of organising a scouting network. He's been chief scout at Millwall for nearly three years.

This goes back a few years! When I came out of the army I was playing a bit of football but I picked up a knee injury that put paid to me. This was mid-'50s. I don't know if I'd have been good enough to play at professional level. Anyway, I never did. But I didn't want to drift away from the game so I started to take an interest in coaching. I began helping out a fellow who had a full FA coaching badge and, although I never did the courses myself, I ended up coaching in South London even though I've always lived in the Wembley area. You know, this fellow said: *I'll run you down there.* I'd watch and listen until one day he couldn't make it and I ended up doing it. This was coaching in schools, and I really started to enjoy it.

142

Wanting to get more involved, I took a referee's badge. I thought: *At least I'll be out there, even if I can't play!* I was only late 20s and I was made up to class one in only four years, which was quite fast going. I got some FA appointments, games with top amateur sides of the time like Leytonstone and Hendon, which were plum jobs for a budding referee. I loved it. I started to ref in the South East Counties League, which I've been on the management committee of now for over 20 years.

At the same time – I've always been a QPR fanatic, it was my nearest team when I was a boy – I was down at Loftus Road, coaching with the kids, keeping myself fit. They let me have the run of the place! And, as I progressed as a ref, I used to do all Rangers' pre-season friendlies. Some of them were smashing games: I remember one against the Italian Olympic XI! And then, one day, the manager – Les Allen – asked me to go down to Portsmouth to watch a game and report on a player. That was the start of everything that's happened since.

I kept refereeing because I loved doing it but, eventually, I got 'shopped'. You weren't supposed to referee and scout. That was the rule and one day, when I tried to pick up a young player, someone wrote to the FA and I had my badge withdrawn. Well, I left it a year and got my badge back but, after a few weeks, I packed it in because the scouting was taking over. I was assistant to the chief scout at QPR for quite a while.

All this time, of course, I'd had a good job. I was a buyer for an electric motor manufacturer. Then Gordon Jago took over at Loftus Road and asked me to go full time as a scout. I went home and scratched my head, wondered what to do. It was my wife said to me: *If you don't have a go, you'll never know.* Well, that was good enough for me. I joined QPR full time. It was a risk then but, with recessions and whatever, who knows what would have happened if I'd stayed in industry? As it is, I've never been out of work since!

I spent six seasons at QPR and then went to Cambridge United with John Docherty when John took over from Ron Atkinson. I was there six years and had quite a lot of success before David Pleat came in for me and I moved to Luton

Town. After about eight years, I think David decided I was past my sell-by date. I had one or two enquiries and was fortunate enough to come to Millwall. I've really enjoyed it here so far. It's a great club to work for.

The higher up you go, the more scouts you'll have working for you. The job's pretty well the same everywhere, though. At Millwall I've got seven or eight people I'll keep busy right through the season with weekend and midweek games, League and non-League. The youth development officer, Allen Batsford, looks out for younger players and has his own people working for him. Some of my scouts are people who've been with me since I was at Luton, others are people who've had a connection with Millwall. Most of them are ex-players, people who've coached or managed. They're all in business for themselves and do scouting because it keeps them involved with the game. They get their expenses so they're not out of pocket but, basically, they just enjoy the involvement.

I'll spend most of my day here in the office, talking on the phone, organising scouts, doing my paperwork and going over reports on players. I watch games, too, and write up reports for the manager on the opposition strengths and weaknesses, set pieces, patterns of play. We'll usually watch opponents at least twice before we play them. Looking for players, you can't have too many contacts, can you? People move around, you can get different points of view on the same player. I've always got someone, somewhere, I can ask about anybody I might be interested in. Every chief scout needs that. And when you've been in the game for 30 years, you get to know people, don't you? Having worked at several clubs gives you a wider perspective too. The job goes on and on. And it's all I really want to do.

Jack Hixon, Scout, Sunderland

Jack Hixon lives in Whitley Bay. He's been scouting in the north-east since 1950 and is perhaps best known as the man who discovered Alan Shearer. In fact, Shearer is just one of dozens of top-class professionals Hixon has helped introduce to the game. Since 1993 he has been working for Sunderland alongside youth director Jim Montgomery. Hixon recommended Montgomery to the club as a promising goalkeeper over 30 years ago.

I was in the Royal Navy and, towards the end of the war, I was serving on HMS *Tobago*. On the same ship was a lad named Billy Elliott who'd played for Bradford Park Avenue and subsequently for Sunderland and England. I was his best man, in fact. Anyhow, in 1950, Billy joined Burnley for £23,000, which was the then record fee for a winger. A little while afterwards, he got in touch with me and said: *If you see any promising players in local football, will you let us know? By all means*, I said, *but I'll not miss a Newcastle home game to do it!* That was sacrosanct. If I wasn't stood at the Gallowgate End, how would they be able to kick off?

I was working for British Rail on shift work, which meant it wasn't always convenient to go to games and I couldn't get too involved. But, at the time, Newcastle were having their magnificent '50s Cup runs. Their League form was terrible, though. I'd stand at home games thinking: *I must be mad putting up with this!* So I got in touch with Burnley and said I'd be prepared to extend the time I put into scouting up here and that was how I really got started.

Until 1957 I worked with a fellow named Charlie Ferguson, Burnley's chief scout in the north-east. Then the

Burnley manager, Alan Brown, moved to Sunderland and Charlie went with him. They asked me to go too but, strange to say, I'd really got to love Burnley. To leave them would have gone against what I felt about loyalty. So I stayed at Burnley, which meant I worked with a wonderful man named Harry Potts. He'd been on Burnley's ground staff as a boy himself and was an ideal professional. As a manager I never heard him abuse anybody. He always had time for people: if I took a lad down to Turf Moor, even if Burnley were playing Manchester United at three o'clock, Harry would be there till two, talking to the parents, making sure they were looked after. Burnley had a great run in the '60s and it was all down to the youth policy.

So I took over as chief scout in the north-east. I didn't work full time: I had a job with a pension I didn't want to lose. But I got a couple of people in to help – George Murray and my cousin Jack Robson – and between us we could cover the whole area. The three of us worked for Burnley together for ten years. At one time we had 25 Geordie pros at the club at the same time! The first player I took to Burnley as chief scout was Arthur Bellamy, who's now the groundsman at Turf Moor. We signed players like Brian O'Neill, Ralph Coates and David Thomas.

It was a wrench when I had to move on from Burnley. I had great satisfaction from my time there. Harry Potts was a great manager and Bob Lord laid the foundations in the boardroom. We won the League, got to the FA Cup final and the European Cup quarter-finals, all with a playing staff that cost £3,000, the price Harry paid for Alex Elder. But a new manager came and our relationship wasn't good and I moved on to Stoke after 17 years at Turf Moor.

It was an unsatisfactory period. I was at Stoke, then Derby, one or two different clubs. In 1974, Lawrie McMenemy asked me if I'd work for Southampton. I thought: *Hell's fire! Southampton? Two strides and I'm in the water! I couldn't get any further away!* But I went down to meet Mr Reader, the chairman, an ex-FIFA referee. From then on it was a very happy relationship. A couple of years ago, though, with the development of centres of excellence, I started to realise there was more satisfaction to be had from working locally. That's why I joined Sunderland. You see, up here now, you can channel lads into the centres of excellence for the clubs nearby. I had a lovely time at Southampton, though. And I think it was good for them, too. Alan Shearer on his own paid for everybody, didn't he?

I'm happy that I've been able to keep up friendships with so many of the players I've been involved with. I always turn up at the weddings and christenings! It says a lot about a man like Alan Shearer that he took the trouble to ring me up from the hospital to say: *It's a girl!* when his second bairn was born.

Scouting's notoriously underpaid but I love football. When I came into it in 1950, it was the cap and muffler game. It's not that any more. When I go into kids' homes now to talk to parents, I'm representing Sunderland Football Club. I have to be able to present myself and the club in a way to let them see things in full perspective. It's not a matter just of going to games and saying: *He can play.* You look at the fundamentals: pace, athleticism, movement – not necessarily their technique: that's what coaches are there for – to work on execution! One thing all scouts have got in common is a love of the game. That's what gets you out watching schoolboy games in the rain in November.

Home

THE STADIUM

The new stadium was the lifeline.

Paul Fletcher

It was like a focal point for everything and I think that's what attracted me.

John Huxley

After the fire, everything changed.

Alan Gilliver

It always annoyed me we had to have the disasters first. It's like waiting for a child to be killed before putting a speed limit on a road.

Cliff Simpson

Paul Fletcher, Chief Executive,
Alfred McAlpine Stadium, Huddersfield Town

One Huddersfield Town fan described it to me as 'like going to watch Town play at Wembley every week'. A remarkable piece of architecture, the Alfred McAlpine stadium is also the model for a future for football. There are general lessons to be learnt from the success of the new stadium since it opened for business in August 1994. There are also, of course, specific reasons why the project at Huddersfield thrived. One is the genuine sense of co-operation amongst those involved fostered by the stadium's chief executive. Paul Fletcher enjoyed a career as a

•PAUL FLETCHER•

•Huddersfield Town•

centre forward that saw him play at all levels during ten years at Burnley. He's been at Huddersfield for just four and has already left his mark.

My career as a player was like being on holiday. I loved every second of it. But I never thought of being a manager. I was just a bread and butter footballer: I didn't understand tactics, that side. But, during the '70s, I saw commercialism come into football. I was at Burnley who were very switched on to all that: lotteries, sportsmen's dinners, banqueting, people using club facilities to bring in revenue other than gate receipts and transfer fees. I wanted to stay in football but, rather than a job where you have to move around and get sacked every two years, I wanted something settled. The commercial side seemed to offer me that.

I left the game for six years and went into marketing to get an understanding of all that, but always with a view to coming back. I believed I had to go in on the bottom rung and work my way up rather than try to trade on my name.

The way I saw it was that I'd had 16 years learning how to take a corner and how to take a penalty, which wouldn't be much help if I was competing against people who'd had 16 years of learning how to earn a living. I was offered a directorship of a company selling franchises. Instead, I bought the first franchise myself: a photography business of all things.

I made that work, sold the business on, and went to work for the parent company and became marketing manager. By that time I felt I was ready to go back into football. Again, rather than trying to start halfway up the ladder, I went into non-League with a club called Colne Dynamos. The great thing about non-League football is that if you don't sell, you don't eat. That's the best experience.

We got to where we'd sold everything we could at Colne, every ground advertising board. My colleague, Mike King, and I were standing on the pitch and everything we could see was sponsored except for a tree in one corner of the ground. Mike's gone: *We'll get someone to sponsor that tree!* I've looked through the *Yellow Pages*: I thought there must be a pub with 'tree' in its name. The only one I could find was 'The Cotton Tree'. We ran into the medical room and started sellotaping bits of cotton-wool to the tree. I phoned the pub and told him we'd discovered a cotton tree at the ground. Well, the fellow's come down and started laughing but he agreed. It got him a big splash in the local paper and was worth £1,000 to the club. That's non-League. You can be a bit daft: whatever it takes to survive.

After a year or so Steve Kindon, another ex-Burnley player and a good mate of mine, put my name forward for the commercial manager's job at Huddersfield. I didn't really want to leave Colne or Lancashire, so I turned it down at first. But two or three weeks later, I sat bolt upright in bed in the middle of the night: *What am I doing?* Really, I knew I should go back into League football. Which I did. And I've never regretted it. That was four years ago now.

Huddersfield really are a sleeping giant – like a Birmingham City – where a bit of success would bring big crowds. When I got here, the commercial set-up was the worst in football: the club didn't even have a licence to open its bars other than on match-days. But it did have one great facility: an empty 51-acre plot of land right next door where the club could relocate to a new ground. Well, that was the challenge: Huddersfield Town would have gone out of business at the old Leeds Road ground but everybody thought we'd never build a new one. We needed £2 million just to make the old ground safe. There was no Jack Walker here. The directors were local businessmen who loved the club but didn't have that kind of money. The new stadium was the lifeline.

What cracked it was the relationship with the council. We went along to meet them and opened out our plans. All we had on the sheet was a pitch. We said: *That's all we want – two acres of grass. What do you, as the council, what does the community want to build around it?* From that moment, we had them on board. And that's why the stadium isn't just a business, it's a community facility. And it's a ground-share, too, but with another sport: rugby league. It's the home of Huddersfield Town on match-days. The rest of the week the stadium's got a life of its own: pop concerts, cinemas, a golf range, a bowling alley. The stadium's a company run by the football club, the rugby club and the council. Everyone designed it and everybody uses it. Nobody's done that before.

Alan Gilliver, Stadium Manager, Bradford City

On 11 May 1985, a fire broke out during a Bradford City home game. Within minutes, Valley Parade's main stand went up in flames and 56 people lost their lives. It would be difficult to overstate the emotional impact of this event, particularly on clubs in the lower divisions where timber stands were, and still are, commonplace. Alan Gilliver, now stadium manager at Valley Parade, was working at the ground on the afternoon of the disaster.

•ALAN GILLIVER•

•Bradford City•

It was horrendous. Horrific, it was. I don't often think about it now. Of course you think about when the day comes round and I can talk about it now but, for a time, I couldn't talk about it at all, you know. My whole family was in it, in the stand: my wife, my daughter. Our daughter, we couldn't find her for ten minutes, she was on the pitch. It was horrific. My last recollection is looking out that window and all there were was just bodies, legs in the air, covered with sheets.

It changed the whole thing, the whole safety aspect in football. In fact, in some respects, they've gone overboard with it but, having said that, you can't be too careful, can you? People, lives, are precious. You know if anyone stands in the aisles on our Kop, people complain. Our fans are excellent: they're trained, attuned to it now. At least something came out of it all. We've a new stadium, purpose-built with safety in mind and everybody, our fans, have got something to show for it. And we've been leaders, in many respects, for a lot of other clubs in terms of safety. They've come and taken what we do here on board: our relationship with our safety team, our steward training and so on. We were police-free on about 14 games during the 1993/94 season.

My playing career started at Huddersfield. I got transferred to Blackburn for £30,000 in 1966 which was an awful lot of money in those days. But I had a bad back when I moved and I had to have a big operation. They had a tribunal about the whole thing and changed all the rules so that, from then on, the onus was on the team buying a player to check he was fit and there could be no comeback to the team that was selling. In my case, which brought about the change, Huddersfield had to pay Rovers back about £18,000 of the fee. Controversy seems to follow me around! I may not be so much remembered for my football but I'm remembered for that!

I played for half a dozen clubs after that, including Bradford, and ended up running a sports club at Brighouse and playing part time for Boston United. I came over here to Bradford to do some coaching with the kids and I found myself playing again, for Bradford's 'A' team in the Lancashire League, aged 35! When I finished, I was out of the game for six or seven years but kept in touch with Bradford City. I was friendly with the chairman then, Bob Martin, who asked me to come and run the commercial set-up here. The floodlights blew down the day after I started in the new job and a fortnight later the club went bust. And I'd moved house to be near the job and just taken on a new mortgage!

That was in 1983 and we've had a few different regimes since then. I'd started out running the bars, finding sponsorship money, that sort of thing, but then they've sacked the groundsman and, because I'd run a sports club, I found myself looking after the pitch, supervising all the kids looking after the ground – you know what it's like, you end up doing it all yourself! I lost count of the hours I was working here.

Obviously, after the fire everything changed. All the new safety legislation came out and they made me stadium manager. Since then, chairmen, directors, chief executives, commercial managers have all come and gone and, through all of it, people have tended to lean towards me a bit because I'm the only one who's been here all the time. But, whatever else I do a bit of, my responsibility for ground safety is paramount. I'm the ground commander and, especially on match-days, it's all down to me.

When I first took on the stadium manager's job, I didn't really know anything. There's been a lot to learn: the legislation, procedures, health and safety here within the club. And, of course, the better the team's doing, the bigger the crowd, the more work there is on the safety side. My office becomes the stadium control room when we've got a match on; CCTV, turnstile counters, exit gate indicators. It all happens here. I do love my football but the only time I'll get to watch a game now is when we're playing away!

Cliff Simpson, Safety Officer, Crewe Alexandra

Cliff Simpson still clearly re-members watching live pictures of the Bradford fire disaster unfolding on television during a quiet Saturday afternoon at Crewe's main fire station. Arthritis and a knee problem forced Simpson to retire from active duty as a fireman in 1991, after 27 years in the Brigade. This is his fifth season as safety officer at Gresty Road.

I've followed Crewe since I moved up here in 1970. After the fire at Bradford, and with Crewe having a timber stand, the club were looking for fire stewards. I was a season ticket-holder and thought this would be a cheaper way of watching the game! We didn't want any payment but volunteered to work as fire stewards. Basically it was a case of knowing what to do if a fire broke out or the alarm went off. My boss at the fire station was doing the ground safety inspection and suggested it to them, and the club was chuffed to bits they could have professional firemen there on match days. It was all cleared with insurances and everything and the Chief saw it as good PR for the Brigade. That's how I first became involved.

At the time I found out I couldn't carry on in the Brigade, the club was looking for someone to do safety work at the ground after Hillsborough and the Taylor Report. I'd never met Gill Palin, the club secretary, although she lived in the same lane as myself. I got a message to come and see her at the office and I assumed it would be something to do with fire stewarding. But she said they were looking for a safety officer and knew I was retiring: *We can't pay much but would you be interested?* There wasn't any other work around in Crewe – the jobs had dried up at Rolls-Royce and British Rail – and I wanted to keep myself occupied, even though this would only be odd days in the week and on match-days.

So, my last six months as a fireman, I used to come in here on my days off to start picking things up about Taylor and what had happened at Bradford. I went to seminars and so on, met the other people on the safety team here: the consultants, the police, the ambulance people – the Fire Brigade I already knew! It was a question of building relationships.

I started on two days a week but, after six months or so, the chairman and Gill asked me to get involved on the Football Trust side, supervising ground developments. And then they made me stadium manager, looking after all the maintenance at the ground. It's near enough full time now and it's been tremendous.

I remember after Hillsborough, as a fan, getting very edgy looking at grounds when I followed Crewe away. This was in the old Fourth Division: it was obvious money hadn't been spent on grounds. Some were in a really bad state. It was sad it took Hillsborough to bring it to the fore, Hillsborough and Bradford, but that's how it's always been: disasters and then legislation coming through afterwards. Not just with football – it's always been like that, certainly with fire legislation in general. It always annoyed me we had to have the disasters first. It's like waiting for a child to be killed before putting a speed limit on a road.

We instituted new safety procedures for the main stand, closed and tidied up the Railway End and looked at stewarding at the ground from the point of view not just of cutting the police bill but of bringing it up to a better standard. The police, the Football League and the Football Licensing Authority all had guidelines which we used to modify our procedures. The big problem was getting stewards to watch the crowd and not the game! We got the procedures in place and then looked at the stewards themselves – their appearance, their attitude, the club equipping them properly – and tried to establish a rapport between them and the supporters. All our stewards are supporters who want to be involved. And the more involved they are, the more responsible they become.

In 1994 we started thinking about stewarding games without the police. We'd been working with the stewards for two years; we were happy, the FLA were happy, the police were happy. We looked at the Scunthorpe game: 150 away fans, no history of trouble, the clubs have a good relationship. The Tuesday before the game, the police match commander said: *You're on your own, mate! I'll be in the control room with you but that'll be it!* It was brilliant. Everybody, every steward, was really geed up for it. It was like a First Night for all of us, brilliant. We've done other games since. We just keep trying to reduce the police presence and doing games without any. I've seen our stewards grow and become more professional in their attitude to the job. Other clubs borrow our stewards for their big games now, you know!

Reg Summers, Groundsman, Liverpool

While Anfield, like all Premiership grounds, has changed beyond recognition to come into line with the Taylor Report, Liverpool's pitch looks much the same as it did in the 1930s. The club has had two head groundsmen since the war. That sense of continuity has been a Liverpool strength for generations in the dressing-room and boardroom, too. However, Reg Summers, the club's present groundsman, is the first to admit his was anything but an Anfield background.

Well I used to be an Evertonian. I've been here 24 years now but when I first started I had a season ticket for Goodison. So, if there was a reserve match here and the weather was good, I used to go over and watch Everton. The last game I saw them play, funny enough, they won 8--0 and I never went again!

Even though I was an Evertonian for years, this is a job which can give you a lot of satisfaction. So, now, the better they do here, the better I feel about it. I suppose I've gradually changed so that now I want these to win everything going. But if we can't win it, I hope Everton do!

What happened was I was working in Jersey for a while and when I came back and was looking for a job, I saw an advert in the *Liverpool Echo*. It was a box number: *Groundsman required for First Division football club*. As I say, I was a fanatic Evertonian and when a letter came back from Liverpool I was a bit sick, to say the least! But I've been lucky. I've seen a lot of great things here over the years, a lot of fantastic players, Dalglish and all these.

I worked on a golf club straight from school for eight years, that's how I picked up the line of work. It's a similar job here, though it's a lot more routine: you've got your match, you put your divots back and mark out the pitch again. It didn't take long to pick up. The chap who was here at the time, Arthur Riley, was here for 54 years. He knew the best way of doing everything because he'd been doing the job for so long. Whatever he did, I copied. Arthur's dead now. He retired about 12 years ago and very little's changed, to be honest.

Like all the top teams, we keep the grass short because we play a fast game and you don't want the ball holding up. And, if it's dry, a splash of water before the game will soften the pitch a little. I suppose different pitches have different characteristics. The pitch at Anfield's very sandy so it drains well. You see some softer pitches cut up a bit when it rains. This stays quite firm – even with heavy rain it's usually only small bits and pieces come up. I just concentrate on this pitch. The only other place I go is to Everton to see the groundsman, Dougie: we're good friends and if they needed anything I'd lend it or the other way round.

I don't really feel a build-up to a game, but the thing that's always on the back of your mind is the chance of really bad weather on a match-day. It's all very well your pitch looking nice, but the most important thing is to be able to play on it on a match-day. We've had a few close calls. We played Wimbledon a fortnight ago and the rain only started just before the game but it was absolutely torrential. Come 20 minutes from the end, they had to push the ball through puddles and we were pretty lucky to finish. If the rain had come half an hour earlier, it really would have been touch and go – and, of course, once the game's kicked off there's not a lot you can do.

I used to stand up there by the directors' box, but now I sit down here and at ground level you do see more, all the divots flying up and that. I do sit here and cringe a bit when it's cutting up. You just live by the weather, really, if every ground had a roof that moved back and forth, this job would be a piece of cake! As it is, if you've got two or three games in a week and it's really bad weather, you just know it's the be-ginning of the end for your pitch! But if everything goes well, you prepare your pitch and you're happy and the team goes out and plays well, wins by three, four or whatever, even if it's only a small part, you feel you've done something towards it.

'The new stadium was the lifeline.' The last game at Huddersfield's historic Leeds Road ground, versus Blackpool, April 1994. The new Alfred McAlpine stadium takes shape next door. See page 151

HUDDERSFIELD TOWN FC

Winners: 'The last couple of years it's all started to click'. Alan Shearer and Chris Sutton celebrate Blackburn's winning of the 1994/5 Premiership. See page 47

LANCASHIRE EVENING TELEGRAPH

And losers: 'Even an Alex Ferguson has had a bad time before it comes good.' Gary Johnson surveys the scene during his last game in charge of a relegation-bound Cambridge United. See page 100

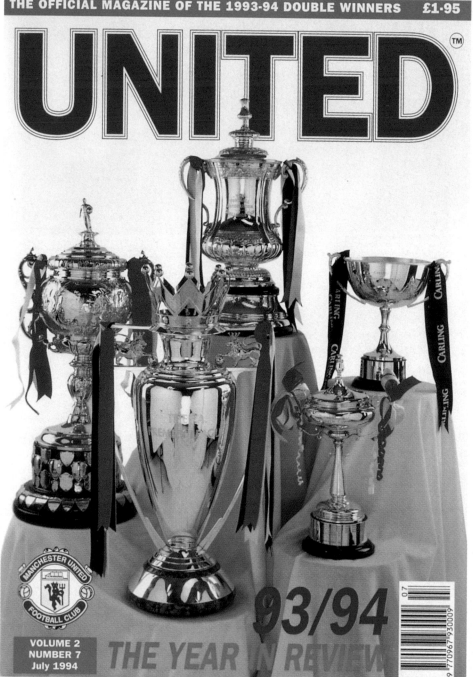

THE OFFICIAL MAGAZINE OF THE 1993-94 DOUBLE WINNERS £1·95

UNITED™

93/94

VOLUME 2
NUMBER 7
July 1994

THE YEAR IN REVIEW

'I don't think there's another operation like it in the country.'
Manchester United's club magazine, the UK's highest circulation
football publication. See page 210

MANCHESTER UNITED FC

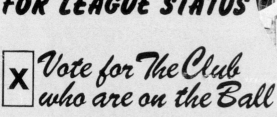

HEREFORD UNITED

FOR LEAGUE STATUS

[X] *Vote for The Club who are on the Ball*

'The night we were elected, there were parties all over Hereford.'
A brochure, written and designed by Ted Woodriffe, as part of Hereford United's campaign for League membership in the early '70s. See Page 288
MRS PAT WOODRIFFE

'There's more to football than match reports and previews.' An early edition of FOUL magazine, the predecessor of the modern fanzine, co-founded by Harry Harris.
See page 285
HARRY HARRIS

Football's Alternative Paper!

Only 12p

Number 28
April 1975

FOUL

DEATH OF SOCCER

IT'S OFFICIAL!

JOIN FOUL'S CAMPAIGN

JAIL THE HIGHBURY 2 NOW!

'My life went to pieces.' One fan overcome by it all after Everton have beaten Wimbledon to stay in the Premiership, May 1994. See page 69

LIVERPOOL DAILY POST & ECHO

It's all about players (1): 'I need to work on everything.' Ross Taylor in action for Arsenal's youth team. See page 39
BILL SMITH

It's all about players (2): 'The player just wants to play football. I try and take care of everything else.' Dennis Bergkamp with Jerome Anderson, the agent instrumental in the Dutch master's transfer to Arsenal in July 1995. See page 300
JEROME ANDERSON

Football for sale (1): 'I can still remember coming down Warwick Road with my dad and tens of thousands of people like us.' Supporters locked out of Old Trafford before a game against Leeds in January 1951. See page 182

MANCHESTER UNITED FC

Football for sale (2): 'Success on the pitch helps, of course, but you've always got Christmas, birthdays for football fans.' Fans queue to get into Manchester United's club shop. See page 210

MANCHESTER UNITED FC

John Huxley, Groundsman, Crewe Alexandra

A diehard Stoke City fan, John Huxley wasn't even sure where Crewe was when Tony Waddington brought him to Gresty Road. Like most groundsmen, Huxley enjoys an affair of the heart with a pitch he's been looking after for the past 18 years.

I've always been interested in football, nothing else. It's my favourite sport. Of course I wanted to play for Stoke. Unfortunately, I played for Port Vale, and that was only a couple of midweek games as an amateur. I never made it as a player. So I worked in the building trade. Now, I always reckoned that apprentices were costing their parents money, so if they didn't seem interested I used to give them a hard time of it. I was working at Bradwell cemetery one time with a lad named Clive, an apprentice joiner. It was pouring with rain and this Clive wouldn't go to the shop for materials even though he had a van. He said it wasn't his job and, in the end, another apprentice had to walk down there, getting soaking wet. Well, from that moment on I gave this Clive rocks. I didn't give him a minute. Anytime he complained, I told him it was for his own good.

Well, time passed and Clive met a girl and went off. He ended up with a job as a maintenance joiner at Stoke City. Years later, one Saturday night, there was a knock on the door and it was big Clive: *All right, Clive? What's the crack? I've got a job for you*, he says. Apart from two years in the RAF, I'd been with the same firm for 21 years so I assumed he meant a 'foreigner', what we call a spare-time job. *No, no*, he said: *I mean a proper job – maintenance at Stoke City. You've got an interview next Wednesday!* As it happened, I'd just started two weeks' holiday. Before I'd gone, I'd asked my firm for a rise: one old penny an hour. They'd said: *Sorry, can't afford to give it to you, pal.*

I bombed down to Stoke on the Wednesday and met Tony Waddington, the manager. He said: *Look, John. There's a job here and you've come highly recommended. All I need to ask is what kind of money you'd expect to earn.* I explained I couldn't afford to take a drop in wages and I showed him my last week's pay slip. He was quiet for a minute and I thought I'd blown it. Finally, he said: *Well, if you're willing to work for this kind of money, you can't blame the firm for paying it you. I'll give you £5 a week more.* That man never knew how close he came to being kissed!

I worked at the Victoria Ground for ten years until Mr Waddington resigned, doing general maintenance. That was everything, really, but not the pitch. It was one man's job to look after the playing surface. The rest of us weren't allowed on it unless Len, the ground manager, wanted help forking the ground or putting divots back in. I think, though, I was a bit ambitious. I thought that looking after the pitch was a job I could do.

Well, after Mr Waddington left, he came down here to Crewe. He phoned and asked me to come and see him. He told me he'd taken over at Crewe Alexandra and wanted me to come and work here, alongside the groundsman, Sid, who was a really good man: *I know you're ambitious – two or three years with Sid and you'll be sound.* Well, much as I loved Stoke City, the atmosphere had changed there and I thought this was an opportunity. I packed in and came to Crewe, even though it was coming down to a club that had had to apply for re-election to the League about five times in the previous seven years. I took the chance.

I'd been here a couple of years when Sid had a heart attack and left. Sid's assistant wasn't great so Tony Waddington said I should take over to stop the pitch being turned into mud. I'd go to Sid and ask his advice and he was great to me. I've been doing it ever since, looking after the pitch here and the training ground, and it's really interesting work. Every day's different, depending on what needs doing or what the gaffer wants. I learnt by watching, I suppose, while I was at Stoke, and from Len and Sid.

I'm lucky here that I've got a manager now who thinks like me, who's as proud of the playing surface as I am. Dario never does anything that'll harm the pitch if he can help it, which means the end of the season isn't a huge renovation job. We can spend a little, but often, to keep it ticking over. We don't worry about our hours or anything, we nurse that pitch and we're chuffed with it. It's how the whole club works, really.

When I was in the building trade, you left things that were permanent. I can go to places now where I worked and say: *I did that*. Maintenance at Stoke, though, wasn't like that: painting, repairing the roof, just odd jobs. But the pitch was different: it was like a focal point for everything and I think that's what attracted me. I decided that was what I wanted to do. I don't want them to know it's me doing it – it's for the club – but I want our supporters to be proud of our pitch.

I'll tell you one story. We played Liverpool down here one pre-season. We'd had a great pre-season and the gaffer was worried that it would all be spoiled by Liverpool coming here and thrashing us. I said we could flood the pitch, you know, turn it to mud to stop them playing their football. But no, Dario didn't want to ruin the pitch. So what we did was let the grass grow long. The morning of the match we put loads of water on it and then rolled it flat so, when Liverpool arrived, it looked lovely. But an hour or so of sunshine dried it out and the grass sprang back up. Come the game, the pitch was so slow they couldn't pass the ball on it. They'd knock the ball and it would just stop dead! We won 2–1 and I was absolutely made up afterwards. Then the door opens and Kenny Dalglish is standing there: *Are you the groundsman? I've got some advice for you: save up and buy a bloody mower!* I looked at him and said: *Mr Dalglish, when I'm working for Liverpool, I'll prepare pitches for Liverpool to play on, but while I'm working here, I'll prepare them for Crewe.* Christ! He slammed the door so hard it nearly came off its hinges. I don't suppose I'll get a job at Ewood Park now! •

Jackie Pitt

Jackie Pitt was an outstanding right-half for Bristol Rovers between the end of the war and the late 1950s. Now 76, Pitt was Rovers' grounds-man at Eastville until the club was forced to leave and has looked after the pitch at Bath's Twerton Park for the past six years.

If they've played the day before, I'll come in of a morning and, if I've got any help, I'll give everybody a fork. We'll start at one end of the pitch and work our way down to the other, forking it and putting divots back.Because we can have three or four games in a week at Twerton Park, the chances are there'll be a match the following day, so I'll just get the pitch rolled and marked out as quick as I can. We're all right then, as long as it doesn't rain! It's very hard work so it's good when I can get a bit of help. Sometimes, though, I'm on my own here, days or a week at a time.

I've been with Bristol Rovers since 1946. I played until I was 38, played over 500 games for the club. I had a couple of years on the coaching staff and then I went on the ground staff. I'm a Wolverhampton boy but I was turned down as a 16-year-old by Wolves and West Brom. I played football and cricket in the forces all through the war and, when I got back from India, a fellow I'd played for in the army came up to Birmingham and asked me if I'd like to come to Rovers. I signed for them and I've been here ever since. I think I'm a Bristolian now!

I really enjoyed my playing career. I could have gone to other clubs but I only found that out after I retired because Rovers had a policy of not buying or selling any players. They didn't tell me about the interest from First Division clubs till I'd stopped playing altogether! But we had a marvellous side:

we won promotion, I got a Football League medal and no one can take that away from me. Football's a great life if you work hard at it. I'll still get a cheer from older supporters if they see me here on a match-day!

The groundsman at Eastville, the old ground, before me was another ex-player, Harry Smith. The club asked me if I'd like to join him: Harry was getting on in years then. I was happy to stay with the club and I learnt the job from Harry, watching what he did, and eventually took over. I've done it ever since and really enjoyed it; I look after the pitch and I've a fellow, Mike Lillington, who'll come in now and again, especially during the summer – to reseed and things like that to do with the actual ground. He's very good. There's special machinery now for all that, too, you don't have to drag things around like I did when we started up.

The first year we came here from Eastville, the pitch was diabolical. It got so waterlogged I can remember Bobby Gould, the manager then, taking his boots off in that goalmouth down there and sinking up to his knees in it! It just hadn't been looked after, it didn't drain. It was upside down: you dug through clay to get to the soil that should have been on top! I pulled all sorts of rubbish – even a big iron bar – out of that ground! We've put hundreds of tons of topsoil and sand on it since we've been here. We had the drainage system put in four years ago and it's nice and firm now, drains lovely. The problem now is we've got no water supply: two half-inch pipes to water the pitch with and no pressure! Mind you, at Eastville it was the opposite: two or three times I remember the river overflowing and the water being six inches from the top of the goalposts – six feet deep. There's a photo of a fellow on the old pitch in a rowing boat!

Nowadays we have more games postponed here because of frost than anything. Obviously, on the day, the decision will be down to the referee. We did used to have some trouble up in that corner. It wouldn't drain and we'd have to have this company up with a hot air cover to dry it out. A while ago, though, I dug it out and pulled out this huge boulder – it was like something out of a volcano! – and we've had no problems since. That was why it wasn't draining. There's an underground spring up there somewhere, too, under the terraces I think. I wish I could tap into it to water the pitch! I don't know about all this fancy scientific stuff. It would cost too much for us, anyway. I just look after the pitch now like I always have. Look at it now, in the sunshine. It's really satisfying seeing it looking like that. Just a pity Bath will go out and train on it tonight but that's something we have to live with, sharing the ground.

It's a job, though, you can't help taking some pride in. I enjoy it even if I am getting a bit old for it now. Trouble is getting a young lad in to learn about it: it's too much like hard work for them! Some winter mornings, the ground's so frozen you can't even kick the divots back and it's that cold you have to run around the pitch a couple of times to warm up before you can start work! I had a great career, played against great players – John Charles, Nat Lofthouse, Ivor Allchurch, Jackie Milburn – and I suppose if I'd been earning what players get today, I'd be driving round in a Rolls-Royce now, but I wouldn't swap anything: it's always been football, football, football with me and I've enjoyed every minute of it.

Jacky Watts, Stadium Tours, Aston Villa

Villa Park is 100 years old in 1997. Jacky Watts has been around the place for three-quarters of that time. The other 25 years he's read up on until it's second nature. It makes two hours in Watts' company walking around one of the country's truly historical stadiums an enlightening way to spend an afternoon whether you're a Villa fan or not.

The first time I came here was in 1922. My brother was ten years older than me and he brought me on his shoulders. I was four. I watched Villa whenever I could, although I played a lot of sport: football, cricket, running, boxing. When I was 21 I got a little job on the turnstile here but I'd only done two games when the war broke out. And the King sent for me: *Jack! We're having a bit of trouble with the Germans!*

I was in the army right through the war. I came out in January 1946. that summer I was playing a bit of cricket – in the same team as 'Mush' Callaghan, who was a stalwart Villa player. He'd been a policeman, won a BM for bravery, and was more or less looking after the ground during the war. He told us a bomb had made a mess at the back of the Witton Lane Stand and some of us from the boys club said we'd go down and help him clear up. When the season got under way, he asked me if I'd like to sweep around the ground after matches and look after the scoreboard. We'd paint the crash bars, snowcem the terraces, anything that needed doing.

I worked 47 years for the same firm, starting out as a sheet metal worker, ending up as a superintendent. But any time I had off, weekends, I'd come over and do odd jobs down here. Apart from a game against Arsenal in the '70s when I was in hospital, I've been at every game here – first team, reserves and youths – since the war.

I retired in 1981 and Villa asked me if I'd take over doing the tours of the ground. They'd had a fellow doing it before but I tried to do the job in my own way: making people feel welcome, trying to entertain them. I'd tell them a few stories and answer as many questions as I could. Especially with youngsters, it came naturally to me because I'd been involved with boys clubs all my life.

The history of the Villa, well, I've lived a lot of it myself. I picked things up being around the place, reading books. It's like arithmetic, you educate your mind to it: I'll sit down and test myself, ask myself who played when, who they beat and what year. The only thing I come unstuck on is the size of the pitch in metres but I tell them I left school in 1932 before I learnt about that!

People phone up for tours. We do them at 10.30 in the morning and 1.30 in the afternoon, and we'll offer them some alternative dates, put one in the diary and confirm it by letter. We put their details down in this book, where they've come from: Yugoslavians, Germans, Danes, Swedes, Americans, Libyans, Chinese, Douglas Hurd! And I'll tell you what makes the job is when you look in the comments and you read something like this, here: *Tour excellent. Jack better than excellent!*

I don't know why it was the Villa for me. My mum was from Hammersmith, an Arsenal supporter, my father was Sunderland. But my brother brought me here and that was it. I wonder if people today enjoy football like we used to when we were young: away on the train, mixing with the home fans, having a drink with them after and telling them where to meet us when they came down to the Villa. Now it's off the coach, into the ground, back on the coach. Where's the day out in that? Football's changed and it's not like it was – the players are cry-babies and games every day of the week – but I still love doing this. It helps out on my pension but I'd do it for love. Without it I'd be sat in my rocking chair or taking the drink!

Kick-off

THE MATCH-DAY STAFF AND MATCH-DAY OFFICIALS

You don't do it if you don't love the game.

Mike Dearing

I've been there 25 years now but I'm still classed as casual.

George Sephton

I sometimes wonder what I might have done with all that energy and time if it hadn't gone on United.

Cliff Butler

It's lovely going down there, knowing everyone after all these years.

Fred Stenner

Kelvin Morton, Referee

Kelvin Morton still lives where he grew up – East Anglia – but commutes to work in North London. If pushed to name the single most important quality in a referee, Morton identifies confidence. His own comes from over 30 years' experience matched with a singularly resilient nature. After nearly ten years as a top-flight referee, 1994/95 was Morton's last on the FA Premiership list. He is now an FA assessor.

•KELVIN MORTON•

•Referee•

I first started refereeing, believe it or not, when I was still a few months short of my 16th birthday. I've always had a great enthusiasm for the game. At the time I was captain of the school second XI and knew all the rules because I'd already studied for the referees' exam. Anyway, I was watching a game and the ref didn't turn up. I was talked into taking his place. I put on the kit which was a terrible fit! And I suppose I did everything wrong from a technical point of view – ran into all the wrong positions – but I really enjoyed it. Everybody was so pleasant to me after the game, I thought: *I must do this again!* There was a little fee: 7/6d. wasn't bad. And I started doing it regularly.

At first my problem was – what shall we call it? – admonishing players. They'd look at me and think: *I've got a son older than you!* That didn't go down too well at village level. I still don't know whether it was good to have started so young. Certainly it's made me quite tough, mentally. Anyway, I took the exam a month or so after that first game and, at first, I was told they only wanted me to do schoolboy football because I was so young. But there was a shortage locally and I ended up doing club games. I was often reffing four games over a weekend as well as playing on Saturday morning for the school! In my first eleven seasons I did a thousand games!

I moved up through the ranks and was a class 1 referee at 21. I was a linesman on the Football Combination list at 23 – I was the youngest in the country. It's funny: now, that wouldn't seem unusual. They're pushing younger men through. But, at the time, they were favouring experience. I sometimes wish I was starting now. I might have got the chance to break through earlier and go on to great things. Then again, I might not have been good enough. You never know, do you?

My stroke of good fortune came in 1970. I went to do a game at March Town. They'd had a terrible ref the week before, according to the club. Well, this game turned out to be a cracker: 4–3 after extra time. I got a few pats on the back afterwards and one fellow was there who was on the management committee of the Eastern Counties League – the foot of the ladder up to top-flight football. He asked me if I had ambitions to go to the top and offered to get me on their list. My own County FA didn't want me to go but this fellow got me a couple of midweek games that didn't clash. Both of them, assessors were there and in the second I did really well. The next season I started in the Jewson League. And then started working my way up, as you do, reffing at one level and running the line at the next level up, until you start reffing at that level and line at the next one up again. By 1980 I was a referee at Football Combination level. In 1982 I went into the Football League as a linesman.

Each level up is a jump. It takes you a while to adjust, to read the game and the speed of the game at the higher levels. Even the kinds of fouls are different in a Division Three game on a compact little pitch, say, to those on the wide open spaces of a Premiership ground. Usually, the game gets quicker and less physical the higher you go. The biggest jump of all is between non-League and full-time professional football, though. The pressure, the demands on your time. It's completely different once you come into the League.

I suppose I put 30 to 40 hours a week into refereeing: games, travelling, training, meetings and so on. That's almost a working week but you have to find it out of your spare time. With work, it balances out. I commute and get into work very early and make up whatever time I have to take off for football. Family time, though, you can never make up and I'm very conscious of that. Fortunately, I've a very supportive family. My wife and daughter came to the game with me last Saturday! My wife was a football fan when I married her – but not quite as involved as she is now! She's great.

The reward of the job is being part of the greatest game in the world. As a referee you've an important part in that. When a game goes well,. there's enormous satisfaction. On the other hand, when a game hasn't gone well there's a tremendous amount of soul-searching: *Was there anything else I could have done?* You take your own satisfaction from a job well done and you must be your own biggest critic when things don't go so well, although not everything is under your control, obviously. I mean, if players want to go round creating mischief, you won't be able to pick everything up. It'd be impossible. But you have people you know and trust within the refereeing fraternity who'll tell you what they thought about a performance in an honest and objective way. The thing is: I'm always the same referee but games are very different. You can only referee the kind of game the players want to have!

Mike Dearing, Linesman

•MIKE DEARING•

•Linesman•

I'm sure I'm not alone in admitting to afternoons in the Lower East Stand at Highbury when a 45-minute session of linesman-baiting has been the highlight of a dull afternoon. Mike Dearing lives in Northolt, Middlesex, works in Brixton and devotes most other waking hours to football. He's now in his third full season as an FA Premiership linesman. The evening we met he was at home watching a tape of the previous evening's live Monday night game.

I used to play for Tooting and Mitcham but I had a bad Achilles tendon problem that got to where I was going into work on Mondays not able to walk. I just carried on playing Sunday football and was a Chelsea season ticket-holder. I think fans, like I was, tend to get 'used' by clubs: they'll take your money but you're not allowed to have an opinion. Well, I think that's wrong. And now, as an official, I still think fans have paid their money and are entitled to have a pop at you! As a linesman, of course, as opposed to the referee, you can't get away from the stick. I remember one game, a night game down at Colchester, where this clown was on at me all night. Nothing to do with football, just personal abuse. Well, I'm all for fans expressing opinions but that was going a bit far. I don't know what the bloke had been reading before the game but he was coming out with some weird stuff! What it comes down to is: you can call me useless, but don't call me a cheat! Seriously, though, all the stick – the verbal abuse, the spitting, whatever – you put up with because you love football, don't you?

I'm a production director of a printing company and, obviously, football pressurises that. Most days, I'm up at five, in work at 6.45. Finish at three. Drive up to, say, Norwich to do a game. Get home about one, 1.30, and up again next morning at five. Come February or March and a little fixture congestion, you can be doing four games a week, so you might have another match to go to the next night. There's meetings and courses, too. They talk about wanting to have full-time officials. I can't see how we could put in more hours than we do now! If I need to do fitness work, I'll go out running at eleven o'clock at night. After all, we're on one-year contracts. One iffy season and we're out. The only thing we might get from being full time would be credibility in the eyes of other people in football who don't recognise the time, effort and thought we put into the game now.

I suppose, not being full time I could chuck it all in, any time there was too much hassle. But to get to this level, you put in a lot of hours, put up with a lot of grief. You don't do it if you don't love the game. The money – we get £125 for a Premiership game, £82.50 in the Football League – isn't really the point.

Anyway, I was 21 when I had to stop playing semi-pro. I got married and got a job over in Ealing. There was a bloke working there, a class 1 referee, who was such a complete football nut he just talked me into taking the referees' exam. I qualified in January 1978 and finished that season refereeing in Sunday football. I remember my first game: Pinner Gas versus Actonian Old Boys in the Chiswick and District League. I made a huge cock-up on an offside after five minutes and I don't really know how I got through the game. I thought: *What am I doing?* It's frightening. It takes ages to learn your positioning. At first you're still playing like a player. But where you need to be to see the game as a ref is completely different.

But I got through it. The camaraderie at the lower levels, between officials, is great and helps a lot. You get involved in societies and so forth. I've still got good friends from those days. I climbed up the ladder into senior non-League football as a class 1 referee. I was lucky: it happened in three seasons. By the time I was reffing in the old Isthmian League in front of 1,500 people – bearing in mind I'd had to be talked into doing it in the first place! – I thought I'd made it. I was on top of the world. By then, you've had the games that make you grow up.

Then, '86/'87, I got a letter from Mr Kelly, when he was at the Football League, inviting me to come on the League Linesmen's list. Completely out of the blue. The first thing I did was rush down to tell the bloke who'd got me reffing in the first place. I was so up there, just thinking of myself, and, of course, he was slaughtered. I'd gone past him and I hadn't realised how that would make him feel. It taught me a bit of humility that did.

You know, the other month, I was doing a European game – Eindhoven versus Bayer Leverkheusen, screened live everywhere in Europe – and me and the other officials were walking round Eindhoven that afternoon. You get such a buzz thinking how far you've come since you first started. For that game I got my 'three lions' from the FA – the top level of appointment – which was the one ambition I had left. For me, that was the equivalent of getting the call to play for England. I can't tell you how proud it made me feel.

Sue Beaumont, Ticket Office Administrator, Huddersfield Town

Sue Beaumont's links with Huddersfield Town go back through her family. Her grandfather reported on the team for the local paper and her parents first took her to Leeds Road in the '60s when Town enjoyed a run in the old First Division. Her husband's a rugby man but their son's interest was Sue's excuse to start watching football again. A year before Huddersfield's move to the new Alfred McAlpine Stadium, she had the opportunity to become more closely involved at 'her' club.

I used to sell electronic scoreboards. Eighteen months ago, thanks to the recession, business wasn't good. I enjoyed the job but it was getting to where I wasn't sure if I was going to be paid at the end of the month. Anyway, I'd been away on holiday and, when I got back, my mum had saved the local papers. I've always been a Huddersfield follower – my little boy is, too – and we wanted to be able to read the news. This was during the close season, just after Neil Warnock became manager, July 1933.

Well, there was an advertisement in one of the papers for an assistant secretary at the football club. It said that part-time applicants would be considered and, at this point, I was three days a week in my job. I thought I'd give it a go. I knew the secretary, Alan Sykes, because his son plays football with my lad but I thought I should apply formally – it's a bit awkward when you know someone, isn't it? – and I wrote a letter. I came down for an interview with Alan. It was all a little confused: things were changing, they needed to set up a new database. But I was lucky enough to get the job.

I had to give notice on my other job, but I began coming

in on my days off to learn about the database. I actually started in the August. The first match-day I was working, my son was selected as the mascot. I was working away in the office but I wanted to be in the stand watching him run out with the team! We had a game against Arsenal just after I started, so things were really busy and they've just snowballed since then. I just took on more and more. I loved it: I liked being at the club more than I did being at home dusting and cleaning, you know! Now we're in the new stadium, I've gone full time. Officially, that is: I was down here full time before that, anyway!

I'm involved with a lot of the supporters' groups, the Young Terriers in particular. I arrange all the mascots. With us doing well, that's a bigger job: we've got away mascots, too, for this season. The Young Terriers have visiting groups who come to our home games and I do all the liaison on that. It's a good day. We usually have about 60 or 70, plus the visiting groups. They meet at 12, have lunch at the sports centre, play football, get a programme and come down to the ground on a bus and all watch the match together. Under-elevens get a free season ticket here, so the whole day just costs about £3 to cover the lunch and whatever.

We've a lot of ticket schemes. We do the family ticket: if you buy two season tickets you get a junior season free. We've done half-season tickets for Christmas presents, which have gone very well. With the move to the new stadium, we did a very good offer for the '94/'95 season and sold more season tickets than ever before: nearly 6,000, which is incredible for a club this size – some of the crowds at Leeds Road, the old ground, were less than 6,000 the season before! The new ground was important, so was the price. But going to Wembley at the end of '93/'94 had an awful lot to do with it. A lot of people came to Wembley who hadn't watched us for a long time. It was such a wonderful day.

Match-day's chaos. We've had a lot of games where we've had to ticket the Kilner Bank – the John Smith stand which has taken over from the East Terrace at Leeds Road as the popular stand – so people are in from nine in the morning. Then, when it's getting really busy around 12, we deal with the match-day staff through here, as well: stewards, gatemen, hospitality staff, car park attendants all come down to collect their badges. People are down to ask about tickets for away games too. And the people who've put their season ticket through the washing machine and: *Can I get a replacement?* Or the wife's gone shopping and they can't get into the house to get their ticket! Then there's all the directors and complimentaries, which we print ourselves, and schools groups that have been organised through Gerry Murphy, the youth development officer.

There was a lot of criticism before we moved but the atmosphere in the new stadium is terrific. Before the first game, no one knew what it would be like, the acoustics and everything. But the noise of the crowd is incredible. Later this season, maybe when Rotherham come down and three sides are open, we could get 16,000 here. I don't know what that'll be like! And what's great, too, is there are more women coming to the new ground than ever went to Leeds Road, and families as well. It's like football's becoming a family day out: we'll sell tickets in fours and sixes, gran or granddad and the kids are coming, too.

George Sephton, Match Announcer, Liverpool

A Liverpool fan for over 40 years, George Sephton works as a freelance computer programmer with Royal Insurance. He's been Anfield's match announcer since 1971.

I used to have season tickets on both sides of Stanley Park. Most of my friends are Evertonians, so I preferred to watch First Division football with them alternate weeks rather than go to Liverpool reserves. That was before I started working at Anfield. Now, I'm like all the casual staff – I've been there 25 years now but I'm still classed as casual! – I can't plan anything else because you never know which day of the week games are going to end up being played and, obviously, I have to be free for the match.

I'm in a funny little niche of my own at Anfield. I really don't 'belong' to anybody. I just turn up and do what I have to do. When I first started going to Liverpool in 1959 there used to be a pipe band trooping up and down the pitch before a game. Some time in the early '60s they got a PA system put in: there'd not been one at all before then, they used to have the half-time scores on boards at the end of the ground. We graduated to the PA system and the then club secretary bought two LPs: Russ Conway and the Black and White Minstrels. They'd play them all the way through, backwards and forwards, so that if you got to the ground early you heard them two or three times!

A year or two later, they actually got an announcer. He lasted a couple of seasons and then came Alan Jackson who's now a presenter on Radio Merseyside. In the middle of the '70/'71 season Alan got an offer to go and work for Manx Radio. He was trying to break into radio at the time, so he explained the situation to the club and said his brother would cover for him, at least till the end of the season. The club were just happy to have someone doing it but Alan's brother wasn't in the same league: I can remember him making an announcement about moving a car one evening just as Tommy Smith was about to take a penalty. He didn't really have the sense of timing. He'd play records at the wrong speed, couldn't get his tongue round the names of European players, you name it! I was at Anfield one night with my wife and said to her: *This guy's an embarrassment!* She said: *It's all right for you to say that, stood down here, I bet you couldn't do it!* Well, I was damn sure I could and when I got home, of course, I wrote the classic letter to the club, you know: *Dear Sir, give us a job! I can do that!* Well, as it happened, they'd just asked this guy to find something else to do with his Saturday afternoons and were wondering what to do next when my letter arrived. I'm not renowned for my sense of timing but that was one masterpiece.

Peter Robinson, who's still the chief executive, dragged me in basically, I think, just to check I didn't have two heads. Even though I had no background in the field, he decided to give me a go rather than advertise. Over the summer, I did start to worry about what I'd let myself in for. I hoped the first game of the season – my first game – would be a reserve match so I could get my feet under the table. It turned out to be Nottingham Forest. I then hoped it wouldn't be on *Match of the Day* or anything. I got on the gantry and there was David Coleman and a full camera crew! I just froze. I thought: *All my friends and workmates are down there in the crowd. I've either got to get on and do this or pack my bags and emigrate to Australia.* I bit down hard and I got away with it, that first day, without any cock-ups. The next day I was in the car with my wife, driving through Bootle, and I stopped and just cried for 20 minutes. My nervous system was just shredded, gone!

Since then I've been okay. It's a strange thing, but there's a point beyond which numbers cease to really mean anything. You get nervous, don't you, doing a speech to a hundred people at a wedding? If it's 150 or 200, it doesn't make much difference. Every now and again, though, the size of a crowd will dawn on you. I was at the Heysel Stadium the night of the disaster there. I was working alongside a local announcer and my counterpart from Turin. After all the trouble – and, unlike the rest of the crowd, we knew the scale of what had happened – UEFA officials came up with the team sheets to say they were going ahead with the game. I couldn't believe it and really didn't want to be a part of risking more lives if trouble flared up again. It got to the point where they had a policeman with a gun pointing at me to say: *Get on with your job.* Phil Neal and the Juventus captain came up and I calmed down. I looked out of the window and all the TV cameras were pointed in our direction because they'd seen the two players up with us. I suddenly realised that there must have been 400 or 500 million people seeing those pictures. I remember thinking: *Well, at least my family will know I'm still in one piece.* Mind you, the PA booth was at the Juventus end of the ground and, as soon as they heard an English voice over the system, we had bricks and bottles flying up towards us. I think I beat Sebastian Coe's 800-metre record getting away from the stadium that night.

Sometimes you sit there and it's very quiet: you can feel the crowd listening to you intently. That doesn't happen very often. Other times, you're sat there and it occurs to you that no one's taking a blind bit of notice of anything you're saying. Then, two days later, someone will come up to you and say: *I agreed with what you said about so-and-so the other afternoon.* And you think: *Good, someone was listening!* My sons used to get messages for me, too: *Tell your dad not to play that Christmas record again!* I do think the crowd takes in what I'm saying if I need to pass on something important.

Until recently I was chairman of the local junior league. I ran junior teams when my kids were young enough to be involved. And that means that some of the other games at Anfield I cover can be very rewarding. Tranmere reserves played here last season with four players who were with me at under-12 level. And the junior cup finals are fantastic: never mind the World Cup, they're the place for real emotion! I just wish one of my teams had made it to Anfield. I could have died a happy man then, couldn't I?

Cliff Butler, Programme Editor, Manchester United

Cliff Butler has been watching Manchester United since he was eight. Indeed, he hasn't missed a first team, youth or reserve team game at Old Trafford since 1965. Butler's enthusiasm for the history and detail of the club and the game has led him, almost inevitably, to do the job of editor of the *United Review*. He took up the position in 1989 after three years as assistant, only the programme's fifth editor since the war.

Like most kids it was my dad initiated me. He was always a football supporter, although, before the war, he was more of a Manchester City fan, I think! He was a POW in the Far East for three-and-a-half years and he came back with a rather jaundiced view of the world. I don't think he took very kindly to City signing a German goalkeeper, Bert Trautman. Otherwise, I might have turned out to be a City fan! As it was, he pushed me towards United, kept telling me that they were the team and that he'd take me down to see them one day.

The first game I can vividly remember was Boxing Day 1958, we played Aston Villa. We were right at the back of the Stretford End paddock and I was only a kid, so it was a question of peering between people's shoulders. But I can remember the sense of occasion. It was a really big adventure for me, coming all the way over from east Manchester where we lived. Straightaway the whole thing had an effect on me: the crowd, the noise, the atmosphere. From then on, I was hooked.

Almost instantly, it was an obsession! And it was a serious thing with me. I started keeping statistics. It was part of history, not just a football match. I started collecting books, programmes, press cuttings. When I left school I wanted to be a joiner, but I got a job in a factory that made lapping boards – things you wind lengths of fabric around in the clothing trade. It was a disappointment but, at the same time, I knew I didn't want a job that would take over and interfere with watching United. The important thing was to have the money to finance the obsession.

I ended up moving from job to job until I worked for ten years as a crane and fork-lift driver in the Port of Manchester. Of course, that brought me close to the ground. I'd started doing stuff for the Supporters' Club and, by now, I was coming into the ground at lunchtimes, answering letters wanting information, writing up the records. It was great. Here I was, an ordinary supporter, welcomed into Old Trafford. But I wasn't a nuisance. I didn't go running after the players or anything. Football was more serious for me than that. I've had my idols – Denis Law still is an idol – but I was more attached to the club than to any individuals.

I started doing articles for the programme. When they offered to pay me, I said I didn't want that but I'd like the title of club statistician. I think my first historical piece for the *United Review* was 20 years ago. After I was made redundant from the Port, I spent more and more time here and ended up with a part-time job in the ticket office, although most of my time was spent helping to put the programme together.

About three years later, in the mid-'80s, it was decided the club should have a museum, and I was taken on full time to set that up. That was my first full-time job at United: curator of the museum. I'd still be doing that, only I kept taking more and more on – at one point I was curator of the museum, programme editor and club photographer – and you can't carry on like that without the job suffering, not at a huge club like this anyway. I wouldn't shed any of the jobs but, eventually, they were shed for me and I was left as programme editor. I wasn't happy at the time but, after all, if you'd sat me down as a kid and asked me what my ultimate ambition would be, I'd have said: *To be editor of the United Review*. It would have been beyond my wildest dreams.

The first programme of the season's the most difficult.

You want it to look fresh. I mean, we're lucky in that the cover isn't a problem. It's instantly recognisable, more or less the same as we've had since 1946. It's an identity, something that belongs to United. It's about two-and-a-half days non-stop collecting the material together. Then it needs proofing and so on. I decide what goes in unless something big breaks and we get the word down from 'upstairs'. Most of the time I'm left to my own devices!

I don't know where I go from here! Just carry on and try to make it better. I've done a couple of books and I'd like to do more of that. I'm an historian, really, and perhaps because of that I tend to dwell in the past too much. I can still remember coming down Warwick Road with my dad and tens of thousands of people just like us, in flat caps and red and white scarves, devoted to United. Those were the people this club was built on when football was a working-class game. I mean, there have always been the haves and have-nots at football but I feel the balance may have gone the other way. Lots of our fans can't get into the ground. I know we've got to generate money and income but I feel that football may be losing its heart along the way. And perhaps that's football just reflecting society as a whole. I think back to those huge crowds, the atmosphere of the '50s and '60s. United are actually more successful now than they were then, but somehow it doesn't feel the same. Maybe that's just me of course. You know, my interest, my obsession, has become my job – the mystique and the sense of release on Saturday can't be the same. I sometimes wonder what I might have done with all that energy and time if it hadn't gone on United!

Emma Hawkey, Programme Editor, Fulham

Emma Hawkey did a degree in English before she found her way behind the scenes at Fulham, the club she had been dragged along to watch as a girl. Hawkey began editing Fulham's programme in 1993 and won the Division Three award for Programme of the Year for the 1994/95 season.

Well, I'm programme editor, mainly, but press officer and a bit of public relations and club administration, too. The thing about a club like Fulham is that we've a very small staff so everyone has to muck in, really, and be flexible. I suppose I drifted into it. I left university wanting to be a sports writer but that didn't happen. I was signing on, actually, at the office just opposite Craven Cottage. I started doing reports on reserve team matches for the programme, as a volunteer, and I've just infiltrated the club since then!

My parents used to come to Fulham and they thought it was a nice place to take the children on a Saturday so I was roped in. Once someone makes a decision like that for you, you're finished! I suppose it would have been better if it had been a more successful club but, in that case, I might not have got so involved. Anyway, it meant I grew up wanting to write and having football as my only area of expertise. It was more *The Observer* I had in mind than the Fulham programme, though!

Anyway, they advertised for a writer and not many people go to reserve games, especially not at Fulham: there'd be me and 20 other people. It was a very sad part of my life! At first I was just doing reports on the reserves but then I started going away and covering first team games. Next thing I was doing interviews and then the club asked me to come in and help in the office. I wanted an interesting job and this was. I liked the fact that people were a bit shocked to find someone like me working in a press box. They were always saying: *Can I help you, madam?* They'd want to know what I was doing and after I told them they'd start explaining the offside rule to me! I enjoyed all that.

I'd never done any journalism before but there was no one else doing it so whatever I wrote went in. One week I'd try to write it like a tabloid, the next week it would be Fulham versus Wigan in the style of a *Sunday Times* feature. I suppose the style I settled on was more like the second of those, with a bit more detail than just quotes and bare description. It took a while to become confident but where, at first, people patronised me and told me the score halfway through a game, it got to where they were asking me who did something or what had just happened. When that started happening at Fulham, I felt I'd found my feet.

When I first started I was a terrible groupie! I'd hang around hoping to bump into players like Gordon Davies and Ray Lewington, smelling the Ralgex as they came out of the dressing-room! I have to say that's worn off a bit now. I know the players now: I've been at the club longer than some of them. I like being able to ring them up to talk about a game, though. And I can do that now without having ten Silk Cuts and a brandy first to steady my nerves.

Before my time, I used to think the programme was a bit boring and I had ambitions for it. Getting control of it was just a process of trying to make myself indispensable. I was given the actual title of 'programme editor' about two years ago. That was when I started being paid, which was nice, as well! I'd been working nine to five, five days a week, for a while but money's very tight at smaller clubs and nobody had actually brought up the question of wages. It was a nice surprise! And I suddenly had a proper job: if people asked me what I did, I could tell them.

We got new printers in and the job got really interesting, not just writing but discussing design and layout, too. I really do think the programme's got better. I've tried to make it read like a magazine. I've recruited some very good volunteer writers, we receive some lovely unsolicited articles and I've got someone who'll do all the stats. It's about a three-day job putting a programme together, assembling the material and then writing to fill in the gaps.

The main drawback is not really being able to criticise anybody or anything. The players are quite vain about which photos and quotes you use! Because it's an in-house magazine, the board don't want you saying the wrong thing which undermines your credibility with the supporters. There's a bit of a bunker mentality because they've had a lot of flak from fans after so many years of failure. It's a pity because everyone's in it together, aren't they? There's a lot of cynicism among supporters and within the club but that's really born out of passion: people are upset about the last 20 years because they care about Fulham and I hope that, through the programme, we can promote the positive side of that. About 70 per cent of our fans buy it, which is an incredibly high proportion: West Ham or Tottenham sell programmes to about 30 per cent of their crowd.

We've got two fanzines at Fulham who used to be ruthless about the programme, saying it had no backbone, printing cartoons of me with this huge nose! We actually played a football match on the pitch here – it's an annual fixture now – to try and sort out our differences. I had half the first team playing for me – players who'd been criticised in the fanzines and wanted to get their own back! – and so we thrashed them. I think they've accepted that we all want the same things for the club now. They don't slag the programme off and I help them when I can.

A while ago, I was offered a press officer job with the British Safety Council. There was a bit of a furore about me going, so Fulham offered me the job of press officer, which hadn't existed before. No money, just an extra title: you can see I really am a hopeless case. I love Fulham and I love being here. I end up answering mail, handling complaints, helping out on the commercial side. Of course, there's no security in jobs at this level of the game. Everything depends on the team's results. I just hope, when the time comes, that all these job titles I've accumulated will look good on my CV!

Eric White, Press Officer and Programme Editor, Brentford

The majority of a Griffin Park home crowd will recognise Eric White. Now retired after a career in insurance, White is deputy president at Brentford. It's an honorary title, recognition in part, at least, for his work as an editor and administrator – on a voluntary basis – for the club he's followed for nearly 60 years.

As press officer, on a match-day I'm responsible for looking after the members of the press, particularly the 'opposing' press because they don't know their way around Griffin Park. A young lad, Brendan, helps me: showing them where to sit, organising phones, sockets for the radio people, printing out a sheet with the team changes. The 'home' journalists know what's going on and, in the Second Division, we don't get the nationals down very often. I do all the statistics for the Press Association, you know, for Teletext and Ceefax, too.

In 1951 – I won't say I was a little lad in shorts but I wasn't as old as I am now! – Brentford Supporters' Club, of which I was a member, set up a scheme for the blind which is here to this day. A chap called Peter Vaughan-Jones and I volunteered to be the first commentators. We'd never done anything like it in our lives but some idiots had to do it and we volunteered!

I suppose we got reasonably known: Peter finished up as a director and I'm deputy president as well as all my other things! Anyway, I've always been interested in statistics. The manager at that time was Malcolm Macdonald – not the English one! Ours was a canny Scot, the only man to score a hat-trick for Celtic against Rangers between the wars – who played here and then came back as manager. He used to write the programme and used to say himself that it was dreadful. He asked me if I'd be interested in doing it instead; do a pilot one, you know, for the board. Well, I did and I suppose it was marginally better than Malcolm's, so I was offered the job.

Over the years the programme's grown from eight pages in black and white to 40 pages in colour. We've got a really good band of volunteer writers, all supporters, none of whom gets paid. It's to their credit we've won quite a few awards. They all do it for the love of the club, although one person – no names, no pack drill – does love to see his name in print and if the printers leave his name off by mistake I know I'm going to get a phone call Monday morning!

It's all for the love of the club, isn't it? I first came here in 1936. Brentford finished fifth in the old First Division that year: we were a top club, eight internationals in the team. The first game I saw was against Wolves, another top side, and we won 5–0. If we'd lost 2–1 I'd probably have gone away and never come back. But I suppose I got hooked.

It's very easy to follow a Liverpool or a Man United, isn't it? I mean, my son used to come here but being a Brentford supporter wasn't too clever at school, I suppose, and he watches Liverpool now. But there's a very nice atmosphere here: it's a very nice community. Nice people, really, I think. There are a lot of people who support Brentford who do a lot of work for the club. Just really nice people.

I've known 16 managers here. Obviously, I've had my favourites – and one threw me out of the dressing-room once – but I've never felt like not doing it because of any aggravation. Near it once or twice! I know I could always walk away from this but there's something keeps me going! One day the knees'll pack up – or the brain'll pack up – or the club will say they want somebody younger to do the job. That'll be fair dos. But Brentford's my club, so it'll always be Brentford.

And the involvement's important. You might say I'm a big fish in a relatively small pond here. I suppose I should have been a journalist, really, but I was in the airforce during the war and when I came out it wasn't easy to go to university.

Or maybe I never really had the courage of my convictions. At least I know now I can write, talk, do commentaries and radio broadcasts. It's all gone into my team! And I'm happy with that.

Fred Stenner, Press Box Assistant, Bristol City

Fred Stenner's a Bristol man through and through. Now in his 70s, he retired 15 years ago and takes great pleasure walking around the city in which he's lived and worked all his life. Every second Saturday Stenner is at Ashton Gate where he's helped several generations of reporters in the Bristol City press box, covering football in every division, since the war.

This is my 50th season at Bristol City. I've been a fan for longer than that. It still only takes me 20 minutes to walk down to Ashton Gate. I was born in this part of Bristol and I've always lived here. Until I retired, I was the telephonist at Bristol magistrates court. My little office down in Bridewell Street was next to Number One court, the crime court where all the main cases happen, so all the main crime reporters called in. I was there 40 years and got a BEM for my service. Absolutely wonderful time. Well, one afternoon, this particular reporter – an Irishman by the name of Joe Gallagher, a famous crime reporter of the time – called in and said: *Fred! How would you like to earn a pound on Saturday?* I said I'd be delighted before I even asked what for: my wages at the time were £2.50 a week. He said he was going out to cover Bristol Rovers for one of the papers and wanted me to phone his copy through from the ground. We arranged to meet out at Eastville.

So, I'm out there on the Saturday and there's no sign of Joe. I recognised Graham Russell, a freelance reporter, and asked if he'd seen him. I went inside the ground and waited in the press box, wandering around looking for him. The players came out to warm up and I still hadn't found him. I was starting to get nervous! I went back down the stairs inside the stand and there, leaning against a brass rail, was Joe Gallagher drunk, absolutely drunk as a coot! I told him they were starting to kick the ball about and he just said: *Oh, you go and write it!* I told him I couldn't so he told me to go and find someone who would write the copy for him if he paid them: *And I owe you a pound, too, don't I?* He pulled out this big roll of notes – I was on £2 and 10 shillings a week, remember – and peeled off the money. I couldn't believe it! But that's how I started, that was my first time.

Graham Russell wrote the report for Joe and I phoned it through. Graham asked me to work for him after that. He left me a press ticket for the next Rovers game a fortnight later: I was so proud, going in at the same gate as the players and the chairman and the other press boys! It was only my second time but that afternoon I ended up phoning copy through for another fellow, too, who was covering the game for two papers. He had one of those names he could turn around, like Henry Don or something, to write as two different reporters. That meant I earned a few bob more for myself and the fellow gave me a lift part way home as well!

This became a regular thing at Eastville, but I was still going down to watch Bristol City every other week. I used to stand on what they called the Mad Corner, under the old clock before they moved it. This was in the old Third Division: we still had 20,000-odd crowds down there. And we were the madhouse in the corner! I had my own high step on the terrace I could stand on only being five foot four. All of us on that step were short-arses! We used to have a laugh.

Eventually, Graham got me working for him at Ashton Gate as well. When I started there, though, the press boys had a row of seats, with little platforms to write on, in front of the main stand. That was all right unless it was raining. Some afternoons the copy got so wet I couldn't read it to phone it through! Later on, when they built the new stand, we got our press box at the back which was fine. I have a bit of trouble getting up all those steps with the teas at half-time nowadays, though!

I was working for Bristol City, of course. I was working for the reporters. When City went up into the old First Division, though, a lad who knew my son was made secretary. He phoned me up and asked me to go down and see him. He wanted me to be press steward – they'd made a lovely new press room – and do all the teas and look after the reporters. I wasn't sure because it meant getting to the ground three hours before the game, and I didn't know what time I'd get home because the managers and players would come through to do interviews afterwards, too. But then he said: *We'll pay you £10 a time!* Oh, it was a lovely job, that one. I looked after everybody, kept the room clean, ran a free bar in there after the matches. That was why I never really knew when I'd get home: while there was a free drink going, the journalists wouldn't want to leave! We had a wonderful time.

That job only lasted while Bristol City were in the First Division, though. After that it all started to fall apart, they near enough went out of business, didn't they? The press room disappeared, they had to cut back wherever they could. I kept going along to help out, of course, especially after I retired from work at the magistrates' court, even though there wasn't money in it any more. I'd get the teas, keep a count on corners and free-kicks for people, phone goals and scorers through. I've known them all up there over the years, even if I'm not so familiar with all the reporters nowadays. I still cart flasks of tea up to the press box at half-time. I'd be there to watch City every other week anyway, wouldn't I? And it's lovely going down there, knowing everyone after all these years.

Dave Bond, Chief Steward, Brentford

Dave Bond drives a black cab and is a Labour councillor in the London Borough of Ealing. Bond is chief steward at Brentford and comes from a Bees family: at one point in the 1980s, as well as Dave, his father was working as a turnstile operator and his two daughters were selling programmes at Griffin Park on match-day. The family subscribe to Brentford's lottery schemes, too.

I've just won £750 on the Griffin Gold! I'm a member of two things here: the Lifeline – which is about £1.50 a week and I share with my father – and Griffin Gold which is £1 a week and I pay for myself. I don't think my dad's going to take too kindly to the fact I've won £750 on the one I pay for myself!

I've been coming to this club since I was five or six. I was born just up the road in South Ealing. You only put into these things to help the club, don't you? I mean, I never gamble but I've been lucky with these lotteries at Brentford!

As I say, I've always been a Brentford fan. In 1976 I was elected as a full-time union official for what was then the Amalgamated Engineering Union. I'd always worked in construction, as a steel erector – quite dangerous work, putting up steel girders. I think I was the youngest-ever full-time official of the AEU. I knew it was going to be a very stressful job and, at the time, I'd got a bit out of the habit of coming down here regularly. I saw an advert in the paper, I think, for Brentford wanting people to work here. I thought it would be a break from all the paperwork and everything in the week.

Anyway, I came down to see Dennis Pigott, who was Mr Brentford here for donkey's years. I came straight from work, I remember, so I was wearing a suit and he said: *Oh, I've got a job for you here, with that suit!* He took me straight down to the players' tunnel and said: *This is your job here. You're now a steward!* And I'm still here!

Obviously, working down there you get to know all the players. They had to come past me to get to the dressing-room so I was a point of contact. I enjoyed that period. It was all very loose back then. People would just turn up: the club probably only knew the match-day staff by a first name. And, to be honest, even when I first started as chief steward I probably just wrote down a dozen or 15 names on the back of a cigarette packet.

The big change, really, was the Bradford fire. Up till then the job was just to make sure people went where they'd paid to go. The emphasis after the fire shifted to crowd safety. I'll give you a simple example. In the old days, every time you broke or lost a lock, you bought a new one. We had dozens of little hooks and keys with little tags. It was the devil's own job to find the right key for a particular lock. At Bradford that afternoon, they couldn't find the bloke with the right key to open the gate at the back of the stand. That was the tragedy of it. The immediate change was uniform locks everywhere in the ground. And every steward has a key.

The whole stewarding operation's now properly organised. People are known to the club, registered, briefed. We're checked by the Fire Brigade, the Football Licensing Authority, Hounslow Council. Training's done by the safety officer, Jill Dawson, and I work under her. It's all a million miles away from 1976 when I started, and rightly so. And the game itself has changed. Clubs have worked hard to get women, children, families coming to football. I was really proud when we won that Best Community Club award a couple of years ago.

I've been lucky, really, to have the opportunity. This club means a lot to me and I never dreamt I would become so involved here. And most of our stewards are like me. You might get ten or eleven quid for four hours on a match-day which helps – you know, a lot of stewards use the job to sponsor going to away games – but I'd say 90-odd per cent of our stewards are just devoted Brentford fans like me.

Phil Coffey, Host, Exec Club, Brentford

Phil Coffey owns an air cargo company with premises on the perimeter road at Heathrow. It's a very busy office: on the wall beside Phil's desk is a well-marked map of the world's air routes. Every match-day afternoon, however, life for the Coffey family is a local business in Braemar Road, Brentford. His wife Denise works at the club's souvenir shop. Phil runs the Exec Club, a members' room at Griffin Park.

I run a thing called the Exec Club: people pay for the use of a bar; sandwiches, biscuits, savouries, tea and coffee. My wife and I run the club for Brentford – no charge, just what it costs us in ingredients. The room gets used for players and their wives and friends, too. We hadn't got anywhere else big enough!

On Friday evening, my wife goes and buys all the stuff to make the sandwiches. Saturday morning, I go down and buy the bread so it's nice and fresh! We start making sandwiches about nine o'clock, me, my wife, my daughter, our son-in-law, package them up and take them down to the ground around 12. My wife goes off to the club shop – she works there on match-days – and my daughter sits on the door to check passes and so on for me. We'll have anything from 60 to 100 people in: our members – who pay! – up one end and guests down at the far end. I suppose, after clearing up and everything, we get away from the ground about an hour after the game. It's an enjoyable day. We all enjoy it. Otherwise we wouldn't do it! And I've been doing this five, six years now, getting to know everybody: our members, the players and their families.

I grew up in Northolt which isn't very far away. I'm a waste of time on remembering dates and scores but I first came to Brentford when I was about eleven. Me and my mate Nobby used to come down on our bikes and I've been coming ever since. Both my daughters started going. My wife used to hate football but, after a while, she decided that if you can't beat them, you know! She's a supporter now, even more involved than I am because she works at the shop in the week, too.

I can't honestly remember how I came to be running the Exec Club! I'd been going to Brentford a long time and I was a member when they had the old Players Bar there. I suppose you meet people. Anyway, some time after Keith Loring came to the club he told me they were going to start this new thing and asked me if I'd like to run it. When I first asked my wife if she fancied doing sandwiches for 100 people every other Saturday she wasn't best pleased! But we've now got it down to a fine art.

I don't know what I'd do without football! You could say we're a real football family. You know, we do the club and go to every away game. If there's football on the telly, it's not like families where one or two'll say: *Oh, no, not football again!* We all pile in to watch together. A Saturday without football, we're lost!

I do really enjoy the involvement. And if I had the money – and you've got to have a lot of money – I'd like to be more involved. Clubs like ours, you can't survive on what you get through the gate – and it's not like the big clubs with TV deals, sponsorships and so on – you have to have people who'll put in some money. Our division, the directors will have to keep putting their hands in their pockets!

But we like being there. We just like Brentford. The atmosphere's good, there's a good camaraderie about the place. A lot of us go out to eat together on Saturday night after games. It's not a club, it's a family. That's the way we feel about it. And you know when you go there like we do, you're doing something to help the club. A couple of years ago, when we got promoted the last game of the season against Peterborough: if you could have seen people's faces, people crying, it was so overwhelming. And you feel you had done a little bit to help towards that. I got a buzz out of that. I mean, we're never going to be a big club but, on the other hand, maybe our enjoyment wouldn't be the same if we were.

Peter Barnes, Social Club Manager, Manchester City

Manchester City's supporters' social club is owned by a brewery – Greenall's – but, sat at one corner of Maine Road in the shadow of the main stand, it belongs – in spirit – to the football club. Absolutely packed with home and away fans before a game, 14 bar staff are kept very busy. The club's run by Peter Barnes, who played for Manchester City and England with distinction during the 1970s and early 1980s. Match-days, however, it's unusual to catch him actually working behind his own bar.

For the past couple of years I've been coaching under-elevens and under-14s at City's School of Excellence and turning out for the Manchester City veterans' team, playing charity games all over the country. I do a bit of radio work, too, for Piccadilly Radio. That's match analysis for most home and a few away games and a phone-in programme for a couple of hours before matches. That's all in addition to running the social club here, which I took over in October '94.

My father played for City in the '50s and I played here in the '70s and '80s, so the family's got 50 years' involvement between us. Working here now is like coming back to my roots and it's doing something I always wanted to do: the licensing trade. I'd only done six weeks over the summer as relief for Scottish and Newcastle and I was looking for my own pub or hotel/restaurant or whatever when I was approached by Greenall's to take over the club. Well, I was already coaching here and doing the radio: I thought it would be an experience, if nothing else! It's a big challenge for me at the moment but I'm really enjoying it.

Funny enough, this is the first time I've had a night off

from the radio and actually been working in the club before a match. You can see how busy it is. It's not like a pub: we've got eight tills going this evening. There's obviously a lot of PR work involved and we've got a big cabaret room at the back with a stage where we do shows and we're going to try to put some bands on. I've taken on an entertainments manager and I hope that side's really going to grow.

I think the relationship between the football club and its fans is the most important in the game. When I first came here in 1972, a snotty-nosed 15-year-old, all the players – apprentices through to senior pros – used to come down here to the social club. All our meals were done in the big room through at the back: 50 or 60 staff having steak and chips on the Monday, chicken and chips on Tuesday. We always knew – it was the same menu every week! It was actually another ex-player – another ex-outside left! – who ran the club then. Roy Clarke was a Welsh international who played in the '50s with Don Revie and my dad. He ran this place for 24 years. Manchester City as a whole was a big family back then.

When Roy Clarke retired, five or six years ago, it cut the link at the social club between supporters and players. I think when Greenall's approached me to take over they were hoping I'd be able to make that attachment again. And I've come in at a good time. Francis Lee's arrived and taken the football club over – I used to clean his boots when he was a player here! – and he's been over here to say he'll do whatever he can to help. It's so important that the club has a link with the supporters, and the supporters with the players. We've been really busy the last few months and I think things are going well.

Obviously, everything revolves around success. If the team does well on the park, playing entertaining football, things snowball from there. And the response here from supporters has been tremendous. I'm frightened to go out behind the bar some days! They all want to stop me: *What about that goal? What about the game next week?* And I don't mind that. I enjoy talking to people about football, which definitely helps in this line of work! It's right that people in the game talk to supporters. Without them, the game won't survive. Football's an entertainment business and you've got to look after the people who pay your wages.

My dad'll usually look in before a game. He's 65 and retired but, since Francis Lee came back, he's been doing part-time scouting for the club. It's using my father's experience: every club's got someone like that, haven't they? An old boy who's been at the place for ages, knows the game inside out. He was a big influence on me when I was a player. I could cry on his shoulder, ask him for advice. He's never run a pub but he advises me about this place, too!

Like I say, this is a challenge for me and I'm really enjoying it at the moment. That's not to say, necessarily, that I'll be like Roy Clarke and be doing it for 25 years. In honesty, my heart probably lies in management or coaching in the future. I think I've got a lot to offer the game. It's good to see people I played with in the England team – Glenn Hoddle, Ray Wilkins, Graham Rix – making a go of it. The game's now about young managers like that and I'd love to have a crack.

Football for Sale

MAKING THE BUSINESS WORK

If you know exactly what you want to do, you can do it very quickly.
Karren Brady

You go anywhere now and people are talking about football. We've got to take advantage of that.
Debra Fraser

There's always something else to do, something else to sell.
Abdul Rashid

For me, the football side is a bonus. I'm there to run the business.
Edward Freedman

Karren Brady, Managing Director, Birmingham City

Had Lord Justice Taylor, while preparing his report after the Hillsborough disaster, needed a single clear example of how English football had gone wrong he might have chosen Birmingham City. Come the late 1980s, St Andrews was a vast, outdated stadium literally falling to pieces around the ears of an administration without the wit or the will to cope with failure on the pitch, hooliganism on the terraces and the pace of change in football's commercial environment. The club was in receivership in 1993 when the unlikely figures of a new owner, David Sullivan, and a 26-year-old managing director, Karren Brady, appeared on the horizon.

I used to run Sport Newspapers – the *Sunday Sport* and the *Daily Sport*. I was there for nearly five years, working mainly on the financial side. The boss, David Sullivan, likes football and I'd spent most of a year looking at several clubs – Luton, Cardiff, Peterborough – he'd been thinking of buying, and, for one reason or another, knocked them back. And then Birmingham City came up and I came, met Terry Cooper who was the manager then, and found that the club was in an absolutely diabolical state. That was actually to its advantage because you could see areas for improvement whereas some clubs, no matter how efficiently they're run, you know are never going to make any money because they get such low gates. Here, crowds of 25,000 aren't out of the question.

We made the decision on a Friday and by the next Friday we'd bought Birmingham from the receivers. Part of the deal was that if David bought a club, I would go in and run it. David left it to me. I'm not an expert – I'm a fan. I've got my opinions, like anyone on the terrace, but I try to keep them to myself on the football side! But on the business side, newspapers and football clubs have a lot in common: editors are like managers, supporters are like readers, sponsors are like advertisers. From a financial point of view, one business is the same as another.

I think it helped, in my job, having a strong sales and marketing rather than a football background. Basically, our business philosophy is not to chase turnover but to chase profit. And everything we make goes back into the club and will do for the next five years at least, I think. Only then might people start to get back some of their investment. In the short term we're aiming to make the club self-financing, so that if we want to spend a million pounds on a player we can take it out of the club rather than continuing to put money in.

Certainly, I have a plan. When I arrived there wasn't a single area of the club that wasn't losing money. I mean, in the first week, we launched a new kit, franchised the catering, bought two new shops, restructured the commercial department and renegotiated our programme arrangements. Within seven days money stopped going out and started coming in. It's just making logical business decisions. After a week, I was nearly in tears but after three months things were running the way I wanted them to. If you know exactly what you want to do, you can do it very quickly.

From the club's point of view, me being a woman has helped because it obviously created a lot of press interest, particularly locally. Personally, I find it very hard to deal with. You know, when it's good it's: *Yes, I am pretty wonderful, aren't I?* But when someone writes something that's really crap, it's hard: you're not trained to deal with the press. Even with my background – I only knew the financial and sales side of it.

In the game itself, it doesn't bother me. I went to an all-boys' school – just 20 girls in the sixth form. Obviously, there are certain practical difficulties: if you want to see a player, say, you can't just go downstairs! But for the most part I just ignore the problems: there's no reason a woman can't do this job. That said, I can't ever see a woman football manager. In that job you have to have the experience. You could be a coach

– a fitness-type person – or a good scout – if you watch enough of anything you can get a feel for it – but, to be a manager, you have to have been involved in playing the game. And women aren't at any high level.

But this job? I love football. I work really long hours whatever I'm doing. Football's been the one hobby I've ever had. Football as my job is like a dream come true. It's like a kid with a Saturday job in a sweetshop and being allowed to eat as many sweets as they want. That's how this is for me!

Keith Loring, Chief Executive, Brentford

Keith Loring started work at Brentford under chairman, Martin Large, in April 1985. Ten years on, while David Webb's young team continues to thrive out on the pitch, Loring and his staff have established a healthy sense of stability behind the scenes at Griffin Park. Forward-thinking and a sound commercial sense are the obvious reasons for Loring's success in the role of chief executive. Vital too, however, is the sense of involvement he fostered amongst Brentford supporters, a policy for which his own background serves as a blueprint. At the end of season 1994/95 Loring left Brentford to take up a similar position at Derby County.

The first time I ever went to football was around 1955. I was eleven and everybody at school was talking about this big game at the Valley. Charlton had been relegated to the old Second Division the year before. Here they were, last game of the season: if they beat or drew with Blackburn Rovers they'd go back up; if Blackburn won, they'd go up. Well, the place was packed. We stood at the front, down near the corner flag. Charlton went 1–0 up, then 4–1 down. Then 4–2, 4–3 with ten minutes to go: you can imagine what the atmosphere was like. Anyway, we lost and Charlton didn't go back up for something like 20 years. But I was hooked. I didn't miss a home game for nine years after that!

I married when I was 21 and moved to Cambridge where I was working for a telecommunications company. Cambridge didn't have a League team then and I hardly saw any football at all. I got into some bad habits, really! About as near to being a professional gambler as you could get. I was coping with this sales job all day and then running poker games every night! One thing it did teach me, though, was to judge people very quickly as to whether they could be trusted or not. I did all right but I was backing horses too, and I was a complete mug at that!

Don't ask me why things change, but I was sat having my hair cut on a Friday afternoon and I saw this ad I liked for a car dealership. I was 28 and I'd been having a good time and doing all right at work but I phoned up, interviewed on the back of an all-night poker game, and ended up selling Mercedes! I really enjoyed it and I suppose the boredom that was behind the gambling disappeared and I just knocked all that on the head. Four years later I was a director of the company.

During that time I met a customer, Reg Smart, who was a director at Cambridge United and I got invited along to watch the game at which the club was celebrating getting into the League. We took a ground advertising board – in fact, that car dealership's still involved with Cambridge 20 years later. Anyway, boredom started setting in again at work and I went part time. I'd been organising things between the company and Cambridge, who were now in the Second Division, and Reg Smart asked me if I would help out up there on my days off. I was a supporter now, wasn't I? We set up this thing called Abbey Action, a supporters' organisation raising money for specific projects at the club. We got into all sorts of weird stuff: we put Jasper Carrott on in a tent and had a concert by the London Symphony Orchestra on the pitch with an appearance from the England squad!

I ended up taking over the commercial department at Cambridge on a consultancy basis and did quite well, got the club a big sponsor and so on. But in those days, to be honest, commercial people tended to be seen as a necessary evil in football. My mate Reg Smart went off the board and I fell out with a couple of the new directors, so I packed it in and just kept doing Abbey Action as a supporter.

I was busy doing other things – I opened a snooker hall in Newmarket with Willie Thorne – when John Docherty, who'd been at Cambridge, phoned and asked if I'd come to Brentford where he was assistant to Frank McLintock. I didn't really fancy it but I went along to meet them out of respect for John, I suppose.

I drove down and met Martin Large, who actually owned 51 per cent of Brentford. He showed me around, and I was very impressed with him but just didn't think the idea was practical. Then John and Frank took me out for a curry and got stuck into me, too. Well, in the end, I joined on a six-month trial basis and, with Martin and Brentford, there was never a sense of this 'necessary evil'. The club got on to a really good run: we went to Wembley in the Freight Rover that year and I ended up – I'm just a fan at heart, remember – sitting in the Royal Box, you know, as a representative of the club.

I got really hooked into the place – we never even talked about the six months! – and I was eventually appointed chief executive. I was still stopping in bed and breakfasts here and my wife Lesley was up in Cambridge but we eventually moved down and lived next door to Griffin Park. Now, on a Sunday, I have to be careful to sit on the sofa in my lounge rather than the armchair because if I'm facing the front window I'm looking straight on to the away supporters' gates and I start thinking: *Oh, we should have done this or that yesterday!* But it's that kind of job. It's a way of life.

Paul Britton, Chief Executive, Bath City

Paul Britton is a thorough professional. Chief executive at Bath City, where he's presided over the longest-running ground-share in the country (with Bristol Rovers) and kept the Vauxhall Conference club afloat in a town with a passion only for rugby, he's also on the Conference League management committee and a Football League committee that monitors ground standards at different levels of the game. A self-confessed 'Corinthian' at heart and in fact, Britton recently left Bath City to become Secretary of the Gloucestershire FA.

•PAUL BRITTON•

•Bath City•

I played football at a young age and had to give up because of injury at 16, 17. I didn't really know what to do. I never had the opportunity to get anywhere as a player, but I wanted the involvement, the week-to-week involvement. All my mates were playing football – you know, only parks football, lucky-to-get-a-ref football – but I'd been told I had to stop. How could I stay involved?

Out of the blue somebody said to me: *Look, the secretary we've got isn't all that keen, why don't you have a crack at it?* And I did. It was a real change. I was working for British Airways as an air engine mechanic – hard physical work – and it was great for me, coming home in the evening to do paperwork, swapping my spanner for a pen! It was something I really enjoyed.

Anyhow, I went along to the AGM of the local league, a thing called the Suburban League, and the chairman stood up and said: *Well, this year's winner of Best Administrated Club is Frenchay Hospital.* Now, I didn't even realise I'd won. But they said: *Oh, you'll have to go up!* I had to go up in front of this big gathering – 185 clubs in the league – and everybody clapped and I picked this two-quid trophy up. The recognition meant the world to me.

Then Mangotsfield United, who were a Western League club, had a bit of a problem with their secretary and so I went there. And in 1986 there was, well this quirk: the other side of football being good to me. I had the call from Littlewoods to tell me that we'd won the pools, a syndicate of four of us off the aircraft.

To cut a long story short, they whisked us off to London with our families – we'd put down *No Publicity*, but it took the Littlewoods representative about ten minutes to talk us out of that! – and wined and dined us for three days. But they wouldn't tell us how much we'd won – they wanted us to be surprised when they pulled the blanket off the big dummy cheque. It was terrible. I remember being awake at four o'clock in the morning before the presentation, listening to the Blue and Royals exercising their horses down in Hyde Park. The suspense! Anyway, on the Wednesday, they wheel us all on to the stage. And they drop the blanket and the figure written along the cheque, the first thing I did was divide it by four! Well, it was over 800 grand – so we've come out with £200,000 apiece. And that was it.

Now, even though that wasn't such a great deal of money – I'd have expected to earn three times that if I'd kept working till I was 65 – nevertheless, with investing wisely, it gave me an opportunity. I decided: *Right, I've had enough of twiddling nuts on the back end of Concorde!* I threw a party at Mangotsfield and said: *You've got me full time!* I could pay myself a salary from investments and do what I'd always wanted to do, which was work in football.

And then I moved to Bath, who were in a terrible state, admin-wise – all at sea. After the first week, I wondered what I'd walked into and whether I could cope with it. But we've gradually turned it round, got a system in place and made the club more efficient as we've gone on.

The Littlewoods money has let me do what I always wanted to do. And I think Bath get the benefit, too. Obviously, I work unpaid. I just get a car through the club. But it's the passion in it. My bank manager says I'm nuts. My portfolio manager says I'm nuts. It creates bedlam with income tax returns. It creates bedlam with the Department of Employment. A lot of people would have said: *Right, we'll take that money and go and sit in the Bahamas for two weeks every year or buy a big house or big cars.* Well, I've not done that. I've condensed the money into a financial package that pays me enough to go off and do the job I've got a passion for.

And I've still got that. In spite of all the hassles and the moans and: *There's no money; we played bad again; our players are rubbish!* Any other job with that much hassle you'd walk away from, but with football you still want to go in every day, every week, every month. We're all the same: me, the girl in the office, the fellow who marks out the pitch. Football survives on moaning! And it's great.

Edward Freedman, Managing Director Merchandising Division, Manchester United

While the team remains reassuringly fallible, even at the peak of its powers, Manchester United's merchandising division has left the rest of football apparently standing still over the past few seasons. A massive new retail development in Manchester, its own radio station, and the biggest-selling football magazine in Britain are some of the more recent developments masterminded by Edward Freedman, the club's director of merchandising. Freedman built up and sold a successful retail clothing business in North London before football became a career in the mid-1980s.

He took up his current position at Old Trafford in 1992.

I'd been a Tottenham supporter since I was a kid, but how I

got involved with the club was rather strange. Just after the Mexico World Cup, a friend of mine – an agent on the Continent – had heard that Spurs might be interested in buying Nico Claesen, the Belgian forward, and asked me to establish contact on his behalf. As it turned out, they bought Nico but the negotiations took quite a long time and I got to know Irving Scholar. He checked me out, I understand, and asked if I'd be prepared to do a job for them on the merchandising side.

At first, it was on a consultancy basis but the thing started to take up so much time – Spurs had taken on Hummel and the whole business was expanding – they asked me to come and do it full time. I was very excited. I could see how unprofessional football clubs were in the field and, after a real battle, we established a very successful merchandising division. We looked at merchandising in a completely different way, not just as a tag-on which the commercial manager had to take responsibility for along with all the other things – match-day hospitality, sponsorship, advertising – which are really a separate business. We tried to stop licensing everything – it had to be better and more profitable to be in full control of our product – and started developing the value of the trademark, the 'brand', if you like. We took responsibility for quality, design and the distribution network ourselves. We produced a catalogue, built up the mail order business. I think we were ahead of anyone else in the country.

I was at Spurs when the takeover happened. I stayed there for nine months but, basically, wasn't very happy with the set-up. There were political conflicts which I didn't want to be on one side of or the other. And I was headhunted by Manchester United. I went up and had a look around. I could see the enormous potential. I'd always lived and worked in London, my family's here, my home, but I very much wanted to leave Spurs at that stage. Football's quite a narrow field and the jobs don't come any better than Man United, potentially the biggest club in the world.

The existing structures at Old Trafford – the football team, the commercial department – were very strong. I think Martin Edwards recognised that merchandising was one area in which they weren't realising their potential. The turnover was about £2 million. After a year, we'd got it up to £5 million. And the last six months alone, now, stands at £6 million. Things have gone very well!

When I arrived, about 85 per cent of the business was selling replica kit. We've now got a 50/50 balance between kit and other items. I can see that trend continuing until we only rely on kit for 15 or 20 per cent of the business. We've got two people working full time on developing new products, our own in-house designer, our own wholesale division, a monthly magazine that's bigger than *Shoot!* or *Match*. A survey we did in the magazine showed that 93 per cent of the readership never comes to the ground, so we're working to develop a huge new market: people who don't actually come to matches. I don't think there's another operation like it in the country.

Although Manchester United are a big club with a huge following, every club, in its own way, could be doing similar things to get more out of their merchandising business. We look at our products without the Man United logo to see if they will stand up in the market for quality and value. If we're happy with them on those terms, then we'll add the extra dimension: the brand, the club crest. All right, we're a big business but every club can look at things on its own scale. There's a lot can be done. It's not just that the club's successful. I've been in merchandising all my life, I was trained in textiles, and we make this side of the business work on its own terms, expanding all the time. Success on the pitch helps, of course, but you've always got Christmas, birthdays for football fans. The occasional Jack Walker or Alan Sugar notwithstanding, football's an expensive business when players cost millions and I'm proud of what we've contributed to the club. And I think we've just scratched the surface at Manchester United.

Look, I'm delighted. I'm a very happy man. I could talk about the actual football all night, couldn't I? I remember Spurs' double side. Watching United do the double was amazing. More interesting than merchandising, anyway! You know, I'm the kind of person who can't walk past kids playing football in the park without stopping to watch. Football's something I've always loved. The danger, of course, is that people get carried away with the football side of things and don't run the business. For me, the football side is a bonus. I'm there to run the business. It's a case of keeping your feet on the ground. I've seen too many sensible businessmen get completely carried away!

Abdul Rashid, Commercial Manager, Aston Villa

Abdul Rashid's story is very much that of the local boy made good. Villa's commercial manager grew up in Lozells and watched his team from the Holte End as a boy. That background perhaps explains why Rashid places so much emphasis on the homely qualities which he and his staff bring to the job of running a big-city Premiership operation at Villa Park. He got his first job, in Villa's club shop, in 1977.

I had a meeting yesterday with Scottish Mutual whom we've been involved with for a couple of years. They recently had a soccer six competition with 800 people down here. They'd already written to say what a success it had been, but yesterday the fellow said that what had really impressed him was that all his people had been made to feel really welcome at Villa Park. By the guy who met them at the gate, by the person who let them into the suite, the people who served the refreshments, the staff looking after the dressing-room areas. Basically, he said, that's something you can't buy. He really appreciated it.

It's an attitude you can only develop over a number of years. If you look at the stability of Aston Villa: the chairman has been here 26 years; I've been associated with the club for 17 or 18 years. What we've tried to do is recognise some of the supporters who can have an input. As a commercial department, we can't operate on a match-day without the volume of match-day staff we have – people who act as hostesses, commissionaires, guides and gofers. They're all supporters: people I may have grown up with, people around the club we've got to know. Instead of keeping them on the outside, we've brought them in. All right, we pay them a few bob which gives us the right to say: *Do this, or do that.* The right to come down on them if something goes wrong. But they don't do it for the money. For them, it's Mark Bosnich calling them George or Steve. For me, this job is a dream come true. I get a bit embarrassed talking about it, really. I used to come here as a schoolboy – I lived nearby – and anytime the gates were open, I was here: first-team games, reserves, youth team. I got to know some of the players. I used to clean some of their cars. While I was a schoolboy, I became a ball-boy at reserve team games and I got to know one or two people in the souvenir shop. I'd help carry boxes around the place, a little job that got me into first-team games free, and I'd help around the place at the games, too.

When I left school, I wanted to be a draughtsman but I quickly found I wasn't good enough. I was offered a full-time job in the souvenir shop, which I took. I helped out on the lottery and looked after the travel club. That was a great time: we won the Championship and, the following year, the European Cup. Then a new commercial manager, Tony Stephens, came in and I joined him as an assistant, and then worked for his successor. I became commercial manager the summer of 1988.

A lot of it's luck, being in the right place at the right time. But you can manipulate that, can't you? I made sure I was always around the place! And, of course, Mr Ellis hasn't employed me because he likes me. He's employed me because he thinks I can make the club a few bob. But it is a dream come true for me. When I was a kid, footballers were like gods to me. Still are, really! Football's a magnet, the stadium and everything, it just draws me. Showing people round, I still get a buzz out of the place: the hairs on the back of my neck stand up!

Most of the staff here at Villa are the same. It's our club and we wouldn't have the same enthusiasm for the job working somewhere else. You know, when I first started working here part time, I was involved downstairs and it wasn't until two weeks after I started full time that I had the nerve to go up to the offices upstairs. They were like an inner sanctum! But I'd always had the ambition. When I started as a souvenir shop assistant I was interviewed for the programme and when the fellow asked me what I wanted to be, I said commercial manager! And I fulfilled that ambition by the time I was 27, 28. Where I go from here now, I don't know.

I don't know how good I'd be away from Villa Park. I suppose if you felt the club was stagnating, not going forward on and off the pitch, it would be easy to become frustrated. But the last couple of seasons we've had the new boxes at Witton Lane, new facilities in Trinity Road. And, of course, the new Holte End. It means there's always something else to do, something else to sell. And one of the great things about working in football is that, although you may think you've got your day all planned out, everything can change with the morning's first phone call: the manager's signing a player and you've got to organise a press conference. The biggest buzz, of course, is match-day. That's when it all comes together. We'll start around nine and I love, come 6.30, seven, when all your guests have gone home, sitting down with the staff to have a beer and talk about how the day has gone. That's a real satisfaction. And, from time to time, like for the Coca-Cola Cup run in 1994, you do detach yourself from the job and we all become just Aston Villa fans again.

Debra Fraser, Marketing Manager, Millwall

Ten years ago, a young black woman growing up in London had no reason to look twice at football. Debra Fraser left college and went off to Italy to work in fashion PR. Football crossed her path pretty well by accident. When Millwall chairman Ray Burr was looking for a marketing manager for the club in its new home in south-east London, Fraser's cool, rational attitude to the game may well have appeared a positive benefit: new ideas were what the new stadium would be all about. She's now in her mid-20s and has been at Millwall for nearly three years.

My first involvement with football was through the agent, Jon Smith, at First Artists. I joined him six years ago as a personal assistant. At the time, Jon was looking after the England team's players' pool. The company was doing really well and after a couple of years I became an account manager, looking after particular sponsors like Trebor and Burtons which got me more directly involved.

After I'd been at First Artists for about four years, an American company called Proset, who make collector cards like Pannini, came over wanting to do football cards. Rather than set up a new company, they launched it through Jon and I did all of it: sorted all the pictures out, got all the clearances and licences. The first set came out and did really well, so Proset decided: *Yes, this is worth doing. We're going to blow Pannini out of the water! We can do it!* So they asked me to set up a new company over here. I did that for two years but then everybody got on the football card bandwagon – Merlin, Pannini, Collection World, Shooting Stars. By our third set, we were doing really badly. Proset pulled out and I was out of a job.

So I was unemployed for the first time since leaving college. My background was in marketing so I wasn't necessarily thinking of staying with football. I hadn't been a football fan as a kid – I sometimes feel a bit of a traitor, especially with some of the other people who work here! But, the job at Millwall came up – I actually heard about it through Jon Smith. The geography of it – I lived in North London – and Millwall's reputation meant I wasn't keen at first. You know, football's got every '-ist' going: the racist thing and it being such a male world, I didn't fancy. But I had two interviews with the chairman, heard about the new stadium and everything, and I suppose realised how exciting the job might be. He said the job wouldn't be easy – and my ears pricked up at that straightaway. And I've been here since.

When I arrived, I couldn't believe how unsophisticated Millwall's – and most other clubs' outside your Arsenals and your Man Uniteds – set-up was. The first six months we were still at Cold Blow Lane and the day I joined they didn't have an office for me so I worked from one of the executive boxes – with no central heating, it was freezing! There wasn't a marketing department as such. But now there's a team of us – and we've got a product to sell: a brand-new stadium, executive boxes, TV coverage and people wanting to get involved. I'm not knocking Cold Blow Lane. I know a lot of people didn't want us to move – but from a business point of view the New Den makes more sense.

At Millwall, we've got a stadium management, Ogden, who are a big American company. I think they came over with a big-scale American philosophy and hoped the New Den would be their flagship venue. But I don't think the ideas quite translated to here. I came in and was told Ogden had budgeted advertising income at a million pounds – stupid figures – and I had to review all that, explain that England was different, and set more realistic targets, which we've reached. Ogden are very good but, at ground level, at a football club, they didn't have that experience. Their strength is in running the stadium as a multi-event venue. And I try and handle the crossover with football. I love the football side but, if anything, I spend more time on the other events – meeting promoters for concerts and so on. First and foremost we're Millwall Football Club but I've got to make sure that the bricks and mortar – the stadium – can be used for other things the rest of the time. We need all that to get money into the club.

We've got to spread out. Football used to be just a male working-class sport and it's not any more. You go anywhere now and people are talking about football. We've got to take advantage of that.

John Holmes, Commercial Manager, Cambridge United

John Holmes describes himself as a cross between a charity worker and Arthur Daley. A lifelong fan of Cambridge United, Holmes was appointed commercial manager in 1989. Since 1994 he has been in business for himself as a commercial consultant, with United as his most important client. Inevitably, most working days continue to see Holmes trying to work the Abbey Stadium oracle in a portakabin in the club car park just off the Newmarket Road.

I've always been the same. Even when I was in the navy I'd manage to get to games. I'd find myself stuck in Gillingham or somewhere and in trouble for not getting back to base. I've always been involved with the football club in some way: selling programmes, working as a steward, whatever. Anyway, I got introduced to a player called Lindsay Smith, who was a youth team player at Arsenal before having a career in the lower divisions. Well, one FA Cup day, I was round his house and met Mark Saggers, who works for Sky

TV now but was then a reporter on the local paper. He asked me if I'd help him out on the statistics side at games, driving him around, doing a bit of radio commentary.

I couldn't believe it. I started finding myself on the team coach. I had to go out and buy myself a new suit and a coat, didn't I? Things were on a bit of a high. Chris Turner was the manager and I'm loving it, aren't I? Little Holmesey is Billy Bigtime! At the time they were looking for someone to do commentaries for the club videos and I've got landed with the job! I was absolutely hopeless, but I loved it. Chris Turner was brilliant, really made you feel part of things. I did that until it became too embarrassing. They used to show the tapes on the team coach on the way to games and the lads would absolutely slaughter me.

I learnt a lot about the club and became accepted as part of the family, if you like. And that included some of the directors: that's the kind of club Cambridge is. The club had never had a commercial department. The last person doing work on that side had been Gary Johnson, who's our manager now, but he'd been running the reserve and youth teams at the same time! Well, we finished just below the Fourth division play-off places and the vice-chairman, Reg Smart, recognised there was some potential. I talked to him and to the new manager then, John Beck, and I took the job as commercial manager. I actually started work the next season, the week before we played at Wembley in the play-off final, five years ago now. I sat down in my new office and said: *Yes!* I had so much enthusiasm, so many ideas, loads of things I wanted to do. There was so much going on in football and nothing happening in Cambridge. The place was surviving – just – as a football club but, from a business point of view, it really needed a kick up the backside.

I won't say I was the most qualified person for the job but I had the enthusiasm and people around me who helped me channel that enthusiasm. We made some mistakes but we had some good times, too. A week into the job, we're at Wembley and there am I on the team bus, driving down Wembley Way. I'm crying, shaking with nerves. Becky's actually let me walk out on the pitch with the team. I'm out there and I hear this little voice: *Dad! Dad!* It's my little boy in the crowd. I've lost it completely. There are players who are going to be playing at Wembley having to put an arm round me to say: *Come on, Holmesey, you soft git! It's all right!*

Well, we won, didn't we? And we then had a fantastic couple of years, which meant there was a lot to do. We actually started building a commercial department while the team was winning the Third Division championship and coming so close to promotion the next season into what was about to become the Premier League. I had to get match sponsors, sponsored cars, a club sponsor, Fujitsu. To this day, for the size of club we are, the level of sponsorship we get is fantastic. I had no background in it, I just used to front it out! Of course, I had a lot to learn. Just because I would spend £40,000 on Cambridge if I had it, I assumed other people would too, just to have the chance to meet the players down here at Raggedy-arsed Rovers! And have 2,000 people see their company's name on our shirts on a Saturday!

I think we've come on leaps and bounds, though. And most of that's down to one thing: the success the team had on the pitch. Our operation here is all about service. We're like a corner shop: friendly, hospitable, good value and we want people's regular custom. If we don't give them what they want, they'll go off to Tesco's, which is Arsenal or Liverpool or Man U. I like the one-on-one, the getting involved, whatever the limitations imposed on us by scale. You know, there's no Jack Walker coming in here! But that's the challenge. We've no tradition of business involvement with football in Cambridge, just as there's not a traditional working-class base to our support to get our gates up over 2,000 or 3,000. I think what we've got to offer is the personal touch, and that's what I know how to do.

Danny McGregor, Commercial Manager, Manchester United

Danny McGregor – Manchester born and bred – has been a United fan since the war. Ten years ago he took over the commercial operation at Old Trafford. With the recent explosion in commercial activity, a separate arm has been established to handle United merchandising, leaving McGregor free to concentrate on match-day sponsorship and hospitality. He also oversees the administration of the club's charity work.

At 17 I volunteered for the Brigade of Guards. This was just before the end of national service: I knew I'd be called up, so I volunteered and got into the brigade I wanted to be in. I was a milkman, and went on from there to being a bread man, delivering Mother's Pride to shops around Manchester. It was the period when the corner shops were beginning to fade and the big multiples were becoming very strong. I took a position as a supervisor and then as an area manager. I made the choice to be an area manager concentrating on the multiples which I thought would put me on the right track for where I wanted my career to go. Really, I thought I was always going to be basically a bread man: my dad had been a milkman and I assumed that was how my life would go. Opportunities presented themselves, though, and I took them and ended up as national accounts manager for Rank Hovis McDougall.

The job took me down to the head office in Slough and I lived in a little place called Minty, near Cirencester, for several years. But I wasn't happy. I couldn't make the bridge between north and south and wanted to be back in my own environment. A chap named David Evans offered me a job with a cleaning group as a national account sales director. I took the job: it got me back to Manchester and the north. The Manchester United chairman, Martin Edwards, was a non-executive director of the company and we met at the monthly board meetings. In 1985 we were on a train going to a dinner together and he offered me the position of commercial manager at Old Trafford. Even though I was born in Moss Side – Manchester City territory – I've always been a United fan. My dad took me to my first game just after the war when United were playing their home games at Maine Road. I saw the first game at Old Trafford, too, when they moved back. So, you can imagine, I didn't take much persuading when the chairman offered me the job at United!

When I first started, there was very little in the way of commercial activity at the club. All the VIP and hospitality packages were sub-contracted out to a Bolton company, Delta Sports. I couldn't really see the sense in dialling 0204 to book hospitality at Manchester United! I approached the chairman and asked to take that side of the business over. He set me a financial target and agreed: we now do VIP hospitality for over 500 people every match-day, which is tremendous business.

My responsibilities on the hospitality side include the match-day sponsor, the VIP packages – we had 25 birthday groups at the last home game! I set up a thing called the Europa Club, which is now the Premier Club – we renamed it after we won the League in 1993: 200 companies who take four or six places as packages at every game. I see the Club Class facilities which have been put in at the back of the new Stretford End: 867 seats. I sell the exec facilities for 832 places and 149 boxes. That gives you an idea of the situation from season to season.

We've always been, for the most part, the top-supported club in the country – certainly over the past 30 years or so – and the supporters have always stood by us. Even when things weren't going so well back in the late '80s, when I took over the hospitality packages, we still managed to sell out. Long may things continue to go as well as they are now: it certainly makes my life easier!

The business has grown out of all recognition. When I came here I was basically on my own. I've now got half a dozen people working with me. We keep having to move into bigger offices! Arranging all the tickets and seating plans is a full-time job. There are all the other arrangements, too, to make it a good day out for people: Norman Whiteside, Wilf McGuiness and Vince Miller go round before games and we'll get a couple of players up afterwards for autographs and photos. All that needs organising. We do it properly because we want people to come back!

We've just started doing weekend breaks: I used to drive up on match-days and the forecourt would be full of people over from Ireland and Scandinavia. I didn't think they should just be dumped at the airport or Liverpool docks and left to find their way to Old Trafford. I went over to see travel agents in Ireland and places like Oslo – we've got 10,000 people in our Norwegian supporters' club! – about arranging packages through the club. We now look after 200 or 300 people a game on weekend breaks from as far away as America and South Africa.

I come in just before eight every morning and have a cup of tea with the laundry girls. The chairman knows we put our hours in, so he doesn't have us clocking on and clocking off! I'll leave Old Trafford at about five, 5.30 unless we've got an evening game when I'll be here until 11.30 or midnight: those are long days!

Whatever's going on, though, I make sure I'll always see the game. On a Saturday, by three o'clock everybody's eaten and in their seats. They can settle down and enjoy themselves and so can I! You know, I'm just a normal lad who left school at 15 without any qualifications and took my chances. I've got three great kids – and an understanding wife! – and I've ended with a job at Man United, the best move I ever made in my life. I just wish my dad had been alive to see it happen.

John Rotheram, Complex Manager, Everton

John Rotheram has been running the catering and hospitality facilities at Everton for over 20 years. Quite apart from the obvious match-day services, the entertainment complex at Goodison Park is one of the biggest in the country. This December, for example, Rotheram's staff will serve getting on for 15,000 Christmas dinners!

When I first came here we couldn't decide on a title for the job I needed to do. We eventually came up with 'complex manager'. We've an entertainment complex here within the stadium which I run. In some ways it's a business within the business of the football club. We've got nine executive suites – hospitality suites – which we let out to the public during the week for things like training courses and conferences. Anything that moves and I can fit in here, I'll take it! All nine are often being used during a day. That means the restaurant will be busy too, where we can cater for up to about 180. We've full-time staff – chefs, kitchen assistants, waiting-on staff, a cashier and supervisors – whom we try and keep busy through the week. Of course everything changes on a match-day. We've 150 staff on a match-day – 250 if you include the bars around the ground which I run now, too. It's like switching on to another kind of job on match-day. Complex is quite a good word to describe it all.

I'm actually a production surveyor by trade, in the building industry, but I'd always been involved with my cricket club. I was the secretary and the licensee: Wavertree Cricket Club. I won't say I didn't enjoy my full-time job, but I always found my relaxation in this kind of business, even on a small scale at Wavertree. It was actually the brewery asked me to come up to Goodison. They were having problems here.

I came up and looked around and saw that the place was wide open: no security, no shutters on anything. I offered to work on it on a part-time basis, which I did. Then, when I'd organised things a bit, I left thinking they didn't need me any more.

After 18 months they decided to refurbish the cabaret lounge and asked me to come back. Again, I said I'd do it on a part-time basis. The opening night we had Faith Brown. There was trouble with the PA system and she must have started her first number eight or nine times! She was a real professional, though, and carried on until we got it right. It was all new, wasn't it? We changed things. We had to. In the long run, the cabaret was bad business. I did a paper on it, recommending the club try and go over to the wedding reception side: fixed prices, guaranteed income. The cabaret acts were great – Tom O'Connor and people like that – but they were the only ones who were making any money out of it!

During the course of working on all that, I came on full time and, after a certain amount of internal wrangling, I got to a situation where I was running things the way I wanted and was answerable direct to the board who, to be fair, have left me alone, really. The potential problems in this game are those to do with drinking and people being on the fiddle. I think the board know there's no problem here.

Going back 15 years or so, we were one of the first clubs to get involved in corporate hospitality and sponsorship. The package we offered back then was for 60 people which made it difficult to sell. We had this big sponsorship lounge, so we split that into two. Match sponsors in one half, tables of eight sold off in the other. Then we took over the players' lounge, too. The thing just grew. It's now obviously very big business. It's not as big an operation as, say, Manchester United, but it's very important and I think our new chairman is looking to expand it. As it is, we'll dine around 500 people on a match-day in different restaurants and lounges. On big games we could do more if we had the space but, generally, you need to remember Liverpool's a rundown area and money's tight. There may not be as much of this kind of business to be had as some people think there is.

A problem we have that would surprise you is how some people in these areas of the ground behave: bad language and all that. They're business people, the few difficult ones, but they're often fairly heavy characters and other people are frightened to complain because these are types you couldn't want to cross. I think you'd find that at a lot of clubs. It's a problem for football I think, trying to establish a family atmosphere when some of the language and behaviour's so bad. People are so intense about football and the aggression just pours out. I think twice about bringing my own son, say, to a derby match. It's no use pretending it doesn't go on. I see it first-hand and it's up here in the lounges and clubs as much as anywhere. It can make you a bit cynical, dealing with people you'd be unwilling to cross. It's hard for my staff, too, who work very hard for not much money, when they look around at what other people in football are earning, when we're all working towards the same point on the balance sheet, aren't we, at the end of the day?

All that aside, though, I do enjoy this job. That's why I've been doing it so long. It's as simple as that: I enjoy it. Every day's different. I get up in the morning looking forward to going to work. Without that, I couldn't do it. It's the kind of job that you can't do if you've not got the desire for it. The fact that it's football makes it different from the same kind of job anywhere else. There's that much going on, I don't often watch the games myself any more. I've got a monitor in my office and just go out now and again for a breath of fresh air! It's not the glamour of football that makes the job for me. It's the fact that the football ensures that the job's always interesting. There's always a fresh challenge.

Tom Walsh, Shop Manager, Liverpool

Tom Walsh is an Irishman born and bred in Liverpool. He's lived and worked his whole life in the city, as a shopkeeper, centre manager and local authority worker. Walsh has been running Liverpool's club shop since 1991.

Evening games – like tonight, against Chelsea – are a completely different situation to a Saturday or Sunday game. On a Saturday almost all our customers are visitors, people who've travelled to the game. Last weekend we had a full house and of the customers in the shop I would say 50 to 60 per cent were from Ireland. I spoke to a group from Tralee who'd come over for a few days: they were going to go and watch another game at Aston Villa on the Monday. We get a lot of Norwegian customers, too, and people who've come up from Wales. The weekends are just phenomenal: last Saturday we took £30,000 over the counter. People are queuing out of the shop and we have a couple of stewards to let people in a few at a time. Evening games, when our crowd's local, we're not nearly so busy.

I've been a shopkeeper all my life but I've only been in this business the last four years. It's completely different to anything I've been in before. If you come in, say, in November, when we've just introduced a training-wear range – tracksuits, joggers, stadium jackets, quite expensive stuff – we'll get customers spending up to £100 when they come to the shop. In March, though, when we've got nothing new here, we'll have just as many customers, the shop is just as busy, but every customer will be spending between £10 and £20. People know what they want: if they come into the shop with £100 in their hand for a new kit and we've run out, they'll leave with the £100 still in their hand. The one thing we do have in common with most shops is the pre-Christmas situation: people just buy everything! Not Christmassy things, just more of the ordinary stuff like replica shirts. Sometimes I think dads all over the country are doing up their kids' bedrooms for Christmas! We'll get lots of orders for five or six rolls of wallpaper, a duvet cover and pillowcase.

It's curious: whenever I get job applications, people always stress that they're lifelong Liverpool supporters. Well, I'm not! My game, really, is Gaelic football. If I watch a match, it'll be Gaelic football in Dublin! I'm not all that interested in professional soccer. If anything, when I was younger, I followed Everton. You'll find that Irish people of my generation in Liverpool tend to be Evertonians because Everton had a team of great Irish players after the war.

So my background isn't really Liverpool Football Club. My background is shopkeeping. I was born over a shop – my mum's corner shop in the south end of Liverpool – and I just grew into it. I never went out to work, just stayed on in the shop. When I did leave, it was to become manager of the Irish Centre in Liverpool which I did for 16 years. Basically, though, that was shopkeeping, too: buying and selling. About four years ago, though, Liverpool were looking for a shop manager. An old friend of mine is involved behind the scenes at Liverpool and thought I was the man for it. I never imagined my future might lie at a professional soccer club but they approached me and made me an offer I couldn't refuse. I must say I don't regret having made the move at all.

I work extremely hard and so do my staff. We're doing a huge level of business: in the first three years I was here, we trebled our turnover which is an incredible expansion, really. Now I haven't worked so hard that I can take all the credit for that! And it's not simply because of the team: those three years were the least successful on the playing side for 30 years. It's a question of having the right merchandise, having it when people want it and working hard to expand the mail order side of the business. Mail order is where we can really grow. Whatever I do in the shop, there won't be more bodies walking around out there to come and buy stuff, but there are thousands of customers out there – in Australia, South Africa and Scandinavia, as well as the UK – to reach by mail order. We've got to exploit that: serve customers overseas who can't get the stuff otherwise, and take business away from shopkeepers in London and Birmingham who are selling Liverpool merchandise. Our replica kit's made by Adidas who estimate that 1,500 shops in the UK stock Liverpool kit. I've got to try and increase our share of that business. Even one per cent increase in the market share means a huge increase to our business.

Whatever I do for a living I'm passionate about. I pride myself on being loyal to my employer, whoever that might be. And, although Liverpool are the last employer I would ever have dreamt of ending up with, I'm as loyal to them as I've been to any employer. I have to say I've never worked for any organisation who were as appreciative of my efforts as the football club have been. You do get employers who hardly notice their staff are there but that isn't the case with Liverpool. I'm a bit surprised to be saying it, but I'm saying it genuinely!

I think the club are quite pleased I'm not interested in football: at three o'clock my staff will all be due their lunch break and go off to the game, while I turn the key in the lock, have a coffee and get on with the work. I think the players are pleased, too, that there's at least one person who doesn't want to tell them how they should be playing! We can chat about their families and kids instead. We're sat here, what, 25 yards from the pitch? I have to admit I haven't been to watch a game there for 30 years! Sometimes that's a bit embarrassing, if I'm talking to someone who's travelled miles to worship at the shrine and whose only regret is they don't live near enough to watch Liverpool every week. But at least I'm not taking up a seat that could be occupied by someone who'll appreciate more than I would! And I understand people's feeling for Liverpool. After all, I travel to Dublin because I feel that way about Gaelic football!

Monday to Friday

THE OFFICE JOB

There's no logic in football.

George Binns

I'm just happy to be in the business that's the most fascinating in the world.

Norman Wilson

It's always been a case of everyone mucking in.

Margaret Poole

You have to learn to change. Everything's so different here now.

Dot Wooldridge

George Binns, Stadium Development Administrator, Huddersfield Town

Before the Alfred McAlpine Stadium opened in August 1994, the Huddersfield Town traditionalists remained sceptical about the need to leave the club's historic Leeds Road ground with its memories of the 1920s when Herbert Chapman's Town won three successive League Championships. George Binns, a traditionalist in many ways himself, having written the club's history during 20-odd years as secretary, has helped Huddersfield into a new ground next door. By late 1994 Leeds Road had been levelled for redevelopment as a retail park, and 12,000 fans were packing the 'Banana' stadium for every Huddersfield home game. Binns was at Wembley in May 1995 to see Huddersfield beat Bristol Rovers and win promotion to Division One.

I'm Huddersfield born and bred. I've lived and worked in the town all my life and I've been involved with the football club – first as a spectator, then as an employee – for 53 years. In the early '40s I was an impressionable youngster who used to walk four miles every other Saturday to watch Town play. In fact, I used to walk across the site of what is now the new stadium. If I'd known then how contaminated the land was, I'd have found another way!

I got involved in football in the late '60s when commercialism in football was negligible: no ground advertising, no sponsorship and catering was a fellow walking round with a tray of pies! A friend of mine was appointed as Huddersfield's first-ever commercial executive and he was looking for someone to help him on match-days, looking after the lottery, the souvenir shop and the food concessions he'd set up. I only did it because he was a friend: it meant I couldn't watch the games!

The beginning of 1969, the secretary who'd been at the club for 15 years was about to retire and I was asked if I was interested in taking over. Now, I was director of a clothing company in Huddersfield and although I loved the sport – lived for it – working in it seemed a dicey business, and I turned it down. Three months later, I was approached again. I met the chairman and the manager and was about to turn it down again when, for some unaccountable reason, I just said: *Yes!* And I remained as club secretary at Leeds Road until four years ago: 23 years.

It's an unpredictable business. There's no logic to football. It's not like any other job where, if you've got a bit upstairs and a good command of what you do (accountancy in my case), within a few weeks you'll have got to grips with 90 per cent of the business. Football, the only way to learn is by experiencing it. However clever you are, it's going to take at least a couple of years to experience all the possibilities. When you start, it takes an hour to do a two-minute job. But I was secretary at Huddersfield while we were top of the old First Division and second from the bottom of the old Fourth. Not ideal, but at least I got the experience.

The job of secretary? Well, in my case at Leeds Road, apart from the playing side, the buck stopped with me. You've got the general administration of three teams – first, reserves and youth; the accounts, the wages, the PAYE, the VAT; insurances, pensions, share dealings, transfers, medical arrangements; fixtures, travelling, match officials; match-day staff – you're talking about over 200 part-time in addition to your full-time staff; catering, internal and external; board meetings; ground maintenance, safety measures; the lotteries, the kit, the shop, advertising, sponsorship; the local FA, the county FA; I even edited the programme for nine years. There's so much. I used to work between 70 and 80 hours a week. If I didn't love the game, I wouldn't have done it, would I? And there are so few highs for every club in the game. When those highs come along – like in a promotion season – they are unbelievable!

I was nearly 60 and thinking I should ease down a bit if I wanted to live any length of time, but I jumped out of the frying pan into the fire! I was seconded to the job of stadium development administrator. I'm the only person that's seen the project progress right through from being a glint in somebody's eye.

The new stadium idea was first contemplated after the fire at Bradford in 1985. That single incident made Huddersfield Town look critically at what we'd always seen as a good, safe stadium. And, trying to look towards the next century, we saw that Leeds Road had a very limited future. What we wanted at the old ground in terms of facilities we could never have found the money to pay for as a small-town Second Division club. We were incredibly lucky that the site next door became available, to relocate, and what we've tried to create is something that will give the football club the opportunity to face a viable future.

I think that clubs who don't follow this kind of route are going to be facing real problems by the turn of the century. I was supposed to be retiring last year but I've got to see this through after having been involved from the seed being sown nearly ten years ago. I don't want to be working 70 hours a week for ever, but I've got to stay involved!

Norman Wilson, Secretary, Tranmere Rovers

Born in Birkenhead, 200 yards from Rovers' training ground, Norman Wilson worked his first day at Tranmere 38 years ago. Since then, at Prenton Park and elsewhere, he's tasted life at the top and bottom of the domestic game. His current appointment as Tranmere secretary began in 1984.

Well, to start with, I'm a company secretary. All football clubs are private limited companies with shareholders, so I have all the responsibilities I would have at any company regarding the application of company law, share transfers, accounts and so on. Of course, football's a specialised industry so I have duties, too, regarding young kids coming into the game, player registrations and contracts, which are becoming more complicated all the time: players may bring in an agent, or a solicitor or an accountant before signing a contract; they want pension plans set up, personal accident insurances – a whole range of things is included in the player's contract. Beyond all that, on the club side, my duties involve match arrangements, liaising with referees and linesmen, police co-operation, stewarding, gatemen, organising medical back-up, doctors, ambulances, paramedics on match-day, segregation of crowds, wages – we've 130 staff here, including bar staff, community staff, the commercial set-up and so on, all the correspondence, board meetings and annual general meetings.

Back in 1957 I was working for British Rail as an accountant. I met a fellow named Peter Farrell, an Irish international, who'd come to Prenton Park to be manager. He was keen to find someone with both a football background and an admin background to help run 'A' and 'B' teams here, there being very little youth football before he came. I came in. After Peter left, Walter Galbraith was manager for a while and then, while Dave Russell was in charge, the then present secretary just got up and walked out of the office one day. I think the strain just got to him. I remember when I first came to Tranmere they said: *Well, you can forget your bowls and your golf!* Football's a life occupation in itself – you've no time for anything else – and you have to be a certain kind of person to be involved with it.

At first, Dave Russell asked me to come in as his assistant while he tried to be manager and secretary, which meant I ended up doing all the secretarial work! Eventually, I was appointed secretary and did that for ten years, by which time I became aware that the commercial side of football was just starting to take off. Everton asked me to come and work for them as commercial secretary and I agreed.

I was at Goodison for three years, including the 1969/70 season when Everton won the League. Although I wasn't commercially minded, as such, I had to put the systems in place that made the commercial practices work. We opened the 300 and 500 Clubs, restaurants, bars, Everton memberships, set up the lottery with a new staff, organised ground advertising and sponsorship. I was lucky to learn about that side of football, in its earliest days, from top-class people. To be honest, though, my heart was more in the football side of the business.

Then, one summer, the secretary of Wrexham – a guy I knew well, Cliff Lloyd – died suddenly and they approached me to take over. So I went back to football, when John Neal was manager at the Racecourse Ground. I had ten really happy years at Wrexham. We were in Europe seven or eight times, playing in Poland, Yugoslavia, Sweden, East Germany, everywhere. One season we got to the quarter-finals of the European Cup Winners Cup and only lost to Anderlecht to a last-minute goal. It was all a great experience and a lot of hard work, too. I remember camping out at the Polish Embassy in London for three days, trying to get us visas! We staged a lot of big international games at Wrexham, too, until new safety regulations meant Wales had to stage all their games at Cardiff Arms Park.

Eventually, though, things got a bit tight financially at Wrexham and they asked me to go part time, which I just couldn't afford to do. So I rejoined Tranmere who were in the depths of depression themselves. They'd had this American chairman come in, planning to revolutionise football, who had found out that it didn't matter how much money you had: there was a big, empty pitch and you could pour it right in! He was trying to sell the ground.

We were very lucky. We'd sold Colin Clarke, with the tribunal setting the fee at £25,000. When I objected to that figure they agreed that Tranmere should get a third of any further transfer fee. A year later, Colin went to Southampton for £325,000. The third of that fee that we got saved Tranmere Rovers, really. We had no overdraft facility, no possibility of raising money on a ground relocation but that £100,000 bought us time. We persuaded Peter Johnson, the owner of Park Foods, to become actively involved through his colleague, our present chairman, Frank Corfe.

When they came in the club was in a bad way. The manager, Frank Worthington, the chief executive, the chief scout all lived elsewhere and were hardly ever here. It was left to myself and the commercial manager to look after the ship. Their first season, we had that frightening final fixture at Exeter which, had we lost it, would have seen us relegated out of the Football League. As it turned out, we scored about ten minutes from time and survived. Since then, we've moved up some 65 League places and been to Wembley half a dozen times!

Peter Johnson and now Frank Corfe have turned things round completely. A new 17,000-capacity all-seater stadium is well under way, we're at the top of the First Division. We've got a strong commercial department, a good youth policy, a great manager in John King. Of course, we're sorry to have lost Peter Johnson to Everton but Frank Corfe, who did much of the day-to-day work all along, has come in as chairman. They were a great team and achieved what they did in seven years simply by applying sound business principles. The relationship between the chairman and the manager is of paramount importance at any club. My job, really, is to support and implement whatever those two people should decide we need to do. I'm just happy to be in a business that's the most fascinating in the world.

Bob Twyford, Administrative Secretary, Bristol Rovers

Bob Twyford was born in Birmingham and, when he was a youngster, was on Wolves' books as an amateur. When he wasn't offered professional terms, Twyford took up a career in the police force. Twenty-five years later, he left to become club secretary at Ashton Gate. He left City after a couple of years and has been with Bristol Rovers since 1986.

I was club secretary at Bristol City for two years and I've been with Rovers for the past nine. About two years ago, my assistant, Ian Wilson, took over as club secretary so that I could concentrate purely on administration: cash books, Football Trust grants, insurances. I edit the club programme as well as writing a lot of it, too! Before that, I was a club secretary for nearly ten years which is a 50- to 60-hour a week job. You've got all the match-day arrangements – officials, stewards, police, fixtures, contracts, League meetings, FA meetings, local FA meetings, responsibility for ground safety. In many ways the club secretary has has finger in every pie in the club and, of course, he's the liaison between the club staff and the board.

It's a job where you never know what you're going to have to handle next. Sharing what is really a non-League ground at Twerton Park just makes things more complicated. I'll never forget coming back from a week's holiday up in Yorkshire, crawling into bed at about two in the morning only for the phone to go. There was this crackling voice on a mobile phone: *Bob! Bob! It's Paul Britton – the secretary at Bath City. The grandstand's on fire at Twerton!* Well, I thought it was a wind-up and hung up! A couple of minutes later, the phone went again: *Bob, it really is me, Paul! The ground's on fire!* Well, I checked with the Bath police – typical ex-copper: never believe anything anyone tells you! – and got down there. It turned out that some Bristol City fans had set the stand on fire. We were there with the fire brigade till eight the next morning.

We had to cancel our next game but we got some temporary seating up ten days later. None of it was covered though, of course. We played Sheffield Wednesday and all their directors ended up standing to watch the game in this little paddock we had at the front. Sod's law: it absolutely poured with rain and the lot of them stood there with their umbrellas and got soaked. They were good as gold about it and even printed a picture of themselves, soaked to the skin, in their next home programme. But when Wednesday got promoted at the end of the season we took the credit for it: we knew they didn't want to have to come back to Twerton Park!

All that was back in 1990. We had to put in the seating, get new floodlights up, bring in portakabins to use as offices and rooms to use on match-days. We laugh about it all now but at the time – well, stress is an over-used word but I didn't really go home or see my wife for a fortnight! And that wasn't just me: it was the same for the directors, the groundsman, the electrician. Then, as club secretary, I had the problem of getting our insurers to pay out, which took nearly two years. All that was made more complicated by being tenants at Twerton, too: our insurances were all contingent on the policies of the owners of the ground being in order which, fortunately, they were. Those were exceptional circumstances but it gives you an idea of what a secretary can end up having to cope with!

Our supporters have been fantastic over the years. Although we only get 5,000 or 6,000 for home games at Twerton Park, we have got one of the biggest away followings in the Second Division and the year we got to the Leyland Daf final at Wembley, we took 33,000 up with us! The supporters' club's always been fantastic with us. In fact, my first office was in the supporters' club building in Stapleton Road near the old ground at Eastville. I can still remember going down there to meet the chairman. We'd agreed on money – I knew my wife would kill me for agreeing to such a tiny salary but I wanted to do the job! – so it was just to have a look round. Well, I pulled up in this car park behind the offices: there was rubbish everywhere, rats running around from the market at the back. I went up this narrow staircase and into a small room with desks crammed in: one for me, one for my assistant, one for the lady who ran the lottery, one for the wages clerk and another one for the part-time typist! It was absolute bedlam, all tatty old furniture. I think the chairman was testing me: if I could stand this, I could stand anything!

Back then, when I started, was Rovers' first season away from Eastville. I suppose the club's so friendly because we've been up against it together for years. The situation when I arrived was that our administrative offices were in Stapleton Road, our training ground was at Hanbrook on the edge of Bristol, the reserves played at Forest Green in Stroud and the first team played in Bath at Twerton Park. Well, nine years on, the offices and training ground are here at the Cadbury's site in Keynsham, the reserves play at Yate Town and the first team's still at Twerton. So we've got it down from four locations to three! One of these days we'll get a new ground of our own and all our problems will be solved, won't they?

Even while I was in the police force, I was always involved with football at amateur and semi-professional level and when the opportunity came along to work in the game at Bristol City I took it. I don't know what it is, but football gets you. Five years ago I had to take a month off with what the doctor diagnosed as nervous exhaustion. He told me: *Your problem, Bob, is that at 52 you should be starting to wind down and, instead, you're still winding up, being involved in that stupid game!* But I've always loved football. although I wasn't quite good enough to ever play at a professional level, when the chance came along, at the age of 45, to get involved, albeit as an administrator, I couldn't let it go!

Margaret Poole, Secretary, Peterborough United

Margaret Poole was 32 when she started working as a volunteer in Peterborough United's commercial department. She's now in her 25th year with the club. Her husband, Derek, after 20-odd years as groundsman, is stadium manager at London Road.

What do I work on? I look after the youth trainees, the youth manager, the assistant manager, the manager and chief executive – Chris Turner, whom I've known since he was an 18-year-old player – and keep an eye on everything that happens in the office. I've been through every department! Basically, people can come to me to ask about almost anything to do with any of the areas I've worked in. I'm not getting any younger so, as we try and get our staff levels up, I'll try and ease back a bit, I think. At the moment, though, it would be a bit difficult to write a job description for me.

I'm Peterborough born and bred. I can remember as a teenager coming to the ground on Boxing Day when that end was just a bank, covered in snow and ice, and sliding down to the bottom of it to watch the football. It must have been in the early '70s I first came down to see if they wanted any help in the commercial office. Ellis Stafford, who'd been a player in Peterborough's Midland League days, ran things from a portakabin which was where the new shop is now. My husband, Derek, and I helped out as volunteers for a couple of years, looking after the Fivepenny Pool on a Saturday, just supporters trying to help the club out.

Noel Cantwell arrived as manager. He'd always been used to having a secretary. The woman he'd had left and so he was looking for a replacement. He interviewed about 17 young ladies but eventually chose me. I suppose I knew my way around the club and I'd done secretarial and accounting work in the past. Really, though, I think it was a backhanded compliment: he thought I was safe – 36, happily married with a daughter – and wasn't going to have my head turned by players, management or anybody else!

I worked for Noel for five years before I moved over to the general office where, as I say, I've done a bit of everything, helping out where I could. Every time a different owner or chairman or manager came in, things would change around. I've just tried to keep my feet on the floor, you know, because we've been top and bottom over the years: promotion, the First Division, a trip to Wembley, through to being within half an hour of the chains going up round the ground and the club going under.

We've always been understaffed at Peterborough and it's always been a case of everybody mucking in, which is why I've had a go at everything from running the lottery to drawing up players' contracts. But we've a company secretary now, Caroline Hand, who came to us from a very good job at Thomas Cook. She's trying to put good business ideas into practice here now. It's difficult to change things in football overnight but we'll get there eventually. It's all very well being like me, where you've picked up 25 per cent of every job and you're able to waffle the rest, but you need a certain amount of discipline in business, don't you? You need to know who's doing what and have the right number of staff to cover the jobs. Then my knowing a bit about every job can really be useful, can't it? And I keep trying to learn more the longer I go on: about business from Caroline, about working with different kinds of people who, in the old days, perhaps, I'd have wanted nothing to do with.

For Derek and myself this is more than a job. You'll laugh but they're trying to get me to take half a day a week off and I don't want to. It's not that I'd be away from the job. It's everything else. Peterborough United is more than a job. Derek's the same, we started here at the same time. We just love the club and love being around the place. We've lived in a club house for years.

Derek and I have been together 40 years and we're best friends too. We know each other well enough that we could see that being so completely locked into the football club might be unhealthy. We like dancing and go off to Blackpool regularly. We've even taken up birdwatching as another way to get out, walk and lose ourselves for a few hours. It's another passion, if you like. We've got the telescopes and binoculars. We'll pack up a picnic, a flask of tea and a flask of whisky and go off and just tramp for miles! We've made a conscious effort to make sure there can be more to life than Peterborough United. The thing is, though, I'm still in the office at eight every morning even though I'm not supposed to start until nine! I've a love affair with the workings of this club and Derek's the same with that pitch; he likes nothing better than it being churned-up mud after a game so he can go out and put it right in time for the next match. And I suppose it's too late for either of us to change now!

Gill Palin, Secretary, Crewe Alexandra

Gill Palin's first brush with the world of professional football was as a mother looking to get back to part-time work. She's now in her 17th year with Crewe Alexandra. Palin's office is upstairs in a small terraced house, opposite the Gresty Road ground, where players and staff alike feel very much at home. The club secretary's now a full-time fan, too, but Palin insists she retains at least some of the common sense she developed in a 'normal life' before football took over.

About 17 years ago, I applied for a job as a shorthand typist/receptionist, 20 hours a week, here. The only live football match I'd ever been to was to watch my son playing at school. I was just after a job. It was advertised at the Job Centre and I could do the work it was asking for. That's how I came to be here.

After about 18 months, the club secretary who'd taken me on wanted to transfer to the commercial side. They advertised his job and it was actually the manager then, Tony Waddington, who said: *Why haven't you put in for it?* I didn't want to work long hours and needed the time for bringing up my family. But he said not to worry about the hours and that he'd suggest me to the board. They gave me the job for three months on trial. Nobody really knew if I could do it, of course, me included. But I've been here ever since and I've taken on the commercial manager's role, little by little, as well.

Right from the start it was very new to me. I'd applied for that original job as much for the interview experience as anything. I'd been at home with the children for a long time and, even though I knew I could do the work, I didn't think I fancied a football club. Almost straightaway, though, because the secretary, Ken Dove, was so busy, I began to take on things like the wages and the away travel. Ken was getting more involved on the commercial side – the lottery had just started – but he was an excellent teacher, a very patient man who always told you everything in the right order. When I became club secretary, Ken moved to another office on the other side of the ground. That meant I was left on my own but, at the same time, I knew I only had to pick up the phone if I needed help with anything.

I suppose it took about six months to find I was only ringing Ken once a week for advice rather than once every five minutes! There's a lot of things which you have to learn to deal with in football. Often, it's the way you deal with them that's different from any other way of life: football politics, if you like. For example, you're often dealing with volunteers, people who do things for the club, and you need to be careful in dealing with them – scouts, cleaners, people who help with looking after the ground and the pitch. You can't do without them but you can't totally rely on them, either! It's cheaper for the club and, in a way, it's better because it means you've got a lot of heart around you. But if they don't turn up, you can't say: *Where the hell were you?* You just have to do it yourself!

There's a lot of passion around a football club, isn't there? Not being a fan myself, it took me by surprise a bit being in the entertainment business and dealing with the public. Even now, I sometimes wonder how people make the time to go to every game, home and away. It's a passion with people, no one counts the cost! They know so much about the game, too.

Over the 17 years, I'd say the club's moved upwards steadily. When I first came here, Crewe were literally a few weeks away from going bust. But someone heard about a government subsidy for businesses in trouble which we applied for and got. And, at the same time, we were starting our lottery which was soon generating £3,500 a week. At that time the income wasn't being used as wisely as it might have been, though: Tony Waddington was manager – a marvellous man whom I'm really glad I had the chance to work with – and he did pay the players quite a lot! But we paid off our debts, got ourselves into a reasonable situation and we've never really gone backwards from there. Since Dario Gradi came as manager, things have got better and better. He's brought in a lot of money through the sale of players. We're financially viable, albeit on a year-by-year basis, which means you can't take things for granted.

A lot of what I've done over the years has been to do with the ground. In a way, the Taylor Report made my life easier. Where before the board might argue over whether to buy a new player or put in a new toilet, now the decision's made for them, isn't it? The ground's unrecognisable now: executive suites, a family stand, good facilities where before you had cinder banks with wooden terracing. I used to go down the side there to open up for board meetings and hope there wouldn't be rats around and the fence hadn't fallen in! I suppose being around the club all day, every day, it's natural I would see what needed doing and want to get involved.

I love football now. I can still remember the first game I went to a couple of months after I started here. I remember how physical the game was – you just don't get that on the telly, do you? – and I was hooked straightaway. I don't just watch us either. I go and watch other people's games, too! I really enjoy the game. I like going to other clubs to see how they do things, to pick up ideas we might use. But nothing's the same as watching your own team. I still remember a Cup game up at Carlisle, ten or 12 years ago, when we were 3–0 down and won 4–3. By the end of the game, I felt physically ill, exhausted: everything had happened and the excitement and the emotion were just unbelievable. Football should be marked as a health hazard! Sometimes during a game I'll have to go round the back of the stand and take a deep breath. It can't be good for you, can it? I have to stand up at games, at home games at any rate, because I can't take the tension – or the cold – sitting down!

David Miles, Assistant Secretary, Arsenal

Arsenal have a reputation for bringing on home-grown young players. It's a policy that's stood the club in good stead off the field, too. David Miles, assistant secretary for the past 12 years, is a good example of a member of staff who's come up through the ranks at Highbury.

There's a little bit of everything will pass across my desk during a day. Every day is different, but take today as an example: first thing this morning, I ran off the club's payroll – that's everybody from the highest paid player down to former employees whose pensions come into Arsenal before we pass them on; then I had to deal with faxes requesting press passes for this weekend's game against Manchester United – we could do with a press box about five times as big as we've got for a game like this, with journalists from abroad as well as this country wanting to be here; then there was working out radio rights for the game with Radio 5 Live, local stations in Manchester and Capital here in London; I got through some general correspondence – every letter we get we respond to whether it's sending out a club brochure to a Junior Gunner or a personal reply if that's appropriate; this afternoon I've got a big meeting with the police about the implementation of the new laws on ticket-touting and, later on, a trustees meeting of the Arsenal Charitable Trust, collating requests for donations.

There are certain things – the payroll for example – where the buck stops with me. If a player thinks he's not been paid all his bonuses it'll be my door he'll be banging on – usually for me to explain why he's got it wrong! In the wider sphere of decision-making, of course, things come down from the board. We've two full-time directors here at the club now, David Dein and Ken Friar, so my line management, if I've got something I'm not sure about, is to bounce the problem off Ken Friar. If something's straightforward, I'll take responsibility myself. Match-days it's much simpler: I'm the match-day safety officer. I've been doing that for the past ten years and I don't have to tell you how important the job is.

We've got 20,000 members of our Junior Gunners club which is something we're very proud of. Personally, I go back to the days of the old Schoolboys Enclosure, under the East Stand. That's where I started in the '60s. In 1971, the year we did the double, I was 16 and due to leave school that summer. I got quite good O-level results and I was thinking about doing A-levels. A friend of my father, Jack Kelsey, the ex-Arsenal goalkeeper, was running the club shop. He told my dad that they were planning to expand the commercial side. In those days 'expansion' meant increasing the staff from three to four! That summer I worked in the club shop and helped with the lottery the club had back then. I'll never forget it: they produced a book – *Arsenal! Arsenal!* – to commemorate the Double. It was a huge thing, full of colour pictures, and sold for £2. As office junior, one of my jobs was to restock the shelves everywhere: carrying pallets of 20 of these bloody books up to the top of the East Stand! That was my first job at Highbury: the boy in the shop.

I come from a family that's three generations of Arsenal fans but I had an open mind about working here. I didn't know what I wanted to do, really, so it was just a job. I worked in the shop for 18 months and it had its perks, me being an Arsenal fan! Then March of 1973 I moved over to the ticket office. My first game was a sixth round Cup-tie against Chelsea – which we won 2–1. It was a massive crowd, a 60,000 sell-out. I'll always remember them saying to me: *Right, you better go outside and pull the shutters down to lock up before the game.* Of course, I didn't know any better: I went outside and nearly got lynched by all the people who couldn't get into the game! I wondered what I'd let myself in for. I worked for a man named Fred Jeeves with another lad, Chris Bell, who's now box office manager at Tottenham. Freddie Jeeves retired a couple of years early and Ken Friar offered me the job. I was box office manager through the late '70s when we had three FA Cup finals and a European Cup Winners-Cup final in three years, which was a very busy time. I can remember working regularly till gone midnight during those Cup runs.

I suppose I was quite young to be offered a job like that. I can only assume that during the time I was working under Freddie they decided I'd be able to handle it. I'm very grateful: it would have been easy for the club to have got someone in from outside. If they'd advertised for a box office manager I'm sure they would have had applications from experienced people elsewhere. They took the risk and let me have a go. And I think it worked out: those Cup finals went very well, except for the fact that we only won one of them!

After those Cup finals, which were the limit to that kind of job, I did wonder whether working in a box office was what I wanted to do for the rest of my life. The honest answer was: *No.* I remember having a conversation with Ken Friar in which I explained that I wanted to try to get involved in new areas. The club at that time was getting bigger and that meant that, while I continued to oversee the box office, I did start to get involved in other things such as selling ground advertising and other stuff on the commercial side. In 1983 I was appointed assistant secretary to work with Ken. Again, it was a job the club could have advertised but they gave me the chance. I still have the same job title today although, obviously, the areas in which I take responsibility have become much wider. I'd now like to think that I'll be here for the rest of my working life. I enjoy what I do up here; I left school on the Friday and started here on the Monday, a boy of 16. That's nearly 24 years.

Joyce Neate, Office Manager, Brentford

The job of office manager at Griffin Park covers a pretty wide brief. Joyce Neate runs reception, handles phone calls and mail, looks after match-day mascots, organises Brentford's Lifeline lottery and works in the ticket collection booth for two-and-a-half hours every other Saturday afternoon. For the majority of Brentford supporters, she's their first point of contact in any dealings with the club.

It's amazing! People always ring up and say: *Hello, is that you, Joyce? Now, you don't know me but I know you!* Do you remember when the Lambada was very popular? Well, we always have music at half-time, you know, between the penalty competitions and the Lifeline draw. I do the draw with Peter Gilham, our match announcer. We get on ever so well, Peter and I. He's always taking the mickey out of me on the pitch, telling me to stop skiving and get on with the draw. One afternoon, they were playing the Lambada and Peter just grabbed me and started doing the dance. It got a big laugh from the crowd and people phoned up that night, mostly to ask if the Lambada demonstration was going to be a regular thing. One little old lady came up to me, though, to say she thought Peter was really rude and that she felt sorry for me!

There's lots of things that go on in the office. You don't come in for a nine to five job. You can't say: *This is my job and that's it*. You've got to be flexible and be prepared to help other people when you've got a small staff at a club like this.

My mum and dad were always Brentford supporters and I first came here in 1947. I met my husband standing over there on the New Road terrace on a Christmas morning: he was just demobbed and came along with his brother and some friends of his that I knew. I made lots of friends on the terraces, you know, growing up with people and their families. Going up to away games in Barrow, leaving on a Friday and getting back Sunday night, you'd sleep on the coach. There were no motorways then! We used to have a laugh.

I used to work for C&A in Kensington. I started as a junior when I was 14 and progressed to personnel officer there. But I saw a job advertised in the programme for a clerk in the lottery office. I just thought: *Fancy working for Brentford!* I'd have been happy sweeping the steps here! So, even though I was really happy at C&A, I applied. I came along for the interview and the fellow was really nice, but the money was so poor compared to what I was earning I said I just couldn't accept and went away feeling really disappointed. Then I got a call to say they'd upped the money a bit and would I reconsider?

The Monday I started, I was dreading it. I thought I wouldn't know a soul but I seemed to know everyone! I felt at home straightaway and I've never looked back. Because you support the club, it's not a job. You do it because you love it. I suppose they must have thought I was mad at C&A but this club just draws you. You're hurt if anyone runs the club or the players down. I've been in all sorts of arguments at away games. Before I worked here, I got in a bit of trouble for hitting a bloke over the head with a brolly. That was back in the '50s. I don't suppose people used to get thrown out in those days, did they?

Of course, the way the club's run has changed

completely over the years: we never used to have all this sponsorship and advertising. The amount of money players get transferred for, football's had to become a business, hasn't it? Keith Loring's been brilliant, worked very hard. And the atmosphere's still very friendly, even though there are more people working here than when I started. Cream cakes and doughnuts are still our downfall!

The only problem, really, is I miss most of the home games. I don't finish in the ticket kiosk till about 3.15 and then there's work to be done in the office. I'm lucky if I catch the odd ten minutes in the second half. That's why I'm always on the supporters' coach to away games. I really enjoy my days out watching Brentford away. The day we got promoted at Peterborough – I couldn't cheer, I just stood there and cried – was just about the best day of my life, I'd say!

Chris Salmon, Secretary, Bishops Stortford

Chris Salmon started working at Bishops Stortford as a part-time cleaner nearly ten years ago. She's now the only other regular member of staff working alongside manager John Radford, who describes her as 'worth a million pounds to a club like this'. Salmon's twin sons, Cliff and James, both play for Bishops Stortford.

There's always been someone in my family who played football: my dad, my uncle, my sons. Whenever we used to go out, we'd always end up at a football match. Not the Chelseas or Tottenhams but local football: my family was involved with Epping Town; my dad played for Woodford Town. When I had my own children, I'd take them up the park on a Saturday to watch people playing.

When we moved from Epping to here, I used to bring the kids up to Bishops Stortford at half-time so we could walk in and watch for free! We'd buy teas and sweets from the little hut down there though, so I thought we paid our way! Before I married, I even had an Arsenal-mad boyfriend for a while, so I watched John Radford play. When I first met him here, I was frightened of him!

Anyway after we moved to Bishops Stortford, I got a letter saying there was a playground for under-fives that was being held at the football club in the mornings. Cliff and James were about four, so I brought them along. I quite liked it and ended up as a member of staff at the playgroup. Then this new manager came along and chucked us out! This fellow whom I'd idolised as a teenager. I had to call him Mr Radford, that's how I'd been brought up, and here he was moaning about the noise and the mess. I don't think he really minded that much but he was wanting to get things better organised at the club and here we were, taking over the main bar and lounge every morning, getting in the way.

He did the playgroup a favour, really. We were in the old clubroom, having to shift chairs and tables up and down stairs, all the equipment. He helped us raise funds for new premises: John let us have a summer fair here and even came down to run the bar. In a way he sort of forced us to get ourselves properly organised. And two boys from that playgroup – my sons – have come through to play for Bishops Stortford!

I got to where I was looking to pack up doing the playgroup. Now I'm not a very confident person: I always think I'm no good at anything. John got me to come down here a couple of mornings a week to do some cleaning. A short while after that, after these little executive boxes had been put in, they needed someone to work as a waitress on match-days. I'd just been a mum. I knew nothing about catering, and adding up – maths – was always my worst subject at school. I thought: *I can't do that!* But I needed the extra money, and it was football, so I agreed. I was so scared the first time. I know it sounds daft, but it really took a lot of courage to walk from the car into the club that afternoon! My heart was thumping,

I felt sick. But once I got in and met the people, I really enjoyed it. And it felt like I'd conquered a fear for myself, doing something I knew nothing about. It was a big step for me, after being at home with the kids and working at the playgroup.

It's gone on from there. I'm here five days a week now. I live here, really! Everything from answering the phone to making up rolls to sell at matches on a Saturday morning. I help run the lottery. All the time it's been a case of having to do new things. At first, I wouldn't answer the phone if John was in the room in case I said the wrong thing. But it's been really good, going from being at home or just with other women at the playgroup into this, where it's all men, really, apart from me. I always say I'm going to be the first woman manager! Seriously, though, I do think it's good if women are involved behind the scenes. We see things in a different way, notice things that need doing: attention to details, maybe, or the way things are presented. Things I don't know how to do, I go off and learn how. When I started in the office, doing invoices and so on, I went off and did a typing course, you know.

Working in football, you do have to be prepared to get your hands dirty. Here anyway! I still clean all the changing-rooms and everything. This is a really important part of my life now, though, and I've got the added pleasure that both my sons are playing here. John's coached them both since they were little – he ran a boys' team from under-nines to under-16s. One of them had a trial recently for England under-18s and that's down to him having been involved here, to the guidance he's had from John. I have to pretend I'm not their mum, though, when they're training and I'm here doing the teas!

Paul Johnson, Travel Manager, Arsenal

Arsenal have a tradition of travelling nationally and abroad with a huge army of away support. Paul Johnson hasn't missed many trips to games since he started following his local team back in the early 1970s. He's worked for the club for nearly 15 years and is now travel manager. With the recent re-development of the North Bank End at Highbury, Johnson and his staff have their own shop window and offices on Avenell Road from which to run one of the country's most sophisticated travel operations.

I was born in Hackney. It's always been Arsenal, supporting them home and away since I was a kid. By travelling so much, I got involved in helping out on supporters' coaches and trains, checking tickets, stewarding, that sort of thing. Well, we're out in Belgium, this is 1981, a horrible night at Winterslag in the UEFA Cup. And we lost. But this bloke come up to me and said: *What do you do for a living?* I told him I was a sales assistant in the West End. He said: Do you like it? *Well, it's all right.* So he goes: *Do you want to work at the Arsenal?* I thought it was a wind-up. I don't suppose we had Beadle in those days but I thought someone was winding me up. But he gave me his card and said: *Come and see me Monday.* Well, I went to see him and started work on the Friday. It turned out he was the fellow who was doing the job I'm doing now.

At first, I was working as a sort of sales assistant, selling rail and match ticket packages, that sort of thing. We've got our own offices and everything now, but back then we were working out of portakabin at the back of the Clock End. I was part time to start with but we were on a roll, weren't we? Three consecutive Cup finals, 1978, '79 and

'80 and, in those days, everybody wanted to travel together. Nowadays, people get a car loaded up and go on their own: it's cheaper than British Rail, isn't it? But then, everybody went together. Some of our lads even put out a record about it – *The Beano* – about a trip to Man United. So, in 1982, I went full time.

As I say, though, it's different now. We've got these new offices with everything on computer and so on but the actual travel side has died right away. Obviously, we still organise all the European trips but, in England, for last week's trip to Leicester, for example, out of 2,000 Arsenal fans only about 200 made the trip with the Travel Club. Especially with the changeover to Railtrack – we can't charter trains now, only carriages and at inflated prices – people prefer to have the freedom of going on their own, don't they? We still sell away tickets to Travel Club members, whether they come with us or not, but bondholders and season ticket-holders go straight through the box office. With public transport prices going up too, we're not so busy during the week. People wait until match-day to sort things out for away games coming up.

It was probably around 1987 I started getting involved on the team travel side. At first it was just booking hotels over the phone and so on. But now it's everything. All the travel arrangements for the team – the reserves and youths, too – the accommodation, transport, meals, everything's down to me. I'll tell you: Friday nights are the worst, if the first team's away and using a new hotel. I'm just waiting for the phone call saying the beds aren't long enough for Tony Adams or Dave Seaman, or the food's no good. It's fair enough, I suppose. The manager wants everything right for the team and I'm the one responsible.

I went on a load of courses, too. At one point, when the travel business – not just football, travel generally – was booming, the idea was for the club to take premises in Gillespie Road and set up as travel agents. The first thing we needed was qualified staff, so off I've gone to British Airways in Gloucester Road and done all the courses. I've got the qualifications to actually manage a travel agency, the diplomas and all that. As it turned out, we couldn't get planning permission for what we wanted to do. We experimented with day trips to Calais and Boulogne but, by then, the recession was starting and the club got cold feet. All the studying's come in handy anyway, though.

It's funny. Well, no, it's not. I don't enjoy going to most games now, I get that much grief from people, from supporters; if they've missed their plane or anything, it's my fault, or prices are too high, seats aren't good enough, whatever it is – and it's personal abuse. I can't have a cup of tea at half-time without someone wanting a row. I went to watch an England match at Wembley the other week, absolutely crap game, but I enjoyed it. I could just sit there and watch and nobody was wanting to have a go at me about anything!

I just love this club, though, and I cannot miss a game. If I can't be there, I'm crawling up the wall. Maybe I'm a sucker for punishment! But then there'll be nights like Anfield in 1989 – Mickey Thomas, bang! – and you think: *This is what it's about.* And Copenhagen last year! Have you seen the grey hairs? We took out 12,000. What a night! And the next morning I wake up and switch on the telly and they've got the team arriving back with the Cup Winners Cup at Stanstead. And I've got the actual thing – the Cup – lying in the bed next to me!

Dot Wooldridge, Personal Assistant to the Manager, Wolverhampton Wanderers

•DOT WOOLDRIDGE•

•Wolverhampton Wanderers•

Dot Wooldridge started work at Molineux as a 15-year-old office junior. Now, 36 years on, she's Graham Taylor's personal assistant, the only current member of staff who's been with Wolves since the 1950s.

My parents first brought me to watch the Wolves when I was about eight. My brother didn't like football – I still don't think he's ever been to a game here! – but I did. I stood on the South Bank with my family and I suppose I've got gold and black in my veins. After I finished school, I did a year's secretarial course at college. I remember the bookkeeping teacher there asking me what I was going to do when I finished. I told him I wanted to work at a football club. He said: *I work at West Bromwich Albion.* I just sort of looked at him: *No, I want to go somewhere they play football, not to West Brom!* He laughed and said: *All right, we'll have none of that!* But it was he who suggested I write in to the Wolves.

As it happened – I suppose it was lucky for me – when I wrote, someone here was seriously ill so Wolves replied and said to come in for an interview. That was on the Saturday. On the Monday they phoned and asked me when I wanted to start. I said: Tomorrow! But they knew I was still at college and told me I should finish there. Well, I went to see the principal and told him that I had the job I really wanted. You can imagine, this was 1959: Wolves were top of the League, the Man United of the day. I said: *You won't stop me, will you?* The principal said: *Well, you'd go anyway, wouldn't you?* They released me and I came here. It was 1959: Stan Cullis was the manager, Billy Wright was captain. Billy Wright said to me when I arrived: *I hope your stay is as long and as happy as mine.* I've been very lucky, haven't I?

The first game at Molineux after I arrived, I had two complimentary tickets. I stood on the South Bank and my parents went in the seats. All the people around me, I was saying: *I work here!* They said: *Don't be silly, what are you doing on the terraces then?* And I pointed over to my mum and dad who were waving from the old Molineux stand. That was the last time I stood on the South Bank until the afternoon before they pulled it down, the Millwall game, when I wanted to go back and stand there again for old times' sake.

Do you know, when I first started work here, there were no ladies on the premises after one o'clock on a match-day? At one, the office closed and the men came in and took over! The only women were those who served the tea and biscuits in the boardroom. For me it was a natural thing, wanting to be here. When I was at school all the other girls, with their pictures of pop stars stuck everywhere, thought I was mad: where they had pop stars, I had Wolves players! And women are welcome to work here on a match-day now: I'll be in at nine and work through till six or seven at night, even longer during the week! Where would they be without us?

I started as office junior, answering mail from fans, that sort of thing. Really, though, I was just hanging around hoping to catch a glimpse of Ron Flowers! I got married in 1963. John's like my youngest son: he'd rather play football than watch. But he put up with me! When we used to go out, people would want to talk to me about the Wolves and he'd just sit back and say: *Get on with it!* But I left here in 1964 to have a family.

Then, in 1972, the assistant secretary at the time rang me and asked if I was looking for a job. The kids were at school and I'd been doing a bit of office cleaning. I said I could only work part time but he said: *Fine!* So I started work in the commercial department, supposedly part time: three days a week. Well, that lasted for three weeks and from then on it was full time for the next ten years.

It was when the commercial side was just starting to take off. When I first came here, Jack Bannister – the Warwickshire cricketer – was what you'd now call the commercial manager. He started the first lottery here in 1960. Jack had gone by the time I joined the commercial department and they'd moved to offices behind the North Bank. At first, it was still just the lottery and a tiny little club shop run by Harvey Andrews, the folk singer, who was a mad Wolves fan. It was from the '70s onwards that I think people started taking the financial side of football seriously and trying to generate money within the club.

In 1982 I moved back over to the football club to help the accountant and in 1984, when he became the club secretary, I became his assistant. That was with Keith Pearson who was here until last year – sorting out travel, match officials, contracts, all sorts of things. Back then, we were the ticket office, too! It was all run from one office: a stadium holding 60,000 people. I worked with all the managers we had, but when Graham Taylor arrived I was amazed at the amount of mail that started coming in. At the time I was covering as club secretary after Keith left. When Tom Finn came from West Ham, Graham said he was going to need someone to concentrate on his work with him and wanted me to do it. I was really pleased: being close to the football side has always been the thing for me. Mind you, when games are on I'm usually working inside with the TV monitor on in the corner, because it's the only time there's a bit of peace and quiet around the place!

I've been here that long now they call me The Year Dot! I love it when lads come back to visit – Tim Flowers, Stan Collymore, Vince Bartram. I've been 'mum' here for a lot of them! Having two boys of my own means I can chat to the young lads now. I love that part of it all. You have to get used to change at a football club: the turnover of players, a manager leaving and a new set of staff coming in. I remember saying to Graham Turner when he left: *The king is dead. Long live the king.* You have to learn to change; everything's so different here now. In 1959 there were five of us full-time staff in the office. Now, I couldn't tell you how many people work here. It isn't just football any more, is it? There's all the business that goes with a stadium like this is now. What's underneath it is home for me, though. Molineux is home.

Peggy Moore, Cook, Tranmere Rovers

Peggy Moore is in her 41st year as an employee at Tranmere Rovers. What she does and where she's worked have fluctuated with the fortunes of the club over the years. Since August 1988, Mrs Moore has been cooking for 60 players and staff at Rovers' Valley Road training complex.

I was working in the greengrocer's opposite the ground, Prenton Park. Tranmere Rovers' offices were next door. I was asked to go and work in the canteens on match-nights. That was in 1954. Then they asked me to look after the offices and, when they transferred over to Prenton Park itself in 1968, I went with them. We were in there until about six years ago when we moved out here to the training ground.

Before I started working for Tranmere, I wasn't interested in football at all. I've done all sorts; cleaning all the executive suites, catering on match-nights for up to 300 people – there were seven of us girls worked together, doing parties and discos at the ground. When they first started having their names on them, I embroidered four complete sets of kit: I've got lovely photos at home of me and all the apprentices wearing tops with their names on! You name it, I've probably done it. It's a bit easier up here, there's less hassle. The whisper is that we'll be going back to Prenton Park, though. They're doing all the building at the ground – new stands, office facilities, everything – and we'll be moving in under what they call the Kop. Everything will be there, the players will train just up the road.

It's a way of life now. I don't know what it is about it, really. My husband's still alive – he's 82. He's retired, so me working here means we've something fresh to talk about every day: I can tell him the gossip and we can discuss what's going on up here. If I was at home all day we'd not have this whole different aspect to our lives. Maybe, as well, it's to do with only having had a daughter and no sons!

You get the odd one you'd not be bothered if you never saw again, but most of the boys are great. You know, with the apprentices, I used to get very upset when they finished and they'd come to tell me they weren't being kept on. I suppose now I've got a bit hardened to it! I still don't like to see them leave, although some of them will come back to visit now and again. But you do get quite close, seeing them nearly every day. You watch some of them change so much. They'll arrive with the attitude that they've made it and then, all of a sudden, you'll see them grow up. They'll realise they've only got two years to prove themselves and they calm down and put their minds to what they're doing.

The boys are different now. Attitudes have changed and the young players – kids in general – are spoilt really. In the old days, during the summer, the apprentices used to have to go and work at the ground, having to really put their backs into something that's not football. The club's not allowed to do that now but I don't think it did the boys any harm doing that kind of work. These days they just get six weeks off in the summer! They still don't get paid very much though: I don't know what they used to get 30 years ago, but they only get about £35 a week now. Still, they're doing a job they like doing, aren't they? It's a hobby as well as a job for them and I suppose it is for me too; I get a real buzz out of working here. I always watch football when I can now, too. I've got four grandchildren and one of them's decided he likes football. He's gone mad for it! They live down in Chepstow and he goes to a soccer school down there, so you never know!

Mary Ellis, Cook, Everton

Allegiance to Everton or Liverpool is a defining element of family life on Merseyside. Mary Ellis can talk through the detail of her extended family and describe every member as a Red or a Blue. Mrs Ellis herself, as a youngster at least, didn't take much interest. Nonetheless, for the past 14 years, she's been cooking and serving meals every day for players and staff at Everton's Bellfield training ground. She's been in charge since 1992.

I used to work at Anfield, just casual work on a match-day, in the tea bars. And when Everton were at home I'd work at Goodison. The lady who used to be in charge here worked the tea bars, too. When she took over here, she asked me to come and work for her. I can't say I was ever a football fan, really, but I had three boys and only the middle one was an Evertonian. The others used to take the mickey, so I stuck up for him. I asked him first before I came to work here: he was about ten, then, and he'd come in with me. That was nearly 15 years ago. Anyway, after a while, my mate retired. They got a chef out from Goodison but the money wasn't good enough for him, being a young lad wanting to take the girls out and that! Then there was another fellow did it part time until about three years ago. When he left they asked me to take over and I got my friend out to help me – Linda, who was working on the bar at Goodison, match-nights and functions.

I've seen a few come and go in my time. I was sad to see Mike Walker, the manager, leave. He'd got me a new kitchen ordered. But, you know, it's like a holiday camp out here. Everybody's friendly. The only thing that gets me sometimes is the kids. They'll all crowd into the kitchen together, wanting orange juice or toast. There'll be 20 of them at the same time and I'm terrified in case they hurt themselves, but they don't understand that, so I have to lock the door to them! But I really enjoy it.

I wanted a job, you know, and I only live up the road, so I can walk in or one of the players will pick me up and give me a lift in the morning. I'm here five days a week, nine until three. When I first came here, we were preparing three-course meals, steaks, chops. Now it's baked potatoes, baked beans, soup, tuna or ham pasta, savoury rice, toast. The first team and the reserves come up first. They're no trouble at all. Then it's the kids. At least on a Thursday they're at college so I get a bit of peace! Any one lunchtime, with players and staff, we'll do up to 60 or 70 meals. The kitchen's just about big enough for Linda and me, but when everyone starts coming in and helping themselves, well, all I can say is I hope I'll get my new kitchen in the close season. This one's 30 years' old!

I don't know, really, about the new kind of diet. In the old days, they'd have steaks, sponge puddings, and they were okay. I mean, I went down to nine stone eating the stuff they have now! I do slip some cheese into their rolls if they ask me for a tray to take on the coach for an away game. It's the physio who'll say what they can and can't have, who's cut out cheese and sausages and that kind of thing. Whatever I serve up, though, it goes! I've got to liking pasta, too. I eat it now instead of bread.

As I say, I've seen people come and go. Sometimes you hear about things going on. You get people talking, all the time: *What's going on down there?* But I just have to say: *I don't know. No comment!* It's interesting when you see a new player come in and, at first, they don't say a word. But a week later it's all changed and they've got to know everybody. I can't say a word against any of the players: they've got respect for me and Linda, they really have. They're really nice. We have a laugh with them, tell them how they don't know they're born, how we're going to ring up the papers about them. But what's really good is that there's something different going on every day. You'll never get bored working here.

I still work at the ground on match-days. It used to be

that you had to work at Anfield and Goodison, it was the same organisation doing it. But, now, Liverpool have got their own arrangement so I just work at Goodison. I had the choice. My sister still works at Anfield as well although she's a catering supervisor at Goodison. She's worked at Anfield since 1972 and she's an Evertonian!

It's a football family, really. I had my brother on the phone from Hong Kong on Sunday, wanting to find out what was going on at Goodison. It's funny: I've got three brothers, the middle one's Liverpudlian, the other two are Everton. Of my three sons, the middle one's Evertonian and the other two are Liverpool. My dad was an Evertonian. You know how it is here. When I was growing up, our parish was all Liverpool. But the next parish, Holy Cross, was all Everton.

I never really bothered with football, myself. I don't watch it now, except on the telly. Mind you, my middle boy, the Evertonian, he lives up in Perth in Scotland now, and follows St Johnstone. Well, we went up to visit and he took us to see them play Rangers. Stuart McCall and Gary Stevens were playing for Rangers. Now, at St Johnstone, they've got this tea lady, Aggie Moffat I think she's called, and she just doesn't care! Apparently, she swore at Graeme Souness when he complained that the tea was late! It gets to half-time in the game and I've squeezed out to go to the toilet and, while I was gone – I think my daughter-in-law arranged it – it's come up on the scoreboard; *Welcome to Mary Ellis, Everton's answer to Aggie Moffat!* And I missed it, stood in this queue waiting to go to the ladies!

Oh, I Say!

TV, RADIO AND THE PRESS

If you can't offer football your enthusiasm then you can't offer anything.
Andy Gray

I think a really good football writer is a pretty wise man in the world of football.

Patrick Barclay

I want to know more about football than anybody else.

Harry Harris

Fantasy Football, the radio, the papers: I'd rather do that than climb ladders every day.

Jeff Astle

John Motson, Commentator, BBC TV

Match of the Day has been the BBC's flagship, in terms of football coverage, for over 30 years. For the past 24 John Motson's commentaries have been as much a part of the programme's identity as the signature tune or studio set. Self-confessedly a frustrated player – he turns out regularly for the TV Commentators Charity XI – Motson has a limitless enthusiasm for the game and his job's relation to it. Although he covers well over 100 games a season for professional reasons – commentary or research – any spare evening still finds him in the stand at Underhill watching Barnet for fun.

I was lucky to get into it when I did. I mean, I started on the local weekly paper in Barnet doing general reporting, you know, court cases and council meetings. They asked me if I wanted to do a bit of football – of course I did! – and I started covering Finchley in the Athenian League, Amateur Cup semi-finals and all that.

After four years in Barnet, I thought I should get on to a provincial paper. I joined the *Morning Telegraph* in Sheffield, which was quite well thought of as a provincial daily with a bit of class about it. While I was up there, the sports editor – my boss – a boy called David Jones, was asked to go into BBC Radio Sheffield, a new station, to start a sports programme. He had a very small budget and no staff as such, so what he used to do was ask the lads on the paper who were covering a match to pop into the studio afterwards and do a radio report. That's how I got into broadcasting, really: it came out of the blue. Then BBC Network Radio down here were advertising for sports people and I joined them in 1968, initially just reading the racing results and putting a few bulletins together. A couple of years later they asked me if I fancied trying my hand at football commentary. I had a bash and they seemed quite pleased. They told me they'd put me on the list and I'd do a game occasionally.

After a couple of seasons, the news came through that Ken Wolstenholme was finishing with *Match of the Day*. They already had Barry Davies and David Coleman, but I got an audition for television and they offered me a job there for a year on a trial basis, to see if I could make the transition from radio to TV. And after a year I signed a contract. Touch wood, I'm still signing them!

The job that cracked it for me was when they gave me a Cup-tie to do: Hereford versus Newcastle. The editor said: *Look, it's Southern League versus First Division – if Newcastle win 1–0 we'll probably only show six or seven minutes.* I was the bottom of the pile that evening, or so they thought. As it turned out, Newcastle did score – Malcolm Macdonald – a few minutes from the end, and I was thinking: *Well, that's it, I'll be the third or fourth feature.* And then this guy, Ronnie Radford, whacked a shot in from 40 yards – goal of the season, goal of my career, really. It took the game into extra time. And then Ricky George – it's amazing, really, he was a mate of mine from Barnet, and I'd travelled down to Hereford with him for the game – came on as sub and scored the winning goal. It was an absolute fairy tale: I ended up on the pitch, interviewing him and Radford. Obviously, the game was made the main match that night. It was the giant-killing of the season. It turned my career, really. They saw I could handle a big game and from then on I started to get better and better matches.

As regard the job itself, working on radio you had a very open brief: given that no one could see anything, your job was to create the pictures and describe everything. I remember when I did my first TV commentary, they kicked off and I thought: *What do I say now?* People could see everything for themselves! I decided I needed to find out more about how the game was played. I went on a couple of coaching courses, made appointments to talk to managers. It was quite daunting, really, meeting people like Shankly, Bill Nicholson, Bertie Mee. And then, of course, the overseas stuff came in,

World Cups and so on. It was doing them made me realise how much of the job is really about straightforward identification. That means going to games, watching endless videos, turning up to watch training sessions – anything you can do that will mean you can pick up the microphone and say: *That's so-and-so and he plays left-back, takes the corners.* That is your base and once you've established that you can go on and add a bit of style and create your own identity.

Andy Gray, Presenter, Sky TV

Andy Gray played for Dundee United, Aston Villa, Everton, West Brom and Glasgow Rangers and represented Scotland 20 times during a memorable playing career. For the past three seasons he has proved to be a trump card in Sky TV's coverage of Premiership football, as a match analyst alongside the commentator and as a presenter in his own right. Without compromising his integrity, Gray has the ability to invest the dullest of 0–0 draws with the significance and complexity of a World Cup final.

After my last season at Rangers, when I finished playing, I was sitting at home – this would be the summer of 1989 – and wondering: *Where next?* I got a phone call from a guy named Andy Melvin, a Scottish lad whom I knew from when he was with STV, to say he was working for a satellite station – BSB it was, then – and that they were putting a team together for all their football broadcasting. They wanted me to be part of that. My initial reaction was: I want to carry on playing. But then I thought about it. I was 33, with a bad knee, and not likely to be playing at top level. So I went down to London and met them. I was very impressed and I agreed to go ahead with it.

That was in August. The station wasn't going to be up and running, though, until the following February. I hung on – played for my mate, Jim Barron, at Cheltenham in the Vauxhall Conference – and started up the next year. I've been doing it ever since. If I'd done anything else it would have had to be management: I love the game and, apart from O-levels, I didn't have any other qualifications. I'd had a go at running a nightclub when I was younger and found out I was no good at business. I had to stay in football, but I hadn't imagined earning a living out of television, even though I'd done bits – match analysis, a quiz show for Central TV – while I was a player.

At first there wasn't that much work – maybe a game at the weekend and another in midweek – and I could combine it with coaching a Villa. I had the chance to become Ron Atkinson's assistant there. But at the end of 1991/92 when Sky won the contract for the Premier League, they came to me and said: *You can't do both jobs, we need you full time.* To be honest, it was an easy decision; the hours weren't as demanding as football and it was a good move financially, too. It's a bit like a football club here. We go to do the live games and it's always the same team, the same bunch of lads, and so we've got that football club mentality; everybody taking the piss out of each other all the time! It's really good in that respect and I've enjoyed it.

My working week starts on a Saturday morning, travelling to the live game to start around eleven. I'll do my research, Richard Keys and I have our chat and we do the game, finishing off around seven. If it's close enough, I'll stay at home in the Midlands overnight. Otherwise, I travel straight on to the Monday night venue. Get to the ground for around three on the Monday. It's an easier job for me – I just do the match – and then Richard and I will hang on to help with the phone-in programme that Jonathan Pierce used to do and Bobby Gould does now. Unless there's a Cup replay or something, I'll have the Tuesday and Wednesday off. I head for London first thing Thursday morning to spend all day working on the *Boot Room* programme which we record Thursday night for transmission on the Friday. Friday I'm free and Saturday I might go to a match – if Villa have a big game – but, to be honest, I see that much football, I'd just as well not on a Saturday!

People always say to me that they can't understand how I can be so enthusiastic about every game I do. But, you know, I wake up in the morning and think: *I'm doing a job that 900 players who stop playing every year would die to do.* I come in, watch a game of football and, sat up there, I never play a bad game! It's great. If you can't offer football your enthusiasm then you can't offer anything, can you? It's the same with players. You look at the greats – Keegan, Dalglish, Law, Greaves, Robson – they're great players, but they're all so enthusiastic, too, about the game. Then, look at the ordinary players in the Premiership: what they lack, more than anything, is that enthusiasm. All I've done is taken that into commentary. Sometimes it's difficult, if a game's so poor there's nothing to get excited about. But that's when the other important thing comes in, which is honesty.

Because we've got the time to do it, Sky's coverage can be much more than terrestrial TV coverage of football ever was. We've taken some stick – particularly from referees – saying we're too intrusive and I'm too critical. But I'd hope I'm constructive with it and I think I just ask the questions that the fans would want answers to. I think if you talk to players and managers they'd say Sky's been good for football and promotes the game in a very positive way. I think we show how good the game is and have actually attracted people to live football at the turnstiles.

I've learnt a lot about putting programmes together, but I'd rather stay this side of the camera: the money's better for a start! Maybe in ten years' time, if people are fed up with looking at me, I might go on to the production side, who knows? I wouldn't mind directing Richard Keys, telling him to shut up and do as he's told! What would tempt me away from here – and I'm really happy doing what I'm doing now – would be the right job back in football. It's still there, the wondering if I could have been a decent manager. If the right job, the big job, came along then, without a doubt, I would be very tempted.

Neil Duncanson, Managing Director, Chrysalis Sport

Hard on the heels of the self-styled major players in televised football are a handful of independent companies who provide everything from the production team for ITV's European Champions League coverage to live pictures of Chinese football for Rupert Murdoch's Asian satellite operation, Star TV. Companies like Grand Slam, TWI and Chrysalis Sport may enjoy a relatively low public profile but the impact they've made – and will increasingly make in the future – cannot be overstated. Neil Duncanson approaches the development of Chrysalis Sport not so much with enthusiasm as with something like religious fervour.

My dad, being a Scot, decided that the first football game I went to would be at Crystal Palace because a mate of his said he could use his season tickets for free! So I went to Palace versus Stoke, September 1969, Palace won 3–1 – Cliff Jackson, two, and Bobby Woodruff – and I was hooked, which for a kid growing up in East London didn't make life very easy. I became a complete nutcase on football, anyway.

A friend of mine's dad was a reporter on the *Daily Telegraph* who used to take us to games. We'd watch him doing his stuff and then we'd get autographs after. I also had an uncle who worked for the BBC, so I had this idea that the press and TV were interesting jobs: I never thought I'd be able to put that and football together, though. In fact, my mate's dad told me that having a job connected to football like his would spoil my enjoyment and I sort of took that to heart at the time.

I went into news – local papers then TV. But when I was

26 I had an idea for a sports programme – *The Fastest Men On Earth* – which I made for ITV. I discovered that, in fact, it beat working for a living, really. I was just racing into work every morning and I've been in sport ever since. There were three of us asked to start a sports department at Chrysalis; four years later, we've got a staff of 60! The idea was to set up a company that could turn its hand to everything: videos, documentaries, series, live coverage.

With the club videos, for example: three, four years ago they were crap, really, and I think, with Arsenal particularly, we turned that round. Instead of just bolting a few goals together, we went behind the scenes, talked seriously to players and managers. Obviously, it took a while before George Graham and the players were convinced we weren't just a bunch of lash artists looking to stitch them up. But we started turning out some good videos, then the magazine on video and now we've got the big screens. In the next five years, I think you'll see the big clubs with their own cable TV stations, too.

The Italian football was what put us in a different league, internationally. And, to be honest, we were lucky! What happened was that Sky had just got the Premier League and had taken their eye off the ball with respect to Italy. There was all the fuss about there being no top-flight football on terrestrial TV. Paul Gascoigne, whom we already had a contract with, had just joined Lazio. We were doing a documentary with Paul about his injury and he was saying how sorry he was about no one seeing the games over here. We rung up the Italians and asked if we could buy Lazio's games. They said: *No, but you can pitch for it all.* We went to Michael Grade at Channel 4 and he thought it was a great idea. We made an offer and got the deal: the first game was a 3–3 draw, about 3½ million watched it, and we were away. Everybody in the game watches it: George Graham started calling me 'his friend from Italy'. It gave us a completely new dimension. And we've not really looked back.

And now there's cable. Wire TV is a cable station owned by the cable operators. It's a couple of years old and at the moment we provide them with four hours of sports coverage every evening. Some of it's live, most of it is packaged. We introduced Dutch football, Brazilian football, a Latin Goals programme. Any football we could get our hands on! What we didn't have was British football which was all tied up elsewhere. There was only one league we could do: the Vauxhall Conference. And it made perfect sense. It had a 'local' feel. Okay, we might have preferred to get the Football League – and maybe one day we'll get it – but the Conference is a good stepping-stone. We started with a round-up and chat, the Conference people were great, and we now do a live game every Tuesday and treat it as seriously as we did the Italian stuff.

By the end of 1996 there'll be more cable subscribers than satellite. And cable could be great for football in the long term because you could offer real regional coverage. I hope we'll get the chance to work with the Football League. In the meantime, working in sport is like a dream come true. I have to pinch myself: *Is someone really paying me to do this?* I'm amazed I've got away with it so far!

Jonathan Pierce, Commentator, Capital Gold Radio

Jonathan Pierce is a regular presenter and commentator for Sky TV, but has made his significant mark as a radio broadcaster. His fever-pitch live match commentaries have genuinely broken the mould in their field. Pierce heads up the award-winning Capital Gold team, the market leader in football coverage for London. He's currently involved in negotiations with the football authorities, whose demands for more revenue from broadcasting rights threaten to limit, or even end, live radio match coverage in the future.

I went to a rugby-playing school down in Bristol, but my dad was involved in football. From 1972 onwards, he worked for Bristol City, video-taping their games. They were one of the first clubs to use video like that, filming games so they could watch them back later. Then he got involved with the FA as their education officer for the South-west, starting up day-release schemes: getting young players to do college courses so they'd have something to fall back on if they didn't make it in football. Dad was at City about three days a week and, when I was 13, I started training with them on a Thursday. The thing was, because it was a rugby school, I couldn't tell anybody about it – not even my mates! If the school had found out they probably would have stopped me playing, which was all I wanted to do.

When I was 14 I broke my leg in a game and was in plaster for about 3½ months. A couple of weeks after the plaster came off I got a letter from Bristol City saying they didn't think I was good enough. I carried on working with my dad on the videos, climbing up ladders on to gantries all over the country! I remember coming up to Arsenal in 1976 for City's first game in the First Division – we won 1–0 – when I was 16. I had grown up with a lot of the players in that team.

Three or four years later, BBC Radio Bristol were looking for someone to cover City's games and the club suggested I did it as someone who was already involved at Ashton Gate. The audition was to commentate to a piece of video of a City game. Of course, my dad supplied the tape! He told me which bit they were using, so I went in, did it, and got the job! I did that for seven or eight years and commentated on Bristol City as they went down from the First to the Fourth Division in four years.

That all went on while I was at university. I came up to the broadcasting school in London, which is now defunct, to learn some of the finer points. The BBC weren't prepared to take me on full time so, at the end of the course, I phoned GWR, the independent station in Bristol. It happened their sports fellow had just been taken into hospital with peritonitis: *Could I start on Monday?* I was with them until 1987 when I left Bristol and came up here to work in London. I started out freelancing on Club Call lines – Arsenal, Birmingham, West Ham. Without me knowing, the Bristol City manager – Terry Cooper – had written a letter to all the manager's about me, which was great. I turned up at Arsenal's training ground at London Colney and George Graham already knew all about me!

I worked for the BBC for about a year and then Capital came in and asked me to set up their sports output on medium wave. We went on air with the Charity Shield in 1988 and our first League game was Wimbledon 1 Arsenal 5, the year Arsenal won the championship, and it went on from there. What were the ideas we went in with on Capital Gold? Well, my first commentaries were on Subbuteo games upstairs at my house when I was a kid, which I put on tape! I used to get really excited! Of course I grew up listening to the BBC and, although I really liked Peter Jones's descriptions and picture-painting and thought that Brian Butler had a great voice, a lot of them were a bit fuddy-duddy, not what football supporters were like. I thought I should be more exciting than that and relate to the fan standing on the terraces. Football's not about understatement: it's a passionate game. I'm a fan and I tried to reflect that in my commentaries. I can remember doing Bristol City in the Freight Rover Trophy at Wembley and getting completely carried away, the tears streaming down my face, while everyone else in the press box sat there in their suits looking at me: *Who is that lunatic?* Richard Park, the programme director at Capital, had heard this and it was what he wanted. There was a huge gap in the market, too: no local station covering the 15 or so teams in the London area. It all started with passion but, although people may talk about the ranting and raving, we do work hard on the writing, the picture-painting, to give an all-embracing portrait of the scene around you. I remember how Stuart Hall used to set the scene on *It's A Knockout* and that's what we're after – drawing the listener in. They say radio's a secondary activity – you probably listen while you're doing something else – and so you have to grab people more than you do on TV. You have to work harder on radio which is probably why I prefer it to TV.

At first we did encounter resistance from football clubs. They couldn't understand what we were doing: *The BBC do this, why do you want to do it as well?* There were technical problems, too, getting lines into all the grounds. We started with coverage of the six First Division sides and over two or three years extended it down through the League. Ironically, over last season we started to devote less time to lower division local clubs so that we could cover Premiership games outside London. It's unfortunate but we found that, after five seasons as the top London football station, we were losing listeners to Radio 5 now and again if they were covering Man United and Blackburn while we had a game with no bearing on the championship. It's sad but it's market-driven: there are probably as many Man United fans in London as there are fans of Millwall, Charlton and Wimbledon put together and we have to reflect that. Partly because of Sky's TV coverage, I think people are getting hooked into 'Big Star' football and we have to accept that: as a result of our change to more coverage of the Premiership, our figures are better than they've ever been.

Football's fashionable again, the players are stars again like they were in the '60s. The danger is that the grass roots are neglected, which is where the stars of the future should come from. We still have reporters at every Barnet match, every Leyton Orient match, but we're an independent station, market-driven by definition, and we have to reflect the modern game.

Geoff Twentyman, Producer, BBC Radio Bristol

•GEOFF TWENTYMAN•

•BBC Radio Bristol•

Geoff Twentyman worked for Girobank on Merseyside and played non-League for Chorley until he was 24 and got the chance to go full time as a player with Preston. In 1986 Bobby Gould brought Twentyman to Bristol Rovers on a free transfer. The remainder of his playing career saw him made club captain and, under Gerry Francis, lead Rovers to promotion and a Wembley final in the Leyland Daf trophy. Twentyman started work at BBC Bristol in February 1993.

I'm sports producer for BBC Radio Bristol. Somerset Sound is our patch as well. Basically, my job description is to oversee sports output on our local station: a four-hour Saturday programme (with another five-hour Sunday cricket programme in the summer), soccer specials for midweek City and Rovers games and reports every morning, lunchtime and afternoon. It's not just football. Rugby's obviously very big in this area and cricket, too. We've got to try and strike a balance in coverage, between Rovers and City, of course, but between the different sports as well. But we'll have up to ten or 12 hours programming devoted to local football during the week.

When I first came into broadcasting as a sports reporter, 90 per cent of my job was taking out the Uher – tape recorder – and getting interviews and so on. Now, as a producer, it's swung the other way: 80 per cent of my job is behind a desk, organising staff, getting lines up to games, running the team. Having said that, every Saturday I get out and about. I love talking to people about sport and I've got this arrangement – it's unique in local radio – where I have access to the managers once in each half during Rovers and City games. I can talk to them on the bench to ask how things are going or to explain tactics or substitutions, you know. And we've had some great moments: I remember a Rovers game where they went from 3–2 down to beating Bradford City 4–3 while I was talking live to the manager. It's good radio. And, of course, the audience like it that we get in that little bit deeper. I talk to the fans as well.

I was club captain at Rovers under Gerry Francis, a respected senior pro. After Gerry left, Martin Dobson, Dennis Rofe and Malcolm Allison all came and went but nobody at the club said a word about the possibility of Geoff Twentyman Esquire crossing the great divide to do a bit of coaching or anything. I was in my thirties and began to wonder what I was going to do if I didn't get a chance of Rovers. If you've been at a club for seven or eight years and they won't invest in you for the future, you're unlikely to get a job elsewhere. So I did a course at Bristol Polytechnic, as it was then. The course was basically tailored to my availability, to learn the technical side of working at a radio station: a couple of afternoons a week.

Anyway, I got the qualification and, at about the same time, a vacancy arose for a sports reporter here. I got permission from Rovers to do one day a week at BBC Bristol and carry on playing. But at 33 I was a squad player and my contract would have been up that July – this was 1993 – so I decided to take the chance on leaving football and going for broadcasting. I was here on a kind of extended trial and got a six-month contract as a reporter that summer.

During that contract, the sports producer left and I applied for the job. It was advertised nationally and I was up against seven other people but, for some reason, they appointed me! So, in the space of a few months I went from playing football to being a radio sports producer. It was ironic, I suppose. I came into another industry, with very little experience, and people gave me the chance that, really, I'd always wanted in football. That's now in the past, though, and I'm really happy with what I'm doing.

I'm looking at a career in broadcasting now. When I was a kid I used to love commentating while I was playing Subbuteo! And, when I was a player, I became used to being a spokesperson. I was club captain and I was on the PFA management committee and always enjoyed being an interviewee. No disrespect to people who do, but I'd hate to have to get up at seven in the morning and go into a factory for eight hours a day. I love being involved with sport and live broadcasting's a great buzz. As a player, what you do is what people see. Now, what I say is what people hear. Either way, people let you know what they think!

I think, on a local level at least, my background was a real stepping-stone. My dad was a player and a scout for Liverpool. People know what I did as a player and certainly the arrangement with the managers, for example, has come about because of that. Even with other sports, I can go down to Bath or Somerset to talk to rugby players or cricketers and I think they feel a little more relaxed talking to someone who's been a professional sportsman. But my background was unusual, too, because I'd had to work for a living before becoming a pro and that meant I'd always taken responsibility for myself and my family. I was sure I never wanted to end up on the scrap-heap, discarded by football. That's why I decided to leave the game when I did. I suppose you could say I've always thought about my future because of my past.

Patrick Barclay, Football Writer, *The Observer*

As a journalist Patrick Barclay was something of a late developer, beginning a 'second life' as a football reporter at 29. His match reports and, more recently, his general reflective football writing have been read in *The Guardian*, *Today* and *The Independent*. Barclay is currently chief football writer for *The Observer*. At its best, his prose can have the transparent simplicity and elegance which he most admires in the game he's reported on for nearly 20 years.

I was lucky. Like everybody, I always wanted to be a footballer. But I realised I had two left feet. Two bitter left feet. So then I wanted to be Kenneth Wolstenholme. But there was only one Kenneth Wolstenholme and he looked as if he was going to go on for ever and, sure enough, he has. So I couldn't be Kenneth Wolstenholme, and John Motson hadn't been invented yet. The next thing I wanted was to be a football writer but that was never going to happen.

I was living in Dundee and that's where I got lucky. The press is a big industry there and I was able to get a start in journalism as a trainee office boy. I worked in Aberdeen and then got a job in Manchester with *The Guardian*, but still on the production side, sub-editing other people's copy, which was really frustrating. But I got married, had kids and, even though I still used to think how great it would have been to be a football writer, I accepted that I earned a decent wage and had a lovely family and a nice house, you know. The bird seemed to have flown.

Then, mid-'70s, new technology came along and *The Guardian* decided it didn't need two production centres and all the production jobs in Manchester, like mine, disappeared. And I just saw a possibility. They offered me another job and I said: *Couldn't I be a football reporter instead?* They told me I'd have to take a cut in pay – I was chief sub-editor by then – and I said: *Great!* I was straight in doing Liverpool, Manchester United, the best football around at the time. Within two weeks I was flying out to cover Manchester City versus Juventus at the Studio Communale in Turin. You know, instant glamour! I thought: *I've done it!* And the last 20 years has just been a question of trying to keep a toehold on that kind of life.

The funny thing about reporting is always that the times in a game when you most want to go crazy are when you need to be concentrating hardest. When a goal goes in and everybody's up going: *Yes!* or *No!* the journalist's thoughts have to be along the lines of: 7, 9, 4 – the numbers on the backs of the last three players involved, so you can log the goal and describe how it happened. It's a bit of a passion killer! Now I can't even watch Dundee, my own team, without checking my watch when a goal goes in.

The job's always been a panic. I've always worried I'm going to be busy doing my re-writes and end up getting locked in the ground – it actually happened to me once at the Bernabeu Stadium in Madrid. Or that I'd be found out: that people would realise I'd not had the basic training as a writer which most reporters get during their careers, and so wouldn't know what to do in a crisis.

I think a really good football writer is a pretty wise man in the world of football. He or she may not know as much about managing as managers, as much about accountancy as chief executives or be able to play like players but, for breadth of knowledge about the game, a good writer will take some beating.

I think I missed out on the best days when football writers could have managers and players as very good friends but that doesn't bother me too much. It's better, perhaps, that their opinions don't get in the way of my opinions. That isn't arrogance. It's just that I can't ever bring myself to talk to someone, take the bloke's time, and then be critical of him. I just can't do that. And people in the game are very suspicious of the press these days anyhow, without much distinction between individual writers.

I don't think I have any real influence on the game. A lot of what I write turns out to be codswallop. Some of it turns out to be ahead of its time and a year or two later someone else picks up the idea and you're frustrated they'd never seen what you wrote. You know, it's like Basil Fawlty: *Specialist subject, the bleedin' obvious!* Any impact you can have is with fans. The Soccer Diary column I started in *The Guardian* played a part in the whole fanzine movement, I think. And you do offer fans something to rub their own opinions against on a Sunday morning!

I wouldn't last five minutes on a mass circulation paper because the one thing I've learnt, that I know as an absolute certainty, is that there are no absolute certainties. Without the mass circulation papers, of course, the likes of me would struggle. We need what they dig up to write about ourselves. I just feel I'm lucky – and prefer – to do what I'm doing now.

Harry Harris, Chief Football Writer, *Daily Mirror*

Harry Harris made an early start as an investigative football journalist. While still a young reporter on an East London local paper, he co-founded *Foul*, the iconoclastic predecessor of the modern fanzine, some 20 years ago. Harris has been the *Daily Mirror*'s chief football writer for the past eleven years and was voted Sports Journalist of the Year in 1994.

I had a trial for Tottenham when I was a teenager and had my worst game ever: saved a penalty but let in five goals! So when I left school, I went into journalism, a local paper in North-east London. It's a harder apprenticeship than most people imagine. I wanted to write about football but, of course, you can't go in as a specialist. Like everybody, I started on news: you know, covering funerals, the women's institute, fires, the lot. But I let people know what I was interested in, turning up at work with a football under my arm, that sort of thing!

Well, I was lucky. There's a big turnover on local papers because, obviously, it's where the nationals come for their staff. Within six months, the sports editor, his assistant and all the reporters had left and, when they looked around, I was there, going: *I'll have a go!* I was sports editor because I was the only one left who knew anything about sport. They gave me a sub-editor to take care of laying out the pages and the technical stuff.

My break into covering professional football was a job for the North London group papers, covering Arsenal from their Wood Green office. Now, I'd grown up a Tottenham fan. After a year or so, the fellow who covered them left and I started reporting on Spurs. This was phenomenal. I was introduced to Bill Nicholson. The great man sits me down and says: *Right, son. What can I do for you?* I suggested we might meet every Monday, so he could talk me through what was happening and I'd have the rest of the week to write it up. *Every Monday?* he said. *I used to see your predecessor once a season!* But he agreed. He was marvellous with me. I made some terrible mistakes but I got to know him very well. One Monday I was half-an-hour late because my watch had stopped. He reached down into a drawer and gave me a gold watch he'd been given by AC Milan after a game and told me not to use that excuse again! But I think there was a mutual respect there. He could see I worked hard. It ended up that all the nationals used to phone me every Thursday for the Spurs news, and that was how I first came to their attention.

I had offers from national papers but I didn't want to leave what was a dream job for me. In the end, for personal reasons, I resigned from that paper and went off to Newcastle to work for a year, which was my first experience of a daily paper. I was covering racing of all things, giving my tips and everything, even though I knew nothing about horses. But I did cover Blyth Spartans run to the fifth round of the Cup, which turned into a very big story.

Even while I was up there, I stayed in touch with Spurs stories. One person I got on very well with and had great respect for was Victor Railton of the old London *Evening News* who had a great feeling for the integrity of the game and taught me a lot about how to deal with people in football. When Vic died of a heart attack, the *Evening News* sports editor phoned me up and asked me to come down. I was with them for six months. That was what journalism was all about: a big broadsheet paper, with a Saturday classified, you know, sending your copy through while the game was still going on, sentence by sentence.

I worked for the *Daily Star*, then for the *Daily Mail*. It was a case of doing match reports and then really having to fight for your own stuff. Stories like the plans to bulldoze Stamford Bridge for a property development, I had to really fight to get space for. That was 13 years ago, I did that story. I think in 20 years' time, if people look back on what I achieved, it would be me trying to cover football from the standpoint of serious investigative journalism.

If you wanted to do stuff other than reports and previews, it meant you had to work long hours. I did stories on Anton Johnson, the Southend guy. I did stuff criticising Robert Maxwell's involvement in football and questioning his motives. Working on stories like that, I'd be at the *Mail* until ten o'clock at night. One night, a flash came on the wires that Maxwell had bought Oxford United. Well, half an hour later I've got through to Maxwell on his mobile – don't ask me how I got the number! – and he was amazed that anyone was picking up the story that late at night. We ended up with an exclusive, quotes from him and everything. He was impressed and actually asked me to come and work for him. I said I wasn't interested, that I valued my independence, and didn't want to work for Pergamon Press. He replied: *Young man, in six months' time, I will buy the* Daily Mirror *and you will be my chief sports writer!* We all had a laugh about it back at the office, but then six months later he bought the *Mirror*. A couple of months after that, ten o'clock at night at the *Mail* office, the phone rings. It's Robert Maxwell. An hour later I was at his office. He said: *You will not leave here until you have joined the Daily Mirror*. He asked me to be sports editor. I said: *No, I want to write about football*. And I left with the job I've got now: chief football writer for the *Mirror*!

The first story I did for them was about the introduction of CCTV into football grounds to combat hooliganism. I think the editor would have preferred a big transfer exclusive, but investigative journalism was the way I wanted to go. I know a lot of people in the game very well and they trust me. If they tell me something in confidence, it's their property and remains confidential. Anything I discover, on the other hand, is my property, which I can write about or use to trade off against people agreeing to talk about other things publicly. I've known for a long time there's more to football journalism than match reports and previews. And I want to know more about football than anybody else. The game gives me a good living and a great deal of pleasure, but so does rooting out any corruption that's in football if and when I can uncover it.

Ted Woodriffe, Freelance Sports Writer

Ted Woodriffe began reporting on Hereford United for the *Leominster News* in 1947. He spent the next half century working and reporting from behind the scenes at Edgar Street. Hugely repected in the town, at the football club and beyond, Ted died suddenly last year but has left a lasting impression on all who knew him.

When I came out of the navy in 1947, after the war, I had a job on the local paper at Leominster, which is just outside Hereford. At that time, all the different kinds of news were scattered through the paper but I managed to put all the sport together on the back page which proved quite popular! Although I played rugby at the weekend, I watched football when I could and started doing pieces on sports personalities. Sport, after all, was what I was really interested in. I then worked for the *Gloucester Citizen* who had a 'Pink 'Un' – a Saturday classified edition – in which I had about five pages on sport to write every week, as well as doing general news reporting Monday to Friday. I joined the *Hereford Times* in 1959. That was just to write about sport!

Hereford United were a Southern League team then, which meant getting up at six o'clock in the morning to catch a train to Gravesend or wherever! During the week, I'd ring every morning to find out what was going on at the club and every Saturday I'd be there, home and away, reporting the match. It was a marvellous time. Len Weston, the chairman, was a real character. Len had his own cider factory in Much Marcle and the team coach would often stop off there after a game and none of us would get home until two or three in the morning if he was in the mood! As the local reporter it was taken for granted that I was 'part of the team'.

Sometimes it was tricky. I had a period when the club didn't want to talk to me because of a critical report I'd written about a particular game. Sometimes Hereford would ask me to wait before printing a particular story I'd dug out, perhaps about a transfer that was still up in the air. Sometimes people would say one thing privately and something else in public, maybe a manager having trouble with his board of directors. But Hereford were always a friendly club and it was a close relationship. Because I was on to them about things every day, I suppose it was inevitable that I'd begin to get involved in other ways.

I started doing the club's programme: I edited that for nearly 30 years. The big thing, though, was when Hereford United decided to go into the Football League. The club programme itself was part of that, in fact. Things like that needed to be right if you were hoping to be elected to the League. Cambridge had been elected during the '60s and the story was that they'd hired a firm to 'sell' the club to the League like a packet of cornflakes. Well, the Hereford chairman – a fellow named Frank Miles it was then – arranged for someone to do the same for us but the chap never showed up. I was having a drink with Frank in a pub around the corner from Edgar Street. I was already doing the programme with a *Times* photographer, Barry Griffiths. I said that we could do the League campaign, too.

We started sending out a newsletter once a week to all the League clubs whom we hoped would vote for us. We produced brochures and put together facts and figures: as a Southern League side we were getting better gates than 23 League clubs! The first year we applied for election we lost out by half a dozen votes to Newport County. It was that close that we came back to Hereford and simply started the campaign all over again. We kept sending stuff out. We even made a little film. That second year, Barrow lost their last game to Exeter City – who were managed by John Newman, a Hereford boy! – and finished bottom of the League. We knew Barrow were vulnerable but we were up against Wigan who'd reached the fourth round of the Cup that season and won the Northern League. We'd had that famous win against

Newcastle in the FA Cup but Wigan, really, had the stronger playing record for the season. We went up to London for the Football League meeting. We were still going round the night before the meeting trying to convince people to vote for us! And we were elected. In 1972 Hereford were elected to the League. It was a tremendously exciting time to be involved. I was doing all this work for the club unpaid while I was working for the paper, sitting up till two o'clock writing up my stories. But, of course, me actually being involved at Edgar Street was good for the *Hereford Times*, too. I took the League campaign on as a personal challenge but it meant I was actually helping make the news I was writing about!

It was a great time for the club and for the town. The night we were elected, there were parties all over Hereford and in our first League season we had an average gate of 10,000. By the time Hereford had established themselves three or four years later, I was running a department with five staff – we had sports pages to get out every evening in those days, two, you see – and all the young lads were wanting to cover League football. I stopped going to away games. You know, things had changed anyway: the comradeship and spirit of the Southern League days was disappearing. The set-up had gone full time and the thing had become a business. I couldn't understand it, really. The strengths of the club, the things that got us into the League, we started to turn our backs on. To be honest, 20 years on, it's disappointing to see the club now: half a million in debt and just battling to stay in the Third Division. And, of course, I feel it that much more because I was so involved in getting Hereford into the League in the first place.

I'm still around Edgar Street all the time because I'm a freelance journalist now doing stories for everyone. I still get involved, too, with the testimonial committees and what-have-you. Over the years, though, the relationship between the club and the likes of me has changed. It's a different world. Apathy's set in, really, and the spirit of the non-League days has disappeared completely. It's difficult to see exactly where United's football future lies.

Jeff Astle, President, West Bromwich Albion Supporters Club

Jeff Astle wore the West Bromwich Albion number nine shirt with pride for eleven years during a memorable domestic and international playing career. He's remained involved at the club ever since and remains 'The King' for West Brom supporters all over the country. More recently, Astle has emerged as a cult figure, his songs a regular feature of BBC2's successful *Fantasy Football* programme.

Teenagers now, young kids, wherever I go, they say: *Dad, look! There's that singer!* A lot of kids now don't recognise me as a footballer. I like to think I was a decent footballer in my prime but now I'm a singer, aren't I? Doesn't matter what match I go to, home or away: *Hey, Jeff! Give us a song! What you singing this week?* Last Saturday I was at the West Brom versus Middlesbrough game. A 20,000 crowd and they wanted me to go on the pitch at half-time to do a presentation. Frank Skinner was with me, so they've introduced him to the crowd and he gets a big ovation. They introduce me: *The singing star!* Frank's doing all that bowing bit and, when I get out there, he's kissed both my feet. The crowd were loving it, you know. My missus came out, and my three daughters – they'd never been all three together at a game before – and two grandsons. They've given us all a standing ovation. A fantastic day out, wasn't it? Just a pity West Brom got beat!

I'm the president of all the West Bromwich Albion supporters' club's branches all over the country. Tony Brown's the vice-president and we go round to all of them, all over the country. We were at a do this week at the Warley Conservative Club. It was a big place: we had about 200 people there. You know, it's a really good night: we tell a few stories and talk to people.

You see, since I finished playing I've always followed West Brom, even while I was playing Southern League at the end of my career. It all started with just going along to supporters' club branches to make presentations and answer a few questions. It's just built up over the years. My heart and soul are still in West Bromwich Albion. Unless I'm doing radio work, I still go to every game home and away. Some games, I do live commentary for Extra AM: I don't mind doing that, I'd be going to the game anyway! It makes me a few quid, too. People say it's a bit unusual, an ex-player like me, following the club everywhere. But it's in my blood now. When I was a boy, my brothers used to take me to Notts County: I was a Nottingham lad. I started my career there, six good years until I was 21. But I was at West Brom then for eleven years. And, you know, they used to say I was King of the Brummie Road. I was idolised at the Hawthorns and so, apart from going off to play a couple of years non-League, I never really left. I like to feel involved. Me and Tony go to every supporters' do we can. They've all got my number and they ring when there's something on.

With the radio, it just came out of the blue. They phoned and asked if I'd be interested in doing a bit. When I was a player I did quite a lot of TV work: I think I was about the only Midlander involved on the international scene at the time so they used to have me on a lot, everything from *Midlands Sport* to *The Golden Shot!* So doing the radio is a natural progression, really, like the column I do for the *Birmingham Mail* on a Monday. It's what I want to write – I'm free to say anything I want about the club or whatever. I chat to a journalist who writes it up for me.

Fantasy Football? Well, Frank's phoned me up and said: *Would you like to come on?* I've found my way down to the studio in London on the day: *Hello, Jeff. Nice to see you. That's what you're singing!* I've gone: *You what? You didn't say anything about singing!* I'd made a record in 1970 with Carl Wayne out of The Move and I was one of the lead vocalists on the one by the 1970 England World Cup squad: *Back Home.* Frank's said he knew I could sing and they thought I could sing this:

Rosemary Goes! Well, I've never been so nervous in my life – I played football in front of over 100,000 people, remember, but this was something else – but it went off all right and now I'm on there every week. Last week it was *Sailing*, wasn't it? They had me dressed up with a costume like a boat and Dave and Frank were chucking fish at me: it was after Cantona had been going on about his sardines! The only one I haven't liked doing was that *Like a Virgin!* It's a woman's song, isn't it, and I didn't like that! Now, I've done a list up for them of my 30 favourite songs and they'll try and build things around the song. It's great and other things start coming in because of *Fantasy Football*. It's a cult following, isn't it?

I've got my own contract cleaning business. We do windows, kitchens, carpets, all sorts. It's seven days a week, really, but at the moment – well, it used to be work and the occasional other thing – now it's other things and, occasionally, work! You know, I'm 52 now and still climbing up three storeys and on to roofs: if I could sell my business for a decent sum, I would now. I'm getting a bit old for all that! *Fantasy Football*, the radio, the papers: I'd rather do that than climb ladders every day!

With the supporters, and with me, there's one day that sticks out in my career. The '68 Cup final. I must have met thousands of people who've said they were stood right behind the goal when my shot went in. That was the highlight for years at the Hawthorns, that game. Only three people in history have ever scored in every round of the Cup: I think that match was made for me. Everton had their chances but I think it was fate that I'd score the only goal. It was 18 May, 27 years ago: *Ee-ay-addio, it's Albion's day!*

> *Best of all, Jeff Astle: for the record up to date,*
> *He'd scored a goal in every round and they add up to eight.*
> *So Everton, let's face it, were unable to decline*
> *To swallow such a bitter pill as Astle's number nine.*
> *Oh, it was Albion's day, what more can we say?*
> *Ee-ay-addio, it's Albion's day!*

Modern Times

THE AGENT, PR AND FOOTBALL IN THE COMMUNITY

The player just wants to play football. I try and take care of everything else.

Jerome Anderson

I love grafting. I love negotiating. I love doing deals.

Eric Hall

My most important role is to build the bridge between the club and the public.

Rachael Heyhoe-Flint

I've always been aware of how powerful a thing the game can be in people's lives.

Alan Sefton

Eric Hall, Agent

Eric Hall grew up in show business. At 12, he went to acting school. At 15, he got his first job in music publishing. A successful career as a publicist, promoter and manager followed. The move into football came eight years ago, almost by chance. Hall is now the most visible example of a new and 'monster' significant player in the business of football: the agent.

You could say I got into this business through Terry Venables, whom I've known for 30 years. I worked very successfully in the music business when I was younger. Among other things, I managed Marc Bolan for the last three years of his life. I'd been involved with a TV show, a tribute to Marc, recorded a year after his death. I came back to London that evening and met up with Terry in town. He dragged me off to Epping, to a function out at a country club. I met this lovely guy. He asked me what I did, I told him and asked what he did. He said: *I'm a football player.* It turned out to be Steve Perryman, who was playing for Spurs at the time. He asked me to be his agent. I said: *Are you mad? I don't understand football!* He said: *That's all right. You don't have to understand football to be an agent!* Well, to be fair, we'd all had a few drinks so I gave him my number and said to ring me if he was interested. I assumed that would be the end of it. About a week later, Steve phoned. We had a meet and I became his agent.

Steve Perryman was such a monster name in football and known as such a shrewd, nice, respectable guy that, even though he was coming to the end of his career then, my name spread quite quickly. Steve was a great passport for me. I started to get phone calls from people. It was: *Steve Perryman's got an agent. Who is this Eric Hall?* I had a big name in the music world, but suddenly I had a name in the football world, too. There were a few agents around then but I was the first agent with a showbiz edge. Because I'd worked as a promotion man in the music industry, I was involved with Steve primarily on the commercial side. I had no idea where it was going to lead. It was just a case of getting him on TV shows, doing publicity and interviews, whatever: things like *Crackerjack*. It never occurred to me that one day I'd be sitting down and negotiating transfer deals.

Steve and I did well. I got him his own radio series on Luxembourg, did a book deal for him. It was great. Then one night I got a phone call from Alan Mullery. I didn't know Alan but I'd heard of him by then! Well, Alan was great friends with the father of a lad named Paul Walsh, who was about to be transferred to Liverpool and didn't have an agent. Alan knew I was Steve's agent – like I said, it was a passport – and knew I must be honest, if nothing else! I met Walshie and became his agent. Four or five weeks later, the deal went through and I'm supposed to go up and meet them all at Liverpool, I thought: *I've never done this! I've done book deals and record deals, but a transfer deal?* Well, negotiating is negotiating, isn't it? I'm a pro. I talked to Steve Perryman about it all and went off and did my first football deal, with Liverpool's chief executive Peter Robinson. I'd found out the basics: salary, signing-on fee and so on. Then it was a case of letting them do the talking! And we met halfway, like you do.

After Walshie, I got to like it. No disrespect to Liverpool or any other club, but I thought: *This is easy!* I started looking around, finding out about players. My family were all Tottenham supporters so I went there a couple of times as a kid. But I'd never really liked football and didn't know anything about it. But I could talk to people: if I saw a kid playing on TV, maybe, I could go and ask someone like Terry Venables for an opinion. And I started to like football, even though I still don't understand it! I'm the one sitting between two blokes at a game and the whistle goes for offside. One of the fellows will say to me: *That's right, that was offside.* I'll go: *Of course it was.* The other one will go: *That was never offside.*

And I'll say: *No, never in a million years!* I like the football world. I like the occasion, too. If I go to football, the actual match is just part of the whole event. I'll go early, have lunch, meet people, graft a bit, and go to the players' bar after and do my shtick there, too.

I look after 35 players now. Some of them are stars and some of them are youngsters with talent. Of course, I look for players but players come to me, too. I took a lad from Chelsea to Blackburn last year, Ian Pearce, who's done very well. Now, Ian's got a mate, Nick Forster, who was playing for Gillingham. His contract was up and his dad got in touch with me. People accuse agents of always chasing the big bucks which, of course, we do to an extent. But we took Nick to Brentford. He could have gone to West Ham or Blackburn who were both interested but, in that case, me and his dad sat down and I advised him not to make such a big jump: *You could go to a Premiership club, but will you play?* All right, he could have got more money – and so could I! – if Nick had gone to a big club straightaway. But you have to take a long-term view. Brentford's a good club and David Webb's a good coach: a year or two's time you can look at the situation again. Football's like showbiz: it's about timing.

Agents have been in showbusiness for years but we're new to football and that's why people are scared of us. But if you ask chairmen or the FA why they don't like agents all they can say is: *You're bad for the game. You pump up the fees.* It's ridiculous. Chris Sutton cost £5 million because that's what Robert Chase wanted for him and that's how much Blackburn were prepared to pay. And players' wages are just in line with that: you pay a film star more than you do a kid working in rep in Southend! People can always say no to an agent. You pay for what you get. Agents are here to stay. Obviously, I help my players. I can help clubs, too, if they're looking for a player or looking to sell one. Ken Bates at Chelsea says about me that I'm a deal maker not a deal breaker. I'm not afraid to walk away from a deal but I've never lost one yet. I love grafting. I love negotiating. I get the same kick out of taking Nick Forster to Brentford as I did from taking John Scales to Liverpool. I love doing deals!

Jerome Anderson, Agent

Jerome Anderson, a half-decent Sunday League centre-forward himself in his time, runs a personal management service for around 35 players from an unprepossessing office above an estate agency in Edgware. A genuine football enthusiast, his clients include Matt Le Tissier, David Rocastle, Ian Walker, Ian Wright, Anders Limpar and Gerry Creaney. He recently appeared before a Commons Select Committee to discuss the future of football from the viewpoint of a participant whose existence the FA has long been unwilling to recognise: the players' agent.

•JEROME ANDERSON•

•Agent•

Football's always been in my life. My dad was a friend of George Eastham. I've still got a pair of his boots: for some reason he liked me as a kid. He knew George Armstrong very well, too. I was about four when he first took me down to watch Arsenal. I think the link first started through my grandfather who was a big Arsenal fan and, in the Billy Wright era, used to make suits for the players. A lot of them used to live in the Southgate area where I grew up. I suppose I grew up in a football environment and I've now started taking my own son, who's four, along to games at Highbury.

While I was waiting for my A-level results – I had a place at University College to study law – I got a job at a bank. As it turned out, they asked me to stay and I'd had enough of studying, to be honest! I was a chief clerk and then they put me in the dealing room – the money markets and all that. As a 21-year-old, that was an amazing experience – exciting, pressured – that's stood me in good stead since, I think. I was there about a year until I was head-hunted by an insurance company and moved into financial management, which is a really important part of the service I offer to players now, probably the most important: players at the top now have the opportunity to set themselves up during a successful career so they don't have to worry about what's going to happen when they reach 35.

It must be ten or eleven years ago, I went along to a shareholders meeting at Arsenal. Towards the end, they said: *Any other matters?* Well, I've stood up at the back and said I wanted to make a point about pre-match entertainment at Highbury: *I think it's absolutely dreadful.* The meeting's given me a standing ovation and Ken Friar said I should see him afterwards. The story's got in the papers – I couldn't believe it! Anyway, I talked to Mr Friar and ended up, for a season or so, playing records and doing the announcements before home matches. Music was my other big thing, you see. I had my own band and all that.

I've never been someone to push myself forward but I did, obviously, meet a few of the players around that time. People knew what I did and asked my advice about mortgages, that sort of thing. A player named Colin Hill was the first, really, to ask me to extend that into what I do now – contracts, commercial activities, everything. Charlie Nicholas, I suppose, was the one who really got the ball rolling. He had a few problems, to say the least, when he first came down to London – understandably, because he was very big news, a 21-year-old down from Glasgow. I think Arsenal fans know how much Charlie achieved down here, whatever people say. He's such a nice fellow, too: really genuine, a real Pied Piper. And, of course, it was Charlie who brought a young 16-year-old along to meet me one day: David Rocastle. Charlie and David are still two of my best friends.

Apart from my family, football's the most important thing in my life. It's a fantastic industry to work in, great people – players, managers, chairmen. There's some great people in football. Players are the people whom fans save all week to go and watch on Saturday. I look at my job as taking all the outside pressures off those players so they can simply concentrate on what they do and there's a satisfaction in doing that job well. The real buzz, though, is when you see a player – whom you may have been involved with since he was a kid – achieve things. You watch someone put on an England shirt or a Scotland shirt or whatever, and there's a real pride in feeling associated with that player.

There's an enormous amount of money in football in this country at the moment. The Sky TV deal took the whole thing into orbit. The rise in players' salaries, particularly at the top, is a result of that: as I've said, players are the people everybody talks about at work and at the pub. I try and advise players about that. But I'm also aware that if the money in the game as a whole isn't managed properly – and, at the moment, it isn't – we're in danger of ending up like Italy, where football's on the verge of bankruptcy. Obviously, the player's my client, he pays my wages and so I may not be welcomed with open arms exactly in boardrooms and managers' offices. But I think people know I try to be fair to all parties. There's no point in asking a club to pay a player twice what I know they're able to afford, is there? All right, there are one or two people running around purporting to be agents who shouldn't be. And if I've got the personal credibility then my official status isn't a problem. But why are we the only country in Europe whose FA doesn't recognise the role agents have to play? Every player has the right to choose someone to represent his interests, hasn't he? The player just wants to play football. I try and take care of everything else.

Jim Pearson, Promotions Manager, Nike

Jim Pearson is promotions manager at Nike, based at their UK headquarters just outside Sunderland. His is a daily involvement with the likes of Ian Wright, Eric Cantona, Ian Rush, Kenny Dalglish and Walter Smith. Pearson's playing career started at St Johnstone where, as an 18-year-old centre-forward, he was part of a memorable European campaign in the early 1970s. He had four successful seasons at Everton before moving to Newcastle where injury limited him to just 12 appearances in two years. Pearson started work for Nike eleven years ago.

I was 26 when I got told my knees had gone and I'd have to pack up playing. I look on the bright side: I'd had ten years at the top level. I'd played for Scotland schoolboys, youth team, under-23s. Apparently, I was first reserve for the 1974 World Cup in Germany. Willie Ormond, who'd been boss at St Johnstone and was the best I ever worked for, was the Scotland manager then. But, anyway, at 27 it all comes to a halt. I've got a wife and a family. Basically, I needed to get a job.

I left it for a couple of months, did a bit of training, and found I could just about manage to play non-League. I'm a football person, I just love the game and a few non-League clubs wanted me to play for them. I ended up at Barrow who were in the Conference. It was great. I was there about a season and a half, great set of lads and I scored lots of goals! It'd be a great day out. But living over here, the travelling was getting to me a bit and Gateshead, who were Northern Premier then, came in. While I was there we won our league and got promotion. It was great, but all this time I'd been working for an insurance company and, really, I'd just been scraping through.

Out of the blue I got a phone call from Nike who were looking to go into football in a big way and wanted someone to head things up on the promotional side. Nike were actually supplying Gateshead with kit at the time and that's how they heard about me. That was 1984 and it kept me in football in a different way. I knew all the players. Now, I'm getting older and I know all the managers! And, at first anyway, I could combine it with playing non-League.

I player-managed at North Shields in the Northern League and then Blyth Spartans, where we only lost four league games in two years before the vice-chairman, who doubled as the club bingo-caller, phoned to say my number was up! I loved that non-League scene. What some pros who come down can't come to terms with is that, at that level, football can't always come first. Lads have got other jobs and commitments beyond the game. But I had a great time: no pressure, great lads, a good social scene. Eventually, I went back to Gateshead to coach – I'd played one game for Workington, couldn't get myself into the box for a cross all afternoon, and realised I was finished playing – and it was unbelievable: just a bunch of local lads but we got promotion to the Conference straight off.

That summer I looked at the fixture list, though: Wycombe, Yeovil, Bath – I knew it wasn't going to work, so I pulled out. I was getting on with the job at Nike which, basically, was to go round the country and use my judgment to sign players on to kit and boot deals with the company. I've tried to develop long-term relationships with people, which I've been able to do with a lot of players: Ian Rush and Ian Wright for example. I work to a strict budget – some people we pay and some we just supply – and look to renew deals every two or four years, often after a major tournament like the European Championships or the World Cup. We've moved into Europe and I'm now involved with the Nigerian national team. It's taken me over to rugby, too, with Scotland, Ireland and England: not my favourite game – but anything physical, I've got to be interested!

In Britain, traditionally, we've done individual players on boot deals. Abroad, it's different: you do team deals, to supply everything. We wanted to do that here and needed a big club to get us under way. Well, they were all fixed up so we had to go to Arsenal! No, seriously, it took a long period of discussions. I make the initial contact then, later on, the marketing director and the MD will get involved. It took about six years to get through to our people in the States how big football is. In the last couple of years things have really taken off.

I've always had a pretty vague job description and that's how I like it. When I came in, John Kane and Brendan Foster, the runners, were doing it and they just said: *You're football. Get on with it!* There's too much to do, three million phone calls a day, but I really enjoy it. I enjoy working with people, talking to people. And the best thing is being in football, albeit in a different way. I should know more about the retail side of things about the manufacturing processes – and I'll have to in the future – but at the moment it's dealing with players, managers, agents. I really do enjoy it. I get to watch a lot of football, too, and in a bit of style!

Rachael Heyhoe-Flint, Public Relations Executive, Wolverhampton Wanderers

Rachael Heyhoe-Flint is perhaps best known for her work during the 1960s and 1970s which put international women's cricket on the world sporting map. A lifelong Wolves fan, she has been involved with the club's public relations since 1990, when Sir Jack Hayward and his son Jonathan, took control at Molineux.

I think my most important role is to build the bridge between the club and the public. Fans can turn to the back page of the paper and find out what's happening on the pitch but people probably don't know what goes on behind the scenes as far as what the club is doing to put something back into the community.

I deal with all the requests for player appearances, donations – financial or in kind – to charity and appearances by our mascot, this giant Wolfie character, who's a sort of cult figure now. We have our own charity, Wolves Aid, which is set up as a charitable trust, and for which I process the applications. I handle the innumerable letters that come in for Sir Jack Hayward. Above all, it's dealing with the players and the community. The PR job behind that is making sure that we get the pictures and the column inches to reflect our involvement in things as different as drug prevention programmes and organ donor schemes. We can do a lot to help raise awareness for a charity or a cause.

I was born in Wolverhampton and I've followed Wolves since 1950. My parents were season ticket-holders. My mother was a PE teacher and my father was the city's director for physical education. I know the club and the city inside out. I was a teacher myself in Wolverhampton before moving over to journalism with the local paper, the *Express and Star*. When I married I became a freelance journalist from which the move into public relations is often a natural progression.

I first met Sir Jack when he was still common-or-garden Jack Hayward back in 1970. I knew of him then as a Wolverhampton man who'd made a lot of money, a British millionaire who aided ailing causes: the SS *Great Britain*, Lundy Island, the Falklands, Chay Blyth's catamarans. At the time I had a tour going to the West Indies with the England women's cricket team. We were all amateurs and had no money. I wrote to Jack Hayward, who responded very positively and became the team's patron for five or six years, until about 1976. At that point, probably because I'd only scored an average of 86.5 runs per inning over the season and had done something to raise awareness and funds for women's cricket, I was summarily axed from the Association!

I think, perhaps, they thought I was getting bigger than the game itself. Jack Hayward saw this happen and thought it was crazy: he'd seen what we'd achieved with the help of his money. He stood down as patron but we stayed in touch and became close family friends. I've known our chairman, Sir Jack's son Jonathan, since he was a 15-year-old Manchester United supporter!

When Jack bought the club five years ago, he knew, of course, that I had links with Wolves – I'd never stopped coming to Molineux – and asked if I might come in to help with public relations. I've become more and more involved: once people know there's a public relations contact, the thing develops. I'll get perhaps a dozen letters a day which I'll sift through. I'd say *Yes* to all of them if I could, but it's just not possible. A lot of people don't realise that footballers are busy and that they're very focused on their job. It's like expecting the managing director of a busy company to pop out every ten minutes to open a fête or present some medals. There's just not always the time.

If you're working as a PR executive in any field, you know you're working for the product. I'm working for the football club. The product has to be known by the public and, quite apart from marketing and advertising, there are ways of getting good PR for absolutely anything. I work here at Wolves through the director of marketing and public affairs and there are some obvious areas I need to keep an eye on, quite apart from those I've already mentioned. For example, each new stand that's opened at Molineux – the Stan Cullis, Billy Wright and Jack Harris grandstands – we've needed a special event for the opening: organising the guests, the dignitaries, the former players, the on- and off-pitch entertainment. I've organised those three openings. I dealt with the visit of the Queen last year to open the stadium, too. It takes a lot of work to get those things right, you know, down to the colour of the fountain pen and the colour of the ink in it!

It's not meant to be a full-time job but I'm not the sort of person who sits there counting the hours I've worked. If there's something that's got to be done, then I'll do it. It gets quieter for me during the close season: I have to plan ahead but I do manage to get a round of golf in over the summer! The job's never very far from my thinking anyway. I adore the club, the whole concept of the place and what it does for the community. A couple of weeks ago, we invited James Eager – the little boy caught up in the crowd violence at Lansdowne Road – to come to a game. David Kelly gave him his Ireland shirt and they led out the teams together in front of 26,000 people. You really felt we'd done something. It's a very warm feeling: that things are right and that everything's right in the world as far as this club is concerned.

Tony Currie, Community Development Officer, Sheffield United

•TONY CURRIE•

•Sheffield United•

Tony Currie was among the most gifted players of his generation, a Londoner who became one of South Yorkshire's favourite sons. When injury finally ended Currie's playing career, he drifted out of football doing odd jobs around London. The Football in the Community programme brought him 'home' to Bramall Lane. After nearly eight years in charge of Sheffield United's programme, Currie now reaches up to 3,000 school kids a year with football courses in the Sheffield area.

I came back up to Sheffield in 1986, when Sheffield United granted me a testimonial. While I was here I met my wife – well, she wasn't my wife then! – and we started living together. We got married in 1989 – a year after I started work here. At the time, though, I didn't have a job. I'd been out of football completely since 1983, apart from playing a few games for Torquay and non-League for Goole. Apart from doing some cab-driving and working in a video shop, just to keep some money coming in, football's all I've ever known. I heard about this job – this would have been in 1987 – and I think the club had more or less earmarked me for it, but I went through the formal procedure of applying for it and started in February 1988.

At the time I wouldn't have wanted to be doing any manager's or coaching jobs. I'd been out of the game and thought it wasn't going to happen for me. I was sceptical. But this job was ideal. The whole idea was to involve ex-professionals with former clubs. The Football in the Community programme was just starting up in this part of Yorkshire. All I really knew was that the job was to involve the whole local community, from senior citizens down to school kids, the unemployed, ethnic groups, everybody. We were thrown in at the deep end, really! We had nothing down on paper. It was a case of going out and looking for the work, ringing schools, approaching the education departments.

At first – and it's never changed – our biggest aim was to go into the schools to work with the 12 and unders. That's 80 per cent of the programme. And we try to bring people into the club. You know, when I was a kid supporting Chelsea, you never saw the players except when they drove past in their cars. I organise kids' parties here now and they'll get a player coming to their party! It makes sense for the club, doesn't it? If I put something on here – a tea dance, a school tour, whoever the people are – the publicity and actually bringing people through the doors means you've a chance that, one day, they'll buy a season ticket.

At first, people were very sceptical. It was hard work to bring them round. I was lucky, I suppose, in that most of the teachers knew me from my playing days. It was probably harder for other people doing the same job elsewhere who didn't have a 'big name'. And with the kids now, I'm as well known as I was in my playing days because of going into the schools! They go home to their mums and dads, saying: *Tony Currie came into our school today.* The mums and dads tell them about me, too. If I'm driving past schools we've been into, I give a little toot and, if the kids are out in the playground, they'll give us a wave. When you take the time to think about that, it's great, it's lovely.

Our target is to get into about 40 of the 200 schools in Sheffield every year. We try and go in for six sessions – one hour-long session per week during the games period. We can take one, two or three classes, depending on the staff we've got. A school we're going to this afternoon, we'll be taking 70 kids. For that, I'll take along five staff, who are young people off the dole whom we train on a recreation and leisure programme funded by the government. I've been to college and what have you so I'm a qualified assessor for Employment Training. It's a demanding job. The more you take on, the more head office seems to bung at you!

After 20 years kicking a ball about, the paperwork was a difficult thing! Of course, the more trainee staff you had, the more paperwork there was, everything from time sheets to monthly appraisals. Up till a couple of years ago, I felt very pressured by all that. Now, though, since the programme's become self-sufficient – it pays for itself, pays my wages, out of money earned from soccer schools and a club we run on Saturdays – I feel much more comfortable with it. I set my own targets. And it's easier now, too, because I've won the club over as well. At first, United weren't too sure about what we were up to, either. They're much more forthcoming with help these days because they've seen what we're doing and how many kids we've got involved. We're accepted now and things are fine.

The seven years in this job have really brought me out of myself. As a player, I was an extrovert on the field and an introvert off it. Seven years ago I wouldn't have said boo to a goose. But running the programme, organising things here, has really brought me out of my shell. I can hold my own a bit now. When I came here it was simply because I wanted to get involved and get myself back on my feet. I hadn't any other motives. Over the past year or so, though, I've been starting to think about management or coaching. I don't want to get to 50 and feel I'd never given it a go. Because I'm close to football again, I can watch other people and see that I could do it. Like I said, I've always been an introvert, kept myself to myself, but doing this job has changed me and a few months ago I started thinking: *Why don't you have a go?*

Alan Sefton, Sports Development Officer, Arsenal

Arsenal have enjoyed a famously successful decade, as a team and as a business. The club's Sport in the Community programme, based at the back of the Old Clock End, has been a less-publicised but equally remarkable achievement over the same period. Alan Sefton – a remarkable man – has run the project since 1987.

Unlike most other clubs, our community scheme is centred on the management of a large sports facility. In fact, having a largely under-used facility was really the reason our scheme got under way, about ten years ago now. There was a sports hall here – the 'College', which had been part of a theological college on the site – which was used more or less exclusively for Arsenal teams, leaving very little opportunity for groups from outside. When we began the scheme, the 'College' was our starting point: developing the facility we already had for community use.

When this end of the ground was redeveloped, I like to think our influence was crucial in getting the club to build a centre with maximum potential. When executive boxes were put into the new South Stand, the club was faced with some difficult choices. Obviously, car parking was crucial: you couldn't sell a box for £120,000 on a ten-year lease without at least one parking space. The original design was for a very small sports hall with car parking around it. We lobbied quite strongly: *How could Arsenal look to the future with a sports hall most primary schools would be ashamed of?* To increase the size of the hall without cutting down on car parking meant building it on stilts and took the price from £400,000 to £900,000. George Graham came over and mapped out the kind of area he needed and we then pushed to widen the hall which would

311

let us use the space more effectively from the community point of view, with enough room for two five-a-side pitches, or three tennis courts or whatever. That took the price up another £500,000!

To their credit, the board took the more expensive option. Obviously, it means there's a better facility for the team and for the Centre of Excellence but it was also – and I think Ken Friar (the managing director) was instrumental in this – that Arsenal's sense of history and sense of responsibility was matched with an awareness that you will never lose out on investment in buildings. For us it means that, while I have to generate sufficient income from the use of the sports hall to cover the whole of our community programme, I don't have to worry about paying the rent, which is usually the main expense in a situation like ours.

I like to think we run a genuinely mixed programme. We've lots going on for which we don't charge or charge very little: schools training, after-school sessions, pensioners' bowls, girls' football, a hockey club – a full community programme. To subsidise that, we can let the space for private or corporate bookings. The hall and the gym are used by the team, too, of course, and by Terry Murphy, the youth development officer, for the Centre of Excellence. The women's team and the supporters' club team used the seven-a-side pitch, and we run soccer schools and Junior Gunners events up here all through the year as well.

The programme at the centre is our base but we also go out from here. We do a games programme every week of the school year in our 12 local primary schools: football, cricket, hockey and tennis. With football, of course, we can offer the kids the chance to take things further through our soccer schools here and, ultimately, Arsenal's Centre of Excellence. We can do the same with hockey through our link with the Old Loughtonians club which is an amazing sporting and social experiment, really, when you consider the backgrounds of our kids: hockey and all that goes with it at a higher level is another world for them!

On the football side, we run short courses in other schools and soccer schools during the holidays in North

London and the surrounding counties. The other important part of our programme is working with trainees. Through the YT, Community Action and Training For Work schemes, we train young people and the unemployed in recreation management and then send them out to work on a variety of community programmes. We're responsible for up to 40 people on training programmes at any one time and take that seriously: they get genuine training rather than being cheap labour. The training – in fact, the whole community programme – is run by half a dozen full-time staff.

Although I didn't come from what you'd call a football background, I've always been aware of how powerful a thing the game can be in people's lives. I was brought up playing sport rather than watching it: *If you're interested in something, go and do it!* I followed Arsenal – I grew up on the double side – but now with the same week-to-week commitment of the regular supporter. I could see, though, the way football excited people, how it could grip them, and always wanted to work in the game in order to try and harness that enthusiasm to benefit the rest of people's lives and the life of the community around them.

I did a law degree and then got on to a recreation management MA course at Loughborough University, which I thought might be a foothold into the area I wanted to be in. It just so happened that the faculty ran a one-week course for League managers which we were asked to help with. I got friendly with Ron Tindall, who'd just been appointed manager of Portsmouth, and arranged to go down there over the summer to do my thesis. Of course, as soon as I got near the football club, I started working on schemes! It was brilliant. We ran a thing through the summer at the local park – I roped in naval cadets, who were at the YMCA where I was staying, to help – and we really had people buzzing. I got all the facilities at the football club opened up for community use. The Portsmouth 'old guard' didn't know what had hit them but Ron Tindall and the club chairman were all for it. We had a fantastic time. I got my thesis in somehow or other – I copied most of it from somebody else's research! – and stayed on at Portsmouth. We were running community schemes –

this was in the mid-'70s, nobody else was doing this stuff! I ended up editing the club programme. We even reactivated Portsmouth's youth team which had been wound up a couple of years earlier! We had a buzz going but there was a management turnaround and the club's priorities changed so I came back to London.

I worked at a project in Kentish Town, Talacre, which was just a tarmac pitch, really, that we used for everything from football to go-karting. As a result of that, after the Brixton riots, the Sports Council drafted me in to run a number of schemes aimed at training local sports workers and involving inner city communities in programmes at local sports centres. Once those were up and running, one of the areas I moved on to was liaison with London football clubs, of which Arsenal were one of the few where we got a community development scheme off the ground. Vic Akers, who already had an association with the club and now manages the women's team, was the first appointment.

When the thing started to expand, taking on trainees and so on, Ken Friar asked me to come in and run things. That was eight years ago and I like to think we've never looked back. In fact, I think we've expanded into areas that weren't covered in our original remit. I'd had a taste of how much could be achieved working through a football club while I was at Portsmouth, so I jumped at the chance to come here. Arsenal are a top club and they've given me carte blanche to develop something that can really make a difference. It's a change to develop community work under a leading brand name, if you like. If there's one slight frustration, it's not being able to generate more enthusiasm among the Arsenal players. Other than that, we've been here a long time and we've become an intrinsic part of the club. What's more, this kind of work is now a part of the game: every club has a community scheme of some description. We work really hard and we really have fun. Working here, working in sport, is a pleasure and a privilege.

INDEX